METHODS AND METHODOLOGIES FOR RESEARCH IN DIGITAL WRITING AND RHETORIC

CENTERING POSITIONALITY IN COMPUTERS AND WRITING SCHOLARSHIP, VOLUME I

T0270671

PRACTICES & POSSIBILITIES

Series Editors: Aimee McClure, Mike Palmquist, and Aleashia Walton

Series Associate Editor: Jagadish Paudel

The Practices & Possibilities Series addresses the full range of practices within the field of Writing Studies, including teaching, learning, research, and theory. From Richard E. Young's taxonomy of "small genres" to Patricia Freitag Ericsson's edited collection on sexual harassment in the academy to Jessie Borgman and Casey McArdle's considerations of teaching online, the books in this series explore issues and ideas of interest to writers, teachers, researchers, and theorists who share an interest in improving existing practices and exploring new possibilities. The series includes both original and republished books. Works in the series are organized topically.

The WAC Clearinghouse and University Press of Colorado are collaborating so that these books will be widely available through free digital distribution and low-cost print editions. The publishers and the series editors are committed to the principle that knowledge should freely circulate and have embraced the use of technology to support open access to scholarly work.

RECENT BOOKS IN THE SERIES

Heather M. Falconer, *Masking Inequality with Good Intentions: Systemic Bias, Counterspaces, and Discourse Acquisition in STEM Education* (2022)

Jessica Nastal, Mya Poe, and Christie Toth (Eds.), *Writing Placement in Two-Year Colleges: The Pursuit of Equity in Postsecondary Education* (2022)

Natalie M. Dorfeld (Ed.), *The Invisible Professor: The Precarious Lives of the New Faculty Majority* (2022)

Aimée Knight, *Community is the Way: Engaged Writing and Designing for Transformative Change* (2022)

Jennifer Clary-Lemon, Derek Mueller, and Kate Pantelides, *Try This: Research Methods for Writers* (2022)

Jessie Borgman and Casey McArdle (Eds.), *PARS in Practice: More Resources and Strategies for Online Writing Instructors* (2021)

Mary Ann Dellinger and D. Alexis Hart (Eds.), *ePortfolios@edu: What We Know, What We Don't Know, And Everything In-Between* (2020)

Jo-Anne Kerr and Ann N. Amicucci (Eds.), *Stories from First-Year Composition: Pedagogies that Foster Student Agency and Writing Identity* (2020)

Patricia Freitag Ericsson, *Sexual Harassment and Cultural Change in Writing Studies* (2020)

Ryan J. Dippre, *Talk, Tools, and Texts: A Logic-in-Use for Studying Lifespan Literate Action Development* (2019)

METHODS AND METHODOLOGIES FOR RESEARCH IN DIGITAL WRITING AND RHETORIC

CENTERING POSITIONALITY IN COMPUTERS AND WRITING SCHOLARSHIP, VOLUME 1

Edited by Crystal VanKooten and Victor Del Hierro

The WAC Clearinghouse
wac.colostate.edu
Fort Collins, Colorado

University Press of Colorado
upcolorado.com
Denver, Colorado

The WAC Clearinghouse, Fort Collins, Colorado 80523

University Press of Colorado, Denver, Colorado 80202

ISBN 978-1-64215-154-1 (PDF) | 978-1-64215-155-8 (ePub) | 978-1-64642-382-8 (pbk.)

DOI 10.37514/PRA-B.2022.1541

Produced in the United States of America

Library of Congress Cataloging-in-Publication Data

Names: VanKooten, Crystal, 1980- editor. | Del Hierro, Victor, 1988– editor.
Title: Methods and methodologies for research in digital writing and rhetoric : centering positionality in computers and writing scholarship / edited by Crystal VanKooten and Victor Del Hierro.
Description: Fort Collins, Colorado : The WAC Clearinghouse ; Denver, Colorado : University Press of Colorado, [2022] | Series: Practices & possibilities | Contains 18 chapters by Ann Shivers-McNair and others. | Includes bibliographical references. | Contents: volume 1. Section 1, The journey and the destination : accessing stories of digital writing researchers ; Section 2, Memory and documentation : digital archives and multimodal methods of preservation — volume 2. Section 3, Ethics and intangibles : unique challenges of digital research ; Section 4, Digital tools for understandinng discourse, process, and writing : languaging across modalities.
Identifiers: LCCN 2022050587 (print) | LCCN 2022050588 (ebook) | ISBN 9781646423828 (v. 1 ; pbk.) | ISBN 9781646423880 (v. 2 ; pbk.) | ISBN 9781642151664 (v. 2 ; PDF) | ISBN 9781642151671 (v. 2 ; ePub) | ISBN 9781642151541 (v. 1 ; PDF) | ISBN 9781642151558 (v. 1 ; ePub)
Subjects: LCSH: Online authorship—Research. | Discourse analysis, Narrative—Research. | Storytelling in mass media—Research. | Internet research.
Classification: LCC PN171.O55 M48 2022 (print) | LCC PN171.O55 (ebook) | DDC 808.0072—dc23/eng/20230111
LC record available at https://lccn.loc.gov/2022050587
LC ebook record available at https://lccn.loc.gov/2022050588

Copyeditor: Tony Magialetti
Designer: Mike Palmquist
Cover Art: Kimmie Fabian Parker. Used with permission.
Series Editors: Aimee McClure, Mike Palmquist, and Aleashia Walton
Series Associate Editor: Jagadish Paudel

The WAC Clearinghouse supports teachers of writing across the disciplines. Hosted by Colorado State University, it brings together scholarly journals and book series as well as resources for teachers who use writing in their courses. This book is available in digital formats for free download at wac.colostate.edu.

Founded in 1965, the University Press of Colorado is a nonprofit cooperative publishing enterprise supported, in part, by Adams State University, Colorado State University, Fort Lewis College, Metropolitan State University of Denver, University of Alaska Fairbanks, University of Colorado, University of Denver, University of Northern Colorado, University of Wyoming, Utah State University, and Western Colorado University. For more information, visit upcolorado.com.

Land Acknowledgment. The Colorado State University Land Acknowledgment can be found at https://landacknowledgment.colostate.edu.

Contents

Acknowledgments

Working on this book has a been a labor of love. I want to thank my co-editor, Crystal for inviting me to join her on this project. We both got a chance to learn a lot on this project and I am grateful for her willingness to be completely collaborative and at the same time pragmatic when necessary. We were thoughtful when we needed to be and moved quickly when we could to move this project along. As soon as we decided on our authors, the only thing we wanted to do was get their work to the field as fast as we could.

Big shout out and love to all of our authors. Without them this collection would not be what it is and I appreciate their patience and energy throughout this project. Thank you for trusting us with your work. Thank you to Kat Stevenson for your editorial work on our project.

Finally, thank you to my partner Laura. Your endless support and love is appreciated and recognized.

– Victor Del Hierro

Thank you to Victor for taking on this project with me and seeing it through, and for teaching me to learn from ways of being and researching that I've paid too little attention to in the past. Thank you to all the authors in the collection for your thoughtful work and willingness to share not only your methods and methodologies, but your identities and experiences. Thank you always to my family and my partner Ben: I couldn't do this without you.

– Crystal VanKooten

METHODS AND METHODOLOGIES FOR RESEARCH IN DIGITAL WRITING AND RHETORIC

CENTERING POSITIONALITY IN COMPUTERS AND WRITING SCHOLARSHIP, VOLUME 1

Introduction

Crystal VanKooten
OAKLAND UNIVERSITY

Victor Del Hierro
UNIVERSITY OF FLORIDA

Coming Together across Computers and Writing: A Playlist as Introduction—Track 1

We find ourselves living and working at such an exciting time in the field of rhetoric and composition and its sub-field of computers and writing—so exciting that this edited collection has developed into two volumes. College students are writing and reading in a wide variety of formats and spaces, and they use computers, phones, and other digital devices to connect to audiences online through words, images, and sounds. Researchers continue to study these and other forms of 21st-century communication, and we too have laptops, cell phones, software programs, digital cameras and microphones, and more to assist us. With the use of digital technologies, though, comes researcher responsibility and new questions. How does the prevalence of the digital in rhetoric and writing affect the questions we ask, the methods we use to answer these questions, the knowledge we make, and the teaching practices we employ?

We developed this edited collection in response to these questions, perceiving a need to revisit where computers and writing today stands in its use of digital methodologies and methods. Drawing on Gesa Kirsch and Patricia A. Sullivan, we define *methodology* as the overarching theoretical approach and design of research, and *methods* as the tangible research practices that are enacted within a study. In this collection, we explore methodologies and methods that are shaped with and through *digital* tools and texts: electronic and computerized tools that allow what Doug Eyman calls "a new form of production enabled by information and communication technologies" (20), and multimodal texts composed with both "fingers and codes" as Angela Haas has described (84). As scholars of digital writing and digital rhetoric, we study communicative products and practices at the intersection of textual production and rhetoric, where a text is defined as any object that can be read or interpreted (Eyman 21), and rhetoric involves practices related to oratory, language, persuasion, style, human action and motivation, ideology, and meaning (Eyman 13–17). Jonathan Alexander and Jacqueline Rhodes further describe digital texts and related practices as having been affected by technological change, as developing over time, and as "enriched

DOI: https://doi.org/10.37514/PRA-B.2022.1541.1.3

by the experiences and traditions of many diverse people and communities" (4). Because of this variety, some difficulty arises, as Eyman notes, when "applying traditional rhetorical theories and methods to new media compositions and networked spaces," and thus "new methods and theories may need to be developed" (18). Specific attention to *how* the digital informs and shapes theories that ground research and the specific methods used is crucial. The authors in this collection provide windows into the process of theory-building and method development for research related to various digital sites, tools, and approaches.

Our conversations about digital methodologies and methods have ultimately been steered by where in the field we stand and what our disciplinary landscape represents. At the outset of this project, both of us wanted to fill the need for a resource for scholars of digital writing and rhetoric: for much of our own research and that of our colleagues, we felt like we were constantly figuring out digital methods and methodologies on our own as we proceeded with our work. We wanted to emphasize that there is a broad landscape of scholars doing important work in digital rhetoric and writing that we knew could provide starting points for others, and we sought to bring some of this work together in one place. As editors, we searched for a balance of chapters that would help us get at granular questions about methods and how they related back to the development of digital methodologies, while seeing how far we could push the possibilities of what could be understood as part of methods and methodologies for digital writing and rhetoric.

One place we often found ourselves coming back to in our discussions was one of our disciplinary homes: computers and writing (C&W). The field and the conference represent the audience we want to speak directly to with this book. For both of us, our work "fits" at C&W. We have presented many times at the computers and writing conference, we have networked there, and we have attended C&W presentations by many authors in this collection. Thus, one of our goals is to highlight voices from C&W. But we also want to expand our methodological discussions and discourses, to shift our attention to diverse scholars and to other parts of the field that might not be our own. C&W, like all conferences in our field, is still overwhelmingly white, but there are many researchers who identify as Black, Indigenous, and people of color (BIPOC) who are designing and implementing digital research related to and aligned with work in C&W.[1] Another goal of this collection, then, is to highlight the voices of BIPOC scholars doing digital work. Finally, we want this collection to speak across and beyond C&W and encourage researchers to look at and listen to a variety of digital research. We both are members of the C&W community, for example, but in the past, we did not interact with each other at the C&W conference: we come from distinct positionalities and different pathways. Perhaps in part because of our differences—our research

---

1.   A note from the publisher: The WAC Clearinghouse practice is to capitalize names of racial and ethnic groups. The editors and contributors to this collection have chosen to capitalize *Black*, *Brown*, and *Indigenous* but not *white*.

interests, the technologies we use, the communities we inhabit and study, our race, age, and gender—we existed in the same academic community for several years without meaningful interaction, inhabiting different corners of the field.

As co-editors of this collection, we now take a different approach: we speak together from a new place, a shared corner, where we highlight our similarities and our differences and use our varying strengths and points-of-view. One of our similarities, for example, is that we both love music. Crystal is a singer; Victor is a DJ. So we frame this introduction as a playlist, juxtaposing and mixing our voices, histories, and positionalities with scholarship to lead you into the chapters to come. We also intentionally use our differences, demonstrating one way that this collection might enter the disciplinary discourse within and adjacent to C&W, and drawing on the collective vision that comes from distinct positions. Crystal approaches this work with strong grounding in composition studies and a desire to seek out digital method/ologies due to the multimodal nature of composition. Victor approaches the collection drawn to the work of BIPOC scholars who have used and developed digital methods and methodologies to trace long histories of technology work in their respective communities. Together, we forge and widen pathways for authors in the collection to share research insights grounded in multimodality, positionality, and community. In volume 1 of the collection, we focus on researchers' stories, exploring how positionality impacts research and vision for the field, as well as how new tools are changing what is possible for digital writing and rhetoric.

Our Histories: How Crystal Learned that Research Inquiry is Always Multimodal—Track 2

The field needs more scholars to share digital writing and research experiences so that others can learn from and build on their mistakes and successes. Thus we begin by each telling our research stories and sharing some context about where we come from personally and professionally. Through conversations with scholars in the field and with each other, we have come to know that thinking critically about identity and positionality in relation to digital methods and methodologies is a crucial part of any discussion on research. We understand that there is no way to fully consider what future technologies await us, yet one constant is the impact of the researcher and their unique and multiple points of experience.

In 2009 as a first-year graduate student, I (Crystal) composed a video to go along with my seminar paper for a course entitled *Introduction to Composition Studies*. My paper explored the use of sound and music in composition studies, providing an overview of work in rhet/comp that demonstrated how sound might be used and emphasized in writing classrooms and in research. I wasn't required to make a video as part of the project, but I felt that writing about the importance of composing with sounds, but including no sounds or music in my paper, wasn't a very appropriate approach. Thus I chose to make a companion video to hand in with my more traditional paper, and in the video, I put songs together with images of musical notes, people singing and playing instruments, and people dancing and moving their bodies. I concluded the video with singing, my voice ringing out a bit awkwardly that "composition needs music." Of course, others in our field had been making such a call already (Halbritter; Selfe; Shankar), but in that moment—my first year of graduate study, my first Ph.D. level seminar paper in rhet/comp, my first attempt at joining the conversation—it seemed amazing and freeing and *fun* to me that I could sing my thesis to my professor, that I could illustrate my argument by lining up photos to the driving beat of a song that I loved and literally got me moving, and that all of this was part of my *writing*.

This story of my first academic video composition demonstrates that research inquiry, critical thinking, and making knowledge are always entwined with multimodal expression, and thus with new (or at least newly accessible) digital technologies for composition. In rhet/comp, we do not always fully acknowledge or explore the multimodal nature of inquiry because of print-centric research traditions, time or technology constraints, lack of training and mentorship for new researchers, or publication venues that favor alphabetic-only composition. But digital technologies that facilitate multimodal inquiry—a laptop, free video editing software, a laptop microphone—were immediately available to me as a grad student and easy to learn how to use, and as I began to use them, I found that the multimodal processes they facilitated stimulated different kinds of thinking and engagement, not to mention a lot of joy. I sat on the bed in my small graduate-student bedroom, hunched over a laptop, lining up images with song beats for *hours*, bobbing my head to the music while I considered the rhetorical qualities of notes, sounds, melodies, and beats. I was sucked into the editing, to the flow, to the hearing and composing and the inquiry.

Thus when it came time to decide what to study for my dissertation project, I knew that multimodal expression of ideas was going to be at the core of my research. My dissertation was a qualitative classroom study in which I observed and interviewed first-year composition students and instructors, looking for evidence of if and how students developed meta-awareness through video composition. To conduct the study, I collected various kinds of digital data: I observed and recorded class sessions, I conducted and recorded one-on-one interviews with students and instructors, and I collected videos that students composed. (To read more about the methods and findings from my dissertation, please reference VanKooten "Identifying . . ."; "Messy Problem-Exploring"; and "'The video was what did it' . . .").

The training I received in how I might approach designing and conducting such a study came from several sources. I took one course in *Qualitative Methods in Educational Research*, where we read about and discussed fundamentals of qualitative inquiry within education: epistemology, validity, reliability, interviews, observations, data analysis, politics, ethics, and the presentation of data. I also took one course in *Multimedia Writing*, in which I composed several videos:

in general. The culmination of this moment was when our English teacher went on some tangent and decided we needed to go back to the basics. Instead of engaging with difficult literature, we would be having vocabulary spelling tests. The whole class groaned at this announcement, and I could not have been more pissed off about having to do a spelling test. After all, we had all already transitioned to writing our papers on computers! Spellcheck would have our backs.

That night, I sat in my room begrudgingly studying for this spelling test while listening to my mp3 player. At some point, I looked at my MPIO FL300, remembered the tiny microphone on the end of the display screen, and suddenly had an idea. Fueled by all my indignation about the spelling test, I held in my hand my tool for rebellion. That night, I schemed to cheat on my test by recording the spelling of each word on the test using this microphone, and then playing back the recording in my ear during the test. Frankly, this instance of rebellion really kickstarted my first experience with a digital tool, helping me begin to understand how to best use these tools for any situation. I recorded drafts, quickly learning that I would need to speak softly but clearly so I could hear the spellings using only one earbud on the side opposite of the teacher's desk. I spelled the words slowly so I could write them while preserving a natural spelling speed. Finally, I had to remember to leave the playback setting on "repeat one track" mode so I could listen back the second time and make sure I spelled everything correctly.

Reflecting on this experience, I could make several connections to scholarly inquiry, including arguments about education, innovation, and lived experiences with digital composing. I could also say this was my first experience with post-humanism, as this mp3 player was just an extension of my own memory as I listened to the sound of my own voice spelling out the words no different than what was happening in the head of any other student in the room. I knew I was cheating, but I felt justified because I felt like I was getting cheated out of an education. Two wrongs may not make a right, but I know this experience set off a continuing relationship I have had with schooling that I continue to grapple with as an educator. This relationship is one of skepticism that is perpetually directed at institutions of learning that are not transparent about their methods and methodologies or about the motivations for the pedagogical decisions that inform schooling. In my experiences of public education, there was hardly any discussion by school officials about the decisions they made. Or at the very least an inkling that my teachers also recognized that there were some cracks in the system. In the example of my AP English class, we were simultaneously supposed to believe that we were gaining a college credit worthy experience while being disciplined with lackluster pedagogy. At all phases of my schooling, I have strived to hack, resist, rebel, and survive by finding solutions to problems that a Chicano studying Hip-Hop might encounter. I have learned which educators are truly invested in helping their students, and which ones are just interested in gatekeeping. I have also learned that there is risk in finding innovative solutions, and that these solutions sometimes don't work, but you can still learn from the experience.

I share this story to locate my experience in digital rhetoric as one that comes from problem solving. Often the problems that I find myself solving are linked directly to not accepting the status quo while simultaneously making sense of the methods and methodologies we gravitate to for our solutions. In this collection, we are excited to highlight work that draws on digital methods and methodologies as tools to solve problems while doing so from lived experiences. We bring knowledges and approaches to our digital methods and methodologies that draw from all our experiences of digital tools and all the ways we have learned to leverage them. Many of the authors in this collection echo the same kind of innovation that draws on lived experience, problem solving, and a rejection of average or getting by. And so, I and my co-authors ask, what problems are you interested in solving? What versions of the status quo are you rejecting? What digital tools are you playing with to go higher?

Who We Are: Crystal's Positionality Statement—Track 4

Many of the authors in this collection powerfully highlight how positionalities and identities intersect with and shape methodology in meaningful—and at times subversive and emancipatory—ways. Scholars of color in the collection, queer scholars, and differently abled scholars, these strong and persuasive voices demonstrate the importance of acknowledging oppression, privilege, and positionality when a researcher speaks and writes. Across the collection, then, you will notice that we have asked all authors to include a positionality statement or a positionality story that links identities and digital methodologies, and Victor and I offer editorial positionality statements here in the introduction. Through writing explicitly about positionality, the authors and editors entered a process of what Jacqueline Royster and Gesa Kirsch label "strategic contemplation" at the intersection of identities and research methodologies and methods. *Strategic contemplation*, a feminist orientation, asks us to "pay attention to how lived experiences shape our perspectives as researchers and those of our research subjects" (Royster and Kirsch 22). Royster and Kirsch remind us that explicit attention to positionality can bring "rich, new dimensions in scholarly work when we deliberately seek to attend to the places where past and present meet, where our embodied experience, intuition, and quiet minds can begin to notice the unnoticed" (22). In the pages that follow, it is our hope that researchers in computers and writing and beyond can learn from these new dimensions together.

I start my positionality statement by introducing myself and the place where I work and live. My name is Crystal VanKooten, and I am a white, cisgender, able-bodied woman. I work as an Associate Professor of Writing and Rhetoric at Oakland University, and I live in Rochester Hills with my family: my partner Ben and my two young kids, Sabrina and Paul. The land on which Oakland University stands is the ancestral, traditional, and contemporary lands of the

Anishinaabe, known as the Three Fires Confederacy, comprised of the Ojibwe, Odawa, and Potawatomi. The land was ceded in the 1807 Treaty of Detroit and makes up southeast Michigan. I recognize these roots to acknowledge that the arts and humanities have been practiced where I live and work long before the arrival of Europeans such as myself.[2] I am half Dutch and half German; I am a Christian; I am a musician (I play piano and love to sing in choir); I am a teacher, a writer, and a video-maker.

I recognize and acknowledge that many aspects of who I am shape the work that I do and the ways that I can do it. Because I am white, straight, cisgender, able-bodied, and Christian, I am privileged in a society and a schooling system that often unfairly recognizes and rewards these qualities as natural or normal. I have benefitted from my white skin, for example, in that I almost always had teachers and professors that looked like me and shared many aspects of my home culture. I fit in at school, and I always loved it, partially because my schooling experiences were dominated by a familiar and comfortable white culture. Now, as a professor in a predominantly white university culture, I am only recently learning to see and prioritize the importance and impact of race in my work—and the dire need to address racial inequities and white supremacy head on—in part through working with and reading the writing of scholars of color such as Victor and other authors in this collection. In 1995, Gesa Kirsch and Joy Ritchie urged feminist researchers to "acknowledge the way race (and for most composition scholars this means examining their whiteness), social class, and other circumstances have structured their own thinking and how that, in turn, has shaped their own questions and interpretations" (10). Today, I see that my white privilege allows me to remain unaware of or even ignore such urging, which can negatively influence the experiences of research participants, my research findings, and the audiences I am able to speak to within the field.

I have benefitted, too, from an able body in my research. I often carry heavy camera and microphone equipment with me, and I freely walk about a classroom research site with a camera in hand. When I compose video products, I see and hear the material I'm working with, and standard video-editing tools generally work well for my body and my abilities. While I am a woman who lives within a patriarchal society, I have experienced few extremely damaging or limiting instances of overt misogyny in my professional and personal life, at least that I am aware of. Because I am married and am a mother, I split my time between family and work, but I receive heavy familial support from my partner and my parents when it comes to childcare, allowing me to focus a great deal of time on my work and scholarship.

These reflections on my identity, positionality, and privileges make clear some of the pathways I've traveled and assistance I've received that have led to and

---

2. I am grateful to Oakland University and the Center for Public Humanities for sharing this land acknowledgment.

facilitated my research and the use of digital methods and methodologies in that research. I share these parts of me while acknowledging, as Kirsch and Ritchie point out, that my experiences are reflections of ideology and culture and that we all inhabit "split selves" where "multiple and often unknowable identities" exist (8). I recognize that these pathways might be open, closed, or partially blocked to other scholars and researchers reading this book, and I commit to working toward opening as many entry points as possible and providing adequate assistance to all who want to engage in similar work.

Who We Are: Victor's Positionality Statement—Track 5

What up doe! What it do? I (Victor) always open my presentations with these greetings because I always want to honor and show love to two Hip-Hop communities that have sustained and nourished me as an academic: Detroit and Houston. Specifically, I want to honor my Southwest Detroit homie Sacramento Knoxx, who inspires and reminds me that Hip-Hop is still about community and resistance. In addition, DJ Screw and Houston Hip-Hop taught me that you can show love to those who came before you while making your own lane and still staying grounded in your community.

I enter this discussion of digital methods and methodologies through Hip-Hop. DJs in Hip-Hop have used records to travel across time and space, listening, learning, and keeping alive records they grew up with as well as records from different eras across all continents. These DJ practices are acts of knowledge making and a practice that I treat as the foundation to my work in Hip-Hop. Furthermore, I credit Hip-Hop for giving me the opportunity to learn how to enact migratory practices as a productive and relational activity. I have learned to find comfort in being a migrant and understanding that migration is my grounding for my relationship to people, culture, and land.

I grew up in the borderlands of El Paso, Texas and Ciudad Juarez, Chihuahua. Growing up, I really did not know the impact crossing back and forth between nation-states had on me. And while reading Chicanx studies scholarship helped it make more sense, it was not until I spent time in Michigan in graduate school making an intentional effort to understand my relationship to land and to Indigenous communities that I started to understand my identity as migratory.

The borderlands taught me about the value of border crossing, Hip-Hop taught me how to respect the spaces you cross into, and migration taught me to be purposeful in my engagements and movements. I draw on this orientation of borders, Hip-Hop, and migration to understand my own positionality and my approach to research. For example, knowing that Hip-Hop is a Black space, I always want to ensure that my movement within Hip-Hop is pro-Black. And while Hip-Hop has embraced me in some spaces, I know that Hip-Hop, like Black people, is not a monolith. So, in every space I engage within Hip-Hop, I do my best to enact a purposeful movement into different spaces. What is purposeful movement and why does it matter? For me, purposeful movement is the foundation to my positionality because it asks me to identify why I am deciding to move into a space and as part of that decision I have to identify whether or not that space is for me. This process is iterative and an important part of my practice of relationship-building.

This brings me back to Hip-Hop, DJs, and the connection to purposeful movement, aka migration. As I have started to play with my own turntables, one of the first revelations made to me was how much data was needed to play records. In addition to what I will call the raw data, the information pressed onto the records, was the information needed to perform as a DJ: how the needle works; the role of the platter; the way to use your hands; the feel of different records. All of these are tools for examining and understanding the raw data on the record. And then there is the part where you commit what is on the record into your own memory: sounds, words, artists, track locations, and so much more. As the hands and the needle physically make their way across the record, you develop a relationship. Hip-Hop taught me how to move over records with purpose by paying attention to language, place, and stories. DJs emphasize this purposeful movement as they develop relationships to records by connecting the physical movements to the content as they apply their analytical frameworks as they listen and compose. A Hip-Hop DJ listens with purpose because their movements require it; this is their digital method.

The ways that Hip-Hop has taught me to listen have been a grounding practice for understanding my own identity and positionality and how it exists in relation to other people, communities, and identities. As a cis-man Chicano, I do my best to be conscious of who and what I embody as I move between spaces and engage with people. I listen for stories because they ground humanization. I pay attention to language, specifically how people describe themselves, their communities, and the places they occupy. When they feel familiar, I make connections, and when there are no connections, I keep listening. When stories sound personal, I respect boundaries. If I did not catch it the first time, I wait for the next time or ask for a rewind. Hip-Hop grounds all my relationships with any kind of knowledge-making experience. I will always make sense of my understanding of scholarship in writing and rhetoric through what Hip-Hop has taught me.

Digital Methods and Methodologies in Computers and Writing—Track 6

In the next several paragraphs, we review prior scholarship within C&W and rhet/comp that has led us to our current moment of collaboration and this collection. Published in 2007, *Digital Writing Research: Technologies, Methodologies, and Ethical Issues* provides a look into several kinds of digital writing research occurring at the start of the 21st century. In their introduction, editors Heidi McKee and Dànielle DeVoss note that there was "little extended and published examination by compositionists of the methodologies used and ethical issues faced when studying writing with/in digital technologies" (12), and they also call attention to an assumption in writing studies that non-digital methods could be applied across digital spaces with little or no changes (13). McKee and DeVoss survey the limited amount of work on digital methods for writing research that had been conducted at the time, mentioning research in the 1980s on writing processes with word processors and computer software, and a few published studies and discussions of methodological approaches in the 1990s (McKee and DeVoss 12–17). The 90s also included calls for new attention to context; to critical, feminist approaches; and to ethnography and empirical work within digital writing research, as well as web-based research in other fields such as technical communication, information architecture, and computer programming (McKee and DeVoss 15–18).

The chapters within the McKee and DeVoss collection offer views into several kinds of digital research that was occurring at the start of the 2000s: research on digital communities (Banks and Eble; De Pew; Sidler), research on global citizens and transnational institutions (Sapienza; Pandey; Smith); research on the activity of writing through digital technologies (Hart-Davidson; Addison; Geisler and Slattery); research on digital texts and multimodal spaces (Blythe; Hilligoss and Williams; Romberger; Kimme Hea; McIntire-Strasburg); and research on the research process and research reports (Blair and Tulley; Burnett, Chandler, and Lopez; Hawkes; Reilly and Eyman; Rickly). Overall, McKee and DeVoss's collection presents wide coverage on a range of research angles and topics within computers and writing, illustrating that the sites and questions for digital writing were changing and that methodologies should be reshaped for these new contexts, technologies, and tools.

At the same time in the mid-2000s, scholars like Adam J. Banks and Angela Haas were developing groundbreaking work bringing together digital and cultural rhetorics. Angela Haas' 2007 "Wampum as Hypertext" brought to the forefront what digital methods and methodologies looked like from an Indigenous perspective, rewriting the history of hypertext while tying it back to embodied practice. Adam J. Banks' 2006 *Race, Rhetoric, and Technology: Searching for Higher Ground* (winner of the 2007 Computers and Writing Distinguished Book Award) and 2011 *Digital Griots: African American Rhetoric in a Multimedia Age* brought African American rhetorics to the center of digital writing. Haas and Banks are representative of the work being done by BIPOC scholars that expands our understanding of digital methods and methodologies. Additionally, Dora Ramirez-Dhoore's 2005 article "The Cyberborderlands: Surfing the Web for Xicanidad" traces early conversations of identity and race on the internet, and Samantha Blackmon's 2004 article "Violent Networks: Historical Access in the Composition Classroom" reminds us that even though computers entered the classroom more frequently, there was still a major digital divide to account for in terms of access and the historical lineage of institutional racism. The genius in all this work is not about identifying new tools for digital writing, but instead connecting longer lineages and discourses to conversations on technology and writing. Banks, Haas, Ramirez-Dhoore, and Blackmon insist on bringing methodologies to digital rhetoric that identify and keep communities at the center.

Since this mid-2000s moment, other scholars have continued to build on these publications in digital writing and rhetoric. We list them briefly here to honor their contributions and to point to how a variety of work related to digital tools has shaped research inquiry in the field. To be blunt, if you haven't read these works and you do digital research, get to reading! First, we have been heavily influenced by the work of scholars in C&W who study writing and rhetoric through video and other related technologies (many of whom are women), listed here in alphabetical order by author name: Megan Adams' use of digital storytelling connected to place; Sarah Arroyo and Bahareh Alaei's visually stunning video remixes; Laura Gonzales's use of video coding software to examine rhetorics of translation; Bump Halbritter and Julie Lindquist's use of video to examine scenes of literacy sponsorship; Alexandra Hidalgo's feminist filmmaking methodology; bonnie lenore kyburz's video experimentation and theorization of film-composition; Lehua Ledbetter's work on YouTube bloggers; Casey Miles' Queer video filmmaking; Andrea Olinger's analysis of visual embodied actions within interviews; Laquana Cooke, Lisa Dusenberry, and Joy Robinson's work on gaming; Ann Shivers-McNair's use of point-of-view (POV) researcher video; and Josie Walwema's studies on intercultural and transnational digital communication.

Overall, these authors demonstrate how digital research tools like a video camera or video editing software function as much more than a "note-taking device," but instead as an integral part of the research ecology that then "demands a retooling of the methodology" (Halbritter and Lindquist 185). We have learned much from technofeminists, as well, who have discussed multimodal methods within a technofeminist research identity (Almjeld and Blair), shown their work through authoring digital dissertations (Adams and Blair), and have extended "conversations in technofeminism, digital rhetorics, and computers and writing, with an increased attention to intersectionality" of race, gender, class, and sex (Haas, Rhodes, and DeVoss).

We also draw from and build on the work from those using digital research and technologies as what Regina Duthely calls a "disruptive political force" (357) to address injustice. Duthely argues that Hip-Hop provides a foundation for digital and multimodal composition in our field, and that we can learn much from online Hip-Hop communities that use digital tools to build community, resist dominance, reaffirm Black experiences, and generate hopeful narratives (355). A.D. Carson's *i used to love to dream* is an apt example, and as the first peer-reviewed rap album, it paves new ground for digital methods related to the presentation of scholarship and simultaneously disrupts dominant forms of discourse within academia and foregrounds Black expression. We are listening, as well, to colleagues from the Sound Studies, Rhetoric, and Writing community and conference who record and mix sound to connect to communities and fight against oppression and injustice (Aguilar, Bravo, Craig, Milburn, Petchauer, Rodriguez, Valenzuela, and Landa-Posas). For these authors, composing and performing with digital tools such as turntables or audio and video editing software is a way to share stories and to disrupt harmful narratives and practices in society.

Extending Work on Digital Methods and Methodologies: Positionalities and Technologies—Track 7

From the history of work on digital methods and methodologies that we present in Track 6, we learn that the digital affects all aspects of research, including methodology and methods. The use of digital technologies for writing research is thus always experiential, contextual, and rhetorical. The authors in this collection are navigating complex experiences, and one way that they build on prior work is that they purposefully—and at length—share methodological stories, experiences, and knowledge gained. They do so with an explicit attention to researcher positionality and how that positionality affects the work. The results are methodological narratives that are personal and professional, individual yet foundational. Our authors, much like Victor with his MPIO FL300, use the digital to solve problems, to challenge the status quo, and to address inequalities. Sometimes they do so by using familiar digital technologies in novel ways, exploring the use of social media, online repositories, a handheld sound recorder, online corpora, or a camera, for example. Other times, they explain the use of relatively new or less familiar technologies such as digital mapping apps, Twitter bots, audio-visual captions, or computer programming code. Overall, the collection usefully combines attention to human positionality and digital technology to dig into important social issues and questions related to writing and rhetoric today. And because our authors have so many important experiences to share and diverse methodological narratives to tell, we have divided the collection into two volumes. In Track 7, we provide an overview of the sections and chapters in each volume.

Telling Research Stories for Activist Ends

In Volume 1, *Section 1—The Journey and the Destination: Accessing Stories of Digital Writing Researchers* focuses on the stories of researchers arriving at their current digital-methodological practices, with attention to how digital methodologies open opportunities for reflective scholarship that is at times activist minded and at others an opportunity to check our privilege. In chapter 1, "Lessons Learned from an Early Career, Five-Year Project with Digital Methods: Accounting for Positionality and Redressing Injustice," Ann Shivers-McNair traces the relationships between bodies, things, contexts, and practices in her experiences as an early-career digital researcher. With careful attention to her own positionality and to networks of relationships with BIPOC women scholars in rhetoric and composition, she describes work on an ethnographic case study of a makerspace where she used video recording and still photography. Specifically, Shivers-Mc-Nair reflects on how digital fabrication technologies like 3D printing and the use of video and photographs for storytelling are intertwined in her work, and how both aspects are often influenced by her own multiple identities and white privilege.

In chapter 2, "Flipping the Table and Redefining the Dissertation Genre with a Digital Chapter," Temptaous Mckoy discusses the methods behind the digital chapter in her award-winning dissertation. Connecting digital publishing with digital methods as fundamental to doing digital scholarship, Mckoy argues that leveraging a wide range of experiences in and out of academia helped her realize the potential of her skill set based in her own lived experience. These skills and practices, including networking, social media strategy, fund-raising, and relationship building, allowed her to utilize a wide range of digital methods to complete her project through an iterative process that eventually led to the digital chapter. By wanting to create a digital publication that would better tell the story of her research, Mckoy was led to the acknowledgment, development, and deployment of her digital methods to complete her research.

In chapter 3, Janine Butler brings together theories of sound, access, interdependency, articulation, and voice to reflect on her methodology and methods, which include the use of audio and video technologies. The chapter, "Strategies for Accessing and Articulating Voices through Digital Writing Research Projects," details processes for accessing a professional voice through signed, captioned, and voiced-over videos; as well as processes for accessing research participants' voices through transcribing and video recording. Butler urges digital writing researchers to join her in further exploring ways to make sounds visible and visuals sonic so that more people might fully access and articulate their writerly voices.

Chapter 4, "'Tell Virgil Write BRICK on my brick': Doctoral Bashments, (Re)Visiting Hiphopography and the Digital Discursivity of the DJ: A Mixed Down Methods Movement," is a reflection from Todd Craig on hiphopography, a term originally coined by James G. Spady, as a research methodology that intermingles with classroom praxis. Hiphopography, for Craig, embraces inclusion through digital resources, always inviting, invoking, and involving participants of Hip-Hop culture into the processes and products of research and teaching. Craig organizes his reflections as a set of tracks, mixing in samples from an online meme, a track from the Buffalo, NY based Hip-Hop collective Griselda, his own theory of Hip-Hop DJ Rhetoric, Nelson Flores and Jonathan Rosa's raciolinguistic theories, and James G. Spady's work on Hip-Hop.

As editors, we wanted to open the collection with these chapters because they emphasized the journey of research. Methods and methodologies are learned, expanded, and understood best through experience. As the authors retrace their research steps, we are grateful to them for sharing their stories. Through their

narratives, Shivers-McNair, Mckoy, Butler, and Craig give us access to their identities and digital research stories in ways that inspire us to build on their work
and learning. Sharing stories is a vulnerable and engaging act that motivated us to
further shape this collection by asking all the authors in the book to acknowledge
their positionalities as they describe their scholarship. We hope you share in our
gratitude to these authors for the stories they provide in their chapters.

New Perspectives, New Tools

Section 2 in Volume 1 contains methodological perspectives that utilize evolving
21st-century digital technologies to document histories, experiences, and phenomena. In the section, entitled *Memory and Documentation: Digital Archives
and Multimodal Methods of Preservation,* the authors explore various applications
and tools for archiving, recording, and mapping that extend current approaches
to looking and listening across time and experiences. In chapter 5, "Digital
Story-Mapping," Eda Özyeşilpınar and Diane Quaglia Beltran employ digital
story-mapping (DSM) as a methodology and method to explore space and place,
embodied storytelling, and multimodal writing in two projects: Özyeşilpınar's
reading of the cartographic narrative within the *Israel in Pictorial Maps* atlas,
and Beltran's writing classroom where students interrogate historical memory on
a university campus. Through these projects, Özyeşilpınar and Beltran demonstrate how DSM offers possibilities for uncovering counterstories and silenced
experiences of under-represented groups.

In chapter 6, "Social Network Analysis and Feminist Methodology," Patricia Fancher and Michael J. Faris explore the question of "who appears?" in two
research projects through social network analysis (SNA). Fancher examines solidarity, inclusion, and exclusion in a community of early 20th-century women
physicians, and Faris presents a citation network analysis of queer rhetoric studies, exploring citation patterns relating to scholars of color. Fancher and Faris
conclude with three feminist methodological principles for the use of SNA, and
they call for more attention to questions of power, embodiment and emotions,
and the complexities of defining and visualizing networks.

Next, Kati Fargo Ahern asks us to consider ethics, ownership, IRB-related
issues, and the consequences of the practice of field recording sounds. In chapter
7, "Recording Nonverbal Sounds: Cultivating Rhetorical Ambivalence in Digital
Methods," Ahern describes field recording as a method, gives details on two sonic
methods projects, and encourages researchers to actively cultivate ambivalence as
they choose whether or not to field record. To assist us in this cultivation, Ahern
offers a heuristic based on Indigenous digital composing and Indigenous sound
studies that includes consideration of sound's purpose, land and space protocols,
relationships, and potential benefit.

In chapter 8, "Digitally Preserving the Home through the Collective: A
Communal Methodology for Filipinx-American Digital Archiving," Stephanie

Mahnke and James Beni Wilson describe the digital archiving of artifacts from the Philippine American Cultural Center of Michigan. Mahnke and Wilson detail communal methods that challenge traditional notions of the archive through seeking balance between the creation of a digital infrastructure for a large set of collections and a community-engaged praxis that attends to narratives and place/space. They discuss grounding their archive in shared identity, communal decision making, local Filipinx history, the cultural center as a physical collective place, intergenerational succession, outreach, access, and financial sustainability.

Bibhushana Poudyal then discusses what minimal computing and community praxis offer digital archival research in chapter 9, "Counter, Contradictory, and Contingent Digital-Storytelling through Minimal Computing and Community-Praxis." Drawing from her experience creating an online archive of images depicting life in Kathmandu, Nepal, Poudyal describes how digital archives can be a dialectical space for deconstructing representations of the Other. She also reflects on openings for working with community members through digital archiving, even as a researcher with few resources, and argues that digital storytellers must learn to pay attention to and reflect the heterogeneities within diverse communities.

Taken together, the researchers in section 2 ask us to consider how mapping and archiving, how recording and networking create a space for preserving and sharing knowledge and for challenging racism and inequalities within the past and the present. The maps, graphs, sounds, and archives they describe help us to visualize and hear digital representations of cultures, events, and locations, and to consider our own roles in the ways we look back and remember in our research and our lives. They help us think about the potential for the digital to preserve—and to alter—the ways the world around us is constructed.

Negotiating Challenges in Digital Research

Digital writing research presents challenges that are contextual, rhetorical, and at times uncharted. While we might imagine that digital writing research presents *new* challenges, and it does, we are reminded that there will always be *people* navigating the technology. In Volume 2, *Section 3—Ethics and Intangibles: Unique Challenges of Digital Research* focuses on complex methodological situations that arose for authors: working with marginalized groups on the web, dealing with online digital aggression, centering Black rhetorics and Hip-Hop DJ practices, negotiating trauma in community engagement projects, and selecting participants within the vastness of the internet. Overall, the authors point to the necessity of continually considering digital ethics when encountering unfamiliar, challenging, or potentially harmful situations. In chapter 10, for example, Constance Haywood draws on her experiences researching online to suggest that Black feminist theory has much to teach digital writing and rhetoric researchers. In "Developing a Black Feminist Research Ethic: A Methodological Approach to

Research in Digital Spaces," Haywood calls rhet/comp researchers to give prioritized attention to the lived experiences of Black women and to the ethics of working with research participants and communities online, especially with those who are multiply marginalized. Black feminism guides and specifies how we might do this, Haywood argues, through critical self-reflection, radical reciprocity, consideration of multiple identities and histories, and a commitment to liberation through protection and privacy.

In chapter 11, "Toward a Feminist Ethic of Self-Care and Protection When Researching Digital Aggression," Erika M. Sparby recounts their experience studying and navigating digital aggression on the popular message board site 4chan. Connecting their work to the growing body of research in writing studies on digital aggression, Sparby highlights the importance of researching digital aggression while acknowledging the inherent potential for harm in doing so. Specifically, Sparby advocates for a feminist ethic of self-care because of the emotional and intellectual toll of working in these at-times dangerous spaces. Sparby offers advice on how to be proactive within this feminist ethic of self-care, including an example of how to contact administrators to help secure support.

In chapter 12, "Reflections on a Hip-Hop DJ Methodology" Eric A. House argues for the centering of Black digital writing and rhetoric practices in our field through Hip-Hop, teasing out what the DJ has to offer pedagogy and research ethics. House illustrates that the Hip-Hop DJ represents a model for digital writing that is situated in a long-standing tradition of multimodal and digital writing practices. By emphasizing DJ practices like the mix, the remix, and the sample, House pushes back on the idea of digital methods and methodologies as new or fresh, but rather sees them as part of a larger rhetorical lineage if we center Black digital writing epistemologies. Ultimately, House argues that foregrounding Hip-Hop DJs in the theorizing of digital writing methods and methodologies goes beyond simply bringing in Hip-Hop, but instead invites a dynamic understanding of the relationship between culture, embodiment, and digital composition.

Shannon Kelly, Eric Rodriguez, Benjamin Lauren, and Stuart Blythe discuss the importance of Trauma Informed (TI) scholarship and its relationship to two community engagement digital writing projects in chapter 13, "Trauma-Informed Scholarship as a Rhetorical Methodology in Digital Research and Design." The authors provide an extensive literature review on TI scholarship and offer a heuristic for conceptualizing a TI approach within digital work. Drawing on two projects as examples, the authors explain how TI scholarship shaped their research designs to prioritize participants and ensure their safety and well-being.

Finally, in chapter 14, "Considerations for Internet Participant Selection: Algorithms, Power Users, Overload, Conventionalization, and Participant Protection" John R. Gallagher discusses the selection of participants in internet research, outlining five challenges: algorithms, power users, overload of possible participants, conventionalization of experiences, and participant protection from online toxic communities. He describes the importance of understanding these challenges while designing a study because while research on the internet can feel unwieldy, careful participant selection aids in understanding internet spaces at a granular level. Ultimately, this granular view helps researchers understand the narratives that users build in their relationships to digital spaces.

Section 3 speaks to the intangible, layered questions that arise as the digital intertwines with human participants and researchers. The people involved in digital writing research have human needs: of representation, protection, safety, and security, and the technologies we use can help to facilitate how we remain aware of and meet these needs, or they might present barriers that can compromise an ethical response. The authors in this section remind us to consider the people *and* the technologies, the original and the remix, as we design and conduct research.

Engaging with Bots, Corpora, Code, and Cameras

In Volume 2's *Section 4—Digital Tools for Understanding Discourse, Process, and Writing: Languaging Across Modalities*, the authors take us back to one of our most powerful technologies: language. In the final section of our collection, we found comfort in our roots in writing studies. At the same time, the authors in this section demonstrate the possibilities of composition when your writing and research tools involve Twitter bots, chunks of code, linguistic patterns, and even fashion. These researchers, with (digital) tools such as bots, corpora, code, and cameras, deeply engage with activism, accessibility, linguistic diversity, and multimodal compositional processes. In chapter 15, "Studying Unknown Unknowns: Lessons from Critical Making on Twitter," Whitney Lew James takes on the work of trying to better understand the relationship between social media, algorithms, and echo chambers. James brilliantly undertakes this project by engaging in the creation of Twitter bots as a method of digital making and data collection. As tools for collecting research, James argues that making bots helps us better understand how they function and how we might utilize them to better understand social media spaces. Finally, James grapples with the complex relationship and associations that bots have as social media menaces as well as with their possibilities for social media activism.

In chapter 16, "Language Policing to Language Curiosity: Using Corpus Analysis to Foreground Linguistic Diversity" Laura Aull argues for a shift in how students engage with language in writing classrooms: from prescribed rules and evaluation to language curiosity and analysis. By centering linguistic diversity as well as linguistic patterns, Aull explains that this shift asks scholars to reimagine how we engage with diverse language practices, not only in terms of language ideologies but also in terms of how we analyze and assess language itself. Furthermore, Aull shows how a corpus approach drawing on linguistic diversity is a method that allows us to put stated beliefs about diversity into action while resisting an urge to return to homogeneity in practice.

In chapter 17, "The Pleasurable Difficulty of Programming," Benjamin Miller calls for a renewed understanding of programming through his experience building digital tools as an enriching collaborative writing process. This chapter hopes to change perceptions of programming code by encouraging non-coders to consider working in both direct collaboration with programmers and indirect collaboration with others as you develop coding literacies. Miller reminds us that all code comes from somewhere, and while you may not directly work side by side with someone, there are collaborators everywhere in online communities or in the code itself. Ultimately, Miller provides a view of composition with a digital tool that aims to both embrace the difficulty of coding while providing an invitation to programming by demystifying the process.

Finally, Christina Rowell dives deep into studying the composing processes of students within a fashion design program. In chapter 18, "Multimodal Methods for Mapping Multimodal Composing Processes," Rowell describes how multimodal process interviews evolved within her study and were born out of collaboration with participants and grounded in feminist theory and research on think-aloud protocols. Rowell details her methods for these interviews, which involve interacting with participants in the composing space, collecting and capturing various kinds of data on video, taking field notes, streamlining and combining data sources in a video editor, and supplementing interview data with various reflections and artifacts. Overall, Rowell calls researchers in writing studies to more carefully attend to the complex ecologies of humans, nonhumans, objects, materials, tools, and environments involved in composing.

Section 4 prompts researchers to make something new—and digital—that helps us better understand different ways of writing and composition. The authors describe their own experiences making and researching, reminding us that writing is ideological, activist, pleasurable, difficult, and always multimodal.

Outro

The chapters in this collection offer insight into designing and approaching research using a wide variety of digital tools and technologies. It is our hope that the chapters in both volumes provide a broad but inclusive cross section of the dynamic work occurring in digital writing and rhetoric studies. What makes digital scholarship digital? What does adding the word "digital" in front of "methods and methodologies" represent for scholars and the discipline? The tools themselves are one aspect of the answers to these questions, albeit an important one. Yet our identities and positionalities, and those of our research participants and collaborators, affect and influence the technologies that mediate our relationships and research. These relationships between humans, technologies, methods, and methodologies determine the results of our efforts towards knowledge-building, problem-solving, and ideally, as many authors in this collection demonstrate, our efforts towards redressing oppression.

As this project developed, we strived as editors to make an impact on digital writing and rhetoric by offering readers a variety of projects with an emphasis on positionalities. We acknowledge that attention to positionality is a common approach within the research designs of multiply marginalized scholars, and we honor this approach as we take it up. We hope that the stories and experiences described in this book offer starting points for those interested in digital writing research, as well as continual access points for those already engaged. We believe that the work represented here is defining what it means to do research in digital writing and rhetoric. Drawing on our own stories and those of our authors, we recognize that a multiplicity of paths can lead you to digital writing research, and so we share these narratives as an invitation to new scholars and an affirmation of those already in the field. We aim to inspire you to go for it, and to give you a little bit of help along the way, as you think about how and why you might learn to use an unfamiliar digital tool, or to reimagine your use of familiar tools for new possibilities.

Works Cited

Adams, Megan. "Affective Connections to Place: Digital Storytelling in the Class-room." *Kairos: A Journal of Rhetoric, Technology, and Pedagogy*, vol. 22, no. 1, 2017, http://kairos.technorhetoric.net/22.1/praxis/adams/index.html.

Adams, Megan, and Kristine Blair. "Digital Dissertations: A Research Story." *Kairos: A Journal of Rhetoric, Technology, and Pedagogy*, vol. 21, no. 1, fall 2016, http://praxis.technorhetoric.net/tiki-index.php?page=PraxisWiki%3A_%3ADigital+Dissertations.

Addison, Joanne. "Mobile Technologies and a Phenomenology of Literacy." McKee and DeVoss, pp. 171–83.

Aguilar, Vanessa J., Stephany Bravo, Todd Craig, Jared D. Milburn, Emery Petchauer, Eric Rodriguez, Cecilia Valenzuela, and Magnolia Landa-Posas. "Testimonios and Turntables: Claiming Our Narratives through Sound and Space." *Kairos: A Journal of Rhetoric, Technology, and Pedagogy*, vol. 26, no. 1, 2021, https://kairos.technorhetoric.net/26.1/topoi/aguilar-et-al/index.html.

Alexander, Jonathan, and Jacqueline Rhodes. "Introduction: What Do We Talk about When We Talk about Digital Writing and Rhetoric?" *The Routledge Handbook of Digital Writing and Rhetoric*, edited by Jonathan Alexander and Jacqueline Rhodes, Routledge, 2018, pp. 1–6.

Alexander, Jonathan, Karen Lunsford, and Carl Whithaus. "Toward Wayfinding: A Metaphor for Understanding Writing Experiences." *Written Communication*, vol. 37, no. 1, Jan. 2020, pp. 104–31.

Almjeld, Jen, and Kristine Blair. "Multimodal Methods for Multimodal Literacies: Establishing a Technofeminist Research Identity." *Composing(Media) = Composing(Embodiment)*, edited by Kristin L. Arola and Anne Frances Wysocki, Utah State UP, 2012, pp. 97–109.

Arroyo, Sarah J., and Bahareh Alaei. "The Dancing Floor." *Kairos: A Journal of Rhetoric, Technology, and Pedagogy*, vol. 17, no. 2, 2013, http://kairos.technorhetoric.net/17.2/topoi/vitanza-kuhn/arroyo_alaei.html.

Banks, Adam J. *Digital Griots: African American Rhetoric in a Multimedia Age.* Southern Illinois UP, 2011.

———. *Race, Rhetoric, and Technology: Searching for Higher Ground.* Routledge, 2006.

Banks, Will, and Michelle Eble. "Digital Spaces, Online Environments, and Human Participant Research: Interfacing with Institutional Review Boards." McKee and DeVoss, pp. 27–47.

Blackmon, Samantha. "Violent Networks: Historical Access in the Compositional Classroom." *Journal of Advanced Composition (JAC)*, vol. 24, no. 4, 2004, pp. 967–72.

Blair, Kris, and Christine Tulley. "Whose Research Is It, Anyway?: The Challenge of Deploying Feminist Methodology in Technological Spaces." McKee and DeVoss, pp. 303–17.

Blythe, Stuart. "Coding Digital Texts and Multimedia." McKee and DeVoss, pp. 203–27.

Burnett, Josh, Sally Chandler, and Jackie Lopez. "A Report from the Digital Contact Zone: Collaborative Research and the Hybridizing of Cultural Mindsets." McKee and DeVoss, pp. 319–36.

Carson, A.D. *i used to love to dream.* University of Michigan Press, 2020, https://doi.org/10.3998/mpub.11738372.

Cooke, Laquana, Lisa Dusenberry, and Joy Robinson. "Gaming Design Thinking: Wicked Problems, Sufficient Solutions, and the Possibility Space of Games." *Technical Communication Quarterly*, vol. 29, no. 4, 2020, pp. 327–40.

De Pew, Kevin. "Through the Eyes of Researchers, Rhetors, and Audiences: Triangulating Data from the Digital Writing Situation." McKee and DeVoss, pp. 49–69.

Duthely, Regina. "Hip-Hop Rhetoric and Multimodal Digital Writing." *The Routledge Handbook of Digital Writing and Rhetoric*, edited by Jonathan Alexander and Jacqueline Rhodes, Routledge, 2018, pp. 352–60.

Eyman, Doug. *Digital Rhetoric: Theory, Method, Practice.* U of Michigan P, 2015, http://hdl.handle.net/2027/spo.13030181.0001.001.

Geisler, Cheryl, and Shaun Slattery. "Capturing the Activity of Digital Writing: Using, Analyzing, and Supplementing Video Screen Capture." McKee and DeVoss, pp. 185–200.

Gonzales, Laura. "Multimodality, Translingualism, and Rhetorical Genre Studies." *Composition Forum*, vol. 31, 2015, http://compositionforum.com/issue/31/multimodality.php.

Haas, Angela M. "Wampum as Hypertext: An American Indian Intellectual Tradition of Multimedia Theory and Practice." *Studies in American Indian Literatures*, vol. 19, no. 4, 2007, pp. 77–100.

Haas, Angela, Jackie Rhodes, and Dànielle Nicole DeVoss. "Introduction by the Guest Editors." *Computers and Composition*, vol. 51, 2019, pp. 1–3.

Halbritter, Bump. "Musical Rhetoric in Integrated-Media Composition." *Computers and Composition*, vol. 23, no. 3, 2006, pp. 317–34.

Halbritter, Bump, and Julie Lindquist. "Time, Lives, and Videotape: Operationalizing Discovery in Scenes of Literacy Sponsorship." *College English*, vol. 75, no. 2, Nov. 2012, pp. 171–98.

Hart-Davidson, William. "Studying the Mediated Action of Composing with Time-Use Diaries." McKee and DeVoss, pp. 153–70.

Hawkes, Lory. "Impact of Invasive Web Technologies on Digital Research." McKee and DeVoss, pp. 337–51.

Hidalgo, Alexandra. *Cámara Retórica: A Feminist Filmmaking Methodology for Rhetoric and Composition*. Computers and Composition Digital Press; Utah State UP, 2017, http://ccdigitalpress.org/camara/.

Hilligoss, Susan, and Sean Williams. "Composition Meets Visual Communication: New Research Questions." McKee and DeVoss, pp. 229–47.

Kimme Hea, Amy. "Riding the Wave: Articulating a Critical Methodology for Web Research Practices." McKee and DeVoss, pp. 269–86.

Kirsch, Gesa E., and Joy S. Ritchie. "Beyond the Personal: Theorizing a Politics of Location in Composition Research." *College Composition and Communication*, vol. 46, no. 1, Feb. 1995, pp. 7–29.

Kirsch, Gesa, and Patricia A. Sullivan, editors. *Methods and Methodology in Composition Research*. Southern Illinois UP, 1992.

kyburz, bonnie lenore. *Cruel Auteurism: Affective Digital Mediations toward Film-Composition*. The WAC Clearinghouse/UP of Colorado, 2019. https://doi.org/10.37514/WRI-B.2019.0025.

Ledbetter, Lehua. "The Rhetorical Work of YouTube's Beauty Community: Relationship-and Identity-Building in User-created Procedural Discourse." *Technical Communication Quarterly*, 2018, vol. 27, no. 4, pp. 287–99.

McIntire-Strasburg, Janice. "Multimedia Research: Difficult Questions with Indefinite Answers." McKee and DeVoss, pp. 287–300.

McKee, Heidi A., and Dànielle Nicole DeVoss, editors. *Digital Writing Research: Technologies, Methodologies, and Ethical Issues*. Hampton Press, 2007.

Miles, Casey. "Butch Rhetoric: Queer Masculinity in Rhetoric and Composition." *Kairos: A Journal of Rhetoric, Technology, and Pedagogy*, vol. 20, no.1, 2015, http://kairos.technorhetoric.net/20.1/disputatio/miles/index.html.

Olinger, Andrea R. "Visual Embodied Actions in Interview-Based Writing Research: A Methodological Argument for Video." *Written Communication*, vol. 37, no. 2, Apr. 2020, pp. 167–207.

Pandey, Iswari. "Researching (with) the Postnational 'Other': Ethics, Methodologies, and Qualitative Studies of Digital Literacy." McKee and DeVoss, pp. 107–25.

Ramirez-Dhoore, Dora. "The Cyberborderland: Surfing the Web for Xicanidad." *Chicana/Latina Studies*, vol. 5, no. 1, 2005, pp. 10–47.

Reilly, Colleen, and Doug Eyman. "Multifaceted Methods for Multimodal Texts: Alternate Approaches to Citation Analysis for Electronic Sources." McKee and DeVoss, pp. 353–75.

Rickly, Rebecca. "Messy Contexts: Research as a Rhetorical Situation." McKee and DeVoss, pp. 377–97.

Robinson, Joy. "Look Before You Lead: Seeing Virtual Teams Through the Lens of Games." *Technical Communication Quarterly*, vol. 25, no. 3, 2016, pp. 178–90.

Romberger, Julia. "An Ecofeminist Methodology: Studying the Ecological Dimensions of the Digital Environment." McKee and DeVoss, pp. 249–67.

Royster, Jacqueline Jones, and Gesa E. Kirsch. *Feminist Rhetorical Practices: New Horizons for Rhetoric, Composition, and Literacy Studies*, Southern Illinois UP, 2012.

Sapienza, Fil. "Ethos and Research Positionality in Studies of Virtual Communities." McKee and DeVoss, pp. 89–106.

Selfe, Cynthia L. "The Movement of Air, the Breath of Meaning: Aurality and Multimodal Composing." *College Composition and Communication*, vol. 60, no. 4, 2009, pp. 616–63.

Shankar, Tara Rosenberger. "Speaking on the Record: A Theory of Composition." *Computers and Composition*, vol. 23, no. 3, 2006, pp. 374–93.

Shivers-McNair, Ann. "3D Interviewing with Researcher POV Video: Bodies and Knowledge in the Making." *Kairos: A Journal of Rhetoric, Technology, and Pedagogy*, vol. 21, no. 2, spring 2017, http://praxis.technorhetoric.net/tiki-index.php?page=PraxisWiki:_:3D%20Interviewing.

Sidler, Michelle. "Playing Scavenger and Gazer with Scientific Discourse: Opportunities and Ethics for Online Research." McKee and DeVoss, pp. 71–86.

Smith, Beatrice. "Researching Hybrid Literacies: Methodological Explorations of 'Ethnography' and the Practices of the Cybertariat." McKee and DeVoss, pp. 127–49.

VanKooten, Crystal, and Angela Berkley. "Messy Problem-Exploring through Video in First-Year Writing: Assessing What Counts." *Computers and Composition*, vol. 40, June 2016, pp. 151–63.

VanKooten, Crystal. "A New Composition, A 21st Century Pedagogy, and the Rhetoric of Music." *Currents in Electronic Literacy*, 2011, https://currents.dwrl.utexas.edu/2011/anewcomposition.html.

———. "A Research Methodology of Interdependence through Video as Method." *Computers and Composition*, vol. 54, Dec. 2019, pp. 1–17.

———. "Identifying Components of Meta-Awareness about Composition: Toward a Theory and Methodology for Writing Studies." *Composition Forum*, vol. 33, spring 2016, http://compositionforum.com/issue/33/meta-awareness.php.

———. "'The Video Was What Did It for Me': Developing Meta-Awareness about Composition across Media." *College English*, vol. 79, no. 1, Sept. 2016, pp. 57–80.

———. *Transfer across Media: Using Digital Video in the Teaching of Writing*. Computers and Composition Digital Press; Utah State UP, 2020, https://ccdigitalpress.org/book/transfer-across-media/index.html.

Walwema, Josephine. "The WHO Health Alert: Communicating a Global Pandemic with WhatsApp." *Journal of Business and Technical Communication*, vol. 35, no. 1, 2020, pp. 35–40.

Section 1. The Journey and the Destination: Accessing Stories of Digital Writing Researchers

Chapter 1. Lessons Learned from an Early Career, Five-Year Project with Digital Methods: Accounting for Positionality and Redressing Injustice

Ann Shivers-McNair
UNIVERSITY OF ARIZONA

> Technology is not just what does the work, it is the work—and that work relies on an ongoing relationship between bodies and things.
>
> – *Angela Haas*

I begin with Angela Haas' reminder that technology is relational ("Race" 291), because this chapter is about the dynamic relations of bodies and things in my engagement with digital research methods as an early-career scholar over a five-year period, from designing my dissertation project to preparing my book for publication with digital components. I also begin by sharing that I am a white, cisgendered, able-bodied woman with the socio-economic privilege of being employed as a tenure-track assistant professor at a large public university, because my multiple dimensions of privilege imbue the dynamic relations of bodies and things in my lived experiences and in the stories I tell. In other words, as Black feminist and Indigenous scholars have long argued (Jones, Haas), I cannot talk about technologies without talking about them in relation to bodies, things, contexts, histories, and practices.

In this chapter, I critically retrace my steps and relations through the last five years as I worked on an ethnographic case study of a makerspace using digital methods (primarily video and photography) as a white, cisgendered, able-bodied woman working as a graduate student and then as a tenure-track faculty member in rhetoric and composition programs in English departments. To resist dominant practices of normalizing the experiences of multiply privileged people in our scholarship and practice, Natasha Jones, Kristen Moore, and Rebecca Walton call for us to examine and account for the 3Ps—positionality, privilege, and power—in our work (220). Therefore, in my retracing, I examine the intersections of my individual privileges with institutional privileges and privileged discourses (both in rhetoric and writing and in the maker movement) as I carried out my work, encountered challenges, and negotiated publishing.

I account for the intersections of privileges and digital technologies and methods in my work and experiences as a white, cisgendered, able-bodied woman in order to create a little more space to resist and redress the ways I (and people

DOI: https://doi.org/10.37514/PRA-B.2022.1541.2.01

like me) benefit from white supremacist, ableist, heterosexism in our engagement with research and technologies, to the exclusion and harm of others. To do this accounting and resisting work, I trace two strands in my work and experience that remained more separate in my thinking and in my practice than they should have, and for longer than they should have:

1. Addressing how relatively recent digital technologies are privileged in the maker movement and in academic spaces, and
2. Using digital tools as a technique for storytelling and locating the embodied researcher gaze.

I trace these strands over a five-year period, from navigating newness and discomfort at the beginning of a project, to navigating attitudes toward technologies in research as well as in the academic job market and publishing process. I conclude with a reflection on learning relationality in research in which I honor the labor of the people from whom I have learned, and I offer takeaways for engaging with digital technologies and methods in research, in mentoring and hiring, and in publishing.

But first, I want to situate my approach to analyzing and telling what I share here in relation to traditions of autoethnography, critical discourse analysis (CDA), and narrative inquiry. As a white researcher, I have a necessarily uncomfortable relationship to autoethnography and to ethnography, which, as Margaret Somerville explains, "emerged in parallel to the colonization of many [I]ndigenous peoples of the world. By the mid-1980s critiques were mounting about the colonizing nature of anthropological knowledge, and the impossibility for the colonizer to represent the lives of the colonized other. In response to the recognition of complicity in the processes of colonization, a fundamental critique of ethnographic practice emerged. The 'death of ethnography' was announced" (10). And yet, as Leigh Patel observes, "even 30 years after the death of ethnography was proclaimed (Somerville, 2013), problematic patterns persist in white researchers pursuing and speaking of research about racially minoritized populations, to presumably white audiences" (55). Patel attributes the continuing of colonizing research practices to the fact that a "privileged population [an upper middle social class that has racialized protection] persists in control of the uppermost spaces of the academy" (55). I am part of that privileged population, and despite my efforts and intentions to resist colonizing research practices, I still participate in and perpetuate them.

As some researchers began seeking to resist or mitigate the colonizing gaze of ethnography toward the end of the twentieth century, a "tradition of auto/ethnography sprang from this response" (Somerville 10). For both white researchers and Black, Indigenous, and people of color (BIPOC) researchers, a critical approach to autoethnography can work against what Steven Alvarez describes as "the colonizing gaze of the decontextualized researcher and the accompanying rhetoric that normalizes a 'universal' viewpoint" (86). Alvarez demonstrates that for BIPOC researchers and communities, autoethnography serves the important function of centering marginalized voices and perspectives. For white researchers and communities like me, autoethnography can serve as a method for critically examining positionality, privilege, and power, as education scholars Julie Pennington and Cynthia Brock model in using autoethnography as a tool for white teachers to critically engage their racial identity. However, as Somerville notes, autoethnography "has been criticized for its inward looking focus" (11), and as a white researcher, I am mindful that simply turning my gaze to my own experience is not inherently just or useful, especially if it only serves to re-center my already-privileged experiences and perspectives.

Therefore, while my approach is informed by the commitment of critical autoethnography to locate and resist "the colonizing gaze of the decontextualized researcher" (Alvarez 86), I also draw on practices from CDA to interrogate the ways that power circulates in and through my actions and experiences. CDA "starts from prevailing social problems" rather than "purely academic or theoretical problems" and "critically analyses those in power, those who are responsible, and those who have the means and the opportunity to solve such problems" (van Dijk 4; qtd. in Wodak 2). In this case, the prevailing social problem is the fact that white academics like me move with unearned ease in research, publishing, and other academic spaces (and, indeed, in all spaces), to the exclusion and harm of BIPOC and multiply marginalized academics and communities. By critically analyzing my own discourses as well as the discourses I engage, I am acknowledging my responsibility for and my opportunity to solve the problems I describe. But here again, there is a danger of an overly-individualistic focus.

This is why I am ultimately guided by Natasha Jones' decolonial approach to narrative inquiry. Jones draws upon and critically resitutates Michael Connelly and Jean Clandinin's definition of narrative inquiry as "'the study of experience as story' (375)," noting that:

> [t]hough the term narrative inquiry was coined in 1990, as JoAnne Banks-Wallace notes, stories have long been a way of making meaning. In fact, oral storytelling traditions that grounded African, African American, and Indigenous communities' ways of being, understanding, and knowing (see scholarship by Wilson; Smith; Banks) are reflected in narrative inquiry as a methodological framework. (519)

In addition to decolonially resitutating the tradition of narrative inquiry, Jones also decolonially resitutates Connelly and Clandinin's three commonplaces of narrative inquiry—place, temporality, and sociality:

> The 'place' commonplace engages with the way that narrative and experience are geographically, physically, spatially, imaginatively, and ideologically constructed (like boundary areas and contact zones). 'Temporality' as a commonplace asserts that events are always shifting and everything is always in transition and in process. Finally, the 'sociality' commonplace

recognizes the collective over the individualistic. Narrative inquiry acknowledges complex, pluralistic, and contextual realities—like those that we find in boundary areas and contact zones. (520)

It is important to note that, as Jones argues, narrative inquiry "calls for us to listen and privilege the particular and lived experiences, especially those of the multiply marginalized" (520). Because my experiences are not marginalized, it is even more important for me to follow Jones' exhortation to acknowledge and cite narrative traditions beyond relatively recent, white, Western approaches and to avoid an individualistic re-centering of my experiences (which also feeds myths of meritocracy) by instead contextualizing myself and my practices in relation to bodies, systems, traditions, and things.

I also want to acknowledge that the (more or less) linear, chronological approach I take in this chapter is only one model. For example, highlighting Indigenous practices, Gabriela Raquel Ríos (2015) models "land-based (or spatial) rather than temporal" meaning making (68). And, as Jones shows, even a temporal approach must account for the fact that "events are always shifting and everything is always in transition and in process" (520). I have chosen a more-or-less temporal approach here because as a graduate student and now as a tenure-track faculty member, academic clocks—years of funding for graduate work, years on the tenure clock—have shaped how, where, and with whom I engage in digital research methods. I also chose this temporal account to complement and contextualize other accounts of digital methods I have published that focus on methods used in a particular place and moment ("Making Knowledge") and on a particular digital technique ("3D Interviewing"). And while my book (*Beyond the Makerspace*) also offers a (more or less) temporal account of my methods, it focuses mostly on the context of the longitudinal study and less on the context of engaging digital and qualitative methods as an early career scholar navigating graduate work, the academic job market, and the tenure process. Therefore, in tracing my engagement with digital methods—especially video recording and still photography—from the beginnings of a dissertation study in 2015 through preparing a book for production in 2020, I reveal and critically examine how my practices and philosophical orientations changed over time and in response not only to my relationships with participants and my engagement with scholarly conversations; but also to my experiences navigating professional processes like preparing and defending a dissertation, going on the academic job market, and publishing articles and a book.

Navigating "Newness" and Discomfort at the Beginning of a Project

Digital methods and technologies were both the subject and the means of my project from its beginnings, though the relationship between the ways they were both the subject and the means was not always as clear to me as it should have been. Specifically, digital methods and technologies were remediating, literally and figuratively, both the subject and the means of my research in two strands that felt separate at first, but that I now realize are inextricably entwined:

1. The privileging of relatively recent digital fabrication technologies (like 3D printing) in the maker movement and in academic spaces, and

2. The use of researcher point-of-view (POV) video and photos as a reflexive ethnographic technique for storytelling and locating the embodied researcher gaze.

The first strand—the privileging of digital fabrication technologies like 3D printing—is what brought me to this project in the first place. I first heard the word "makerspace" in a conversation at the 2014 Cultural Rhetorics Conference with David Sheridan. Scholars like Sheridan were already making connections between the increasingly widespread digital fabrication technologies at the center of the maker movement (such as 3D printing) and writing studies. As Sheridan argues, describing projects that included 3D printing, fabricated rhetoric and "three-dimensional compositions shape attitudes, beliefs, values, behaviors, and identities—all of the 'stuff' of culture" and thus engaging critically with 3D rhetoric "potentially increases our power to shape culture for the better" (262). In 2014, I was new both to the maker movement and to conversations about 3D rhetoric and about multimodality more generally. I perceived that those conversations were increasingly moving to the mainstream (read white-stream) of writing studies—even though scholars like Adam Banks and Angela Haas have shown us that multimodal making practices like remixing, grounded in the practice of Black DJs (Banks *Digital*), and hypertext, practiced in Indigenous wampum belts long before being "invented" by Westerners (Haas "Wampum"), long predate composition studies' interest in them and are often harmfully appropriated and touted as "new" in white/Western-dominated perspectives.

I felt a mix of unease and curiosity about that "newness" in relation to maker technologies. I was both intrigued by and skeptical of the maker movement's goal to democratize innovation by making "makers" of people who might not otherwise have the training, access to technologies and tools, or inspiration (Hatch). I was intrigued because I heard echoes of that democratizing aim in conversations about relatively new media and technologies in writing studies—for example, in conversations about coding as a fundamental literacy. But I was skeptical because I was quickly realizing that not only was the maker movement itself dominated by men (documented, for example, in a 2015 press sheet from Maker Media and in a 2016 maker survey conducted by Hackster.io), but also, as scholars like Debbie Chachra point out, the very definitions of making privileged by the contemporary maker movement have a gendered history that renders invisible the kinds of making work—like caregiving—traditionally associated with women.

I felt that unease and curiosity when I started visiting a local makerspace in early 2015. When I first visited the Seattle makerspace (located on the ancestral, traditional, and contemporary lands of the Duwamish and Coastal Salish Peoples) that would become the starting point of my longitudinal study in February 2015, the CEO of the makerspace greeted me warmly and immediately asked, "What do you want to make?" Seeing a 3D printer, laser cutter, and computer-numerical control (CNC) router for the first time all at once, and in a space where I was the only woman, I had no idea how to answer. I was a writer, a crocheter, a hobbyist baker—but I didn't feel like a "maker" in that moment. I left feeling overwhelmed, but also determined to try to understand more about the ways that identifying as a "maker" (or not) in a makerspace was a function of complex relations of bodies, technologies, and practices. In my dissertation prospectus, I wrote the following:

> I want to attend to the ways in which acts of making are acts of mattering. What comes to matter, and what is excluded from mattering, in acts of making? After all, 3D printed objects, wearable electronics, and laser-cut boxes are not the only things made in a makerspace. Machines and tools are made and remade. Networks and connections are made and remade. Meanings are made and remade. Makers are made and remade. Like the increasingly technology-rich, networked environments in which writing is made, makerspaces are sites of entangled making that include words, objects, humans, machines, and connections. Answering the question "what are you making?" (or the permutations of that question, including "what can we make?," "who can make?," and "how can we make?") draws our attention not only to the objects, technologies, and practices of making, but also to the bodies and desires that are made to matter and to those that are excluded from mattering.

My identification as an outsider to the maker movement (because of my gender identity and my lack of experience with digital fabrication technologies) was important not only to my orientation to the privileging of maker technologies as the subject of my project, but also to my orientation to the research methods in my project.

This brings me to the second strand of digital technologies and methods remediating my project—particularly ethnographic methods with which, as I have explained, I have a necessarily troubled relationship as a white researcher. Despite having previously sworn off ethnography, there I was, in 2015, beginning an ethnographically informed case study. I rationalized that my positionality—at once safe and welcome in the majority-white makerspace as a function of my race, yet also uncomfortable in the majority-men makerspace as a function of my gender identity—might allow me to inhabit a critical perspective on the discourses and practices of power circulating in the makerspace and the maker movement.

And while I certainly sympathize with the perspectives of women who avoid men-dominated makerspaces (such as the members of a feminist makerspace in Seattle, not far from the one I studied, that Sarah Fox, Rachel Rose Ulgado, and Daniela Rosner have described), I also came to realize that I underestimated the extent to which my white privilege would mitigate the discomfort I felt from my underrepresented gender identity and lack of digital fabrication experience.

This is, as legal scholar and Critical Race Theorist Kimberlé Crenshaw has been arguing for decades, a symptom of the realities of the layers of discrimination or privilege people experience because of the intersections of their identities ("Demarginalizing"). In a way, my experience—specifically, the way my white privilege mitigated the discomfort of being often the only woman-identified person in a makerspace—is a photo negative of the discrimination experience of an African American woman that inspired Crenshaw's theory of intersectionality. Crenshaw explains that a judge dismissed the case of the African American woman, Emma DeGraffenreid, arguing that because the employer who had refused to hire her had hired other African Americans and other women, DeGraffenreid could claim neither race nor gender discrimination. But, as Crenshaw points out, "the African Americans that were hired, usually for industrial jobs, maintenance jobs, were all men. And the women that were hired, usually for secretarial or front-office work, were all white. Only if the court was able to see how these policies came together would he [the judge] be able to see the double discrimination that Emma DeGraffenreid was facing" ("Urgency"). While DeGraffenreid's identities as a Black woman rendered her doubly discriminated against in a workplace and invisible to a court of law, my identities as a white woman afforded me safety and goodwill in a space where I had no expertise or connections. My presence was never questioned, even though I was not a paying customer nor a contributor to the work of the space, and my utter lack of knowledge about the technologies and processes in the space was met with patience and the benefit of the doubt.

But despite the ways in which my white privilege mitigated my experience from the beginning, in 2015, my discomfort and unfamiliarity in the space were the primary frames for my experiences and interactions. I spent most of 2015 learning how to relate to the people and the digital technologies in the makerspace, and (perhaps ironically, given the preponderance of digital technologies I was observing) relying primarily on pencil and paper for recording my interactions and observations in words and sketches. I did not feel comfortable taking extensive photos or videos when I was still learning how to interact with people without disturbing or distracting them, how to understand what I was observing, and how to know where it was safe to stand and move. But as the months went by and my discomfort and unfamiliarity began to diminish, I began taking more photos and videos to record the ever-changing configurations and interactions of people and technologies in the space, in part because I felt like I had earned enough trust to ask permission to do so, but also because I did not want to lose that unfamiliarity entirely.

Unfamiliarity attuned me to the partiality of my perspective, to resist a decon-textualized or omniscient gaze. In the words of Lucy Suchman, whose work I was introduced to by Angela Haas, I sought a "located accountability": as Such-man explains, "it is precisely the fact that our vision of the world is a vision from somewhere—that it is inextricably based in an embodied, and therefore partial perspective—which makes us personally responsible for it" (96). In that sense, taking photos and videos helped me remember not only what I experienced but also that my experiences were located in my embodied perspective. As I wrote in my dissertation prospectus, "My own involvement—observing, interacting, taking notes and pictures, filming, asking questions, moving around—is not an elicitation of a phenomenon; it is part of the phenomenon."

And just as the locatedness and partiality of my perspective as a woman in a majority (and often entirely) men-identified space had informed my decision to engage in a critically-oriented ethnographic project in the first place, the located-ness and partiality of my perspective also informed my practices of digital video and photography, because I felt like these techniques allowed me to turn a crit-ically informed gaze both on the practices of men in the space and on my own participation in the space. In my use of digital video and photography, I drew on a tradition of visual research methods in rhetoric and writing studies (McKee and DeVoss; Hawisher, Selfe, Berry, and Skjulstad) in my use of digital video and photography. Specifically, I was inspired by Laura Gonzales' work with video to record not only what people said about multimodal writing but also how they gestured and physically engaged. I realized it was important to attend not only to what people said but also to what people did in a makerspace, where rhetorics circulated in words, movements, and objects. And that included my own words and actions (Gonzales "Multimodality"). By the end of 2015, I had begun vid-eo-recording interactions with a head-mounted camera to account for embod-ied interactions, including my researcher positionality. I drew on traditions like "walking with video" in sensory ethnography (Pink) to guide my procedures and techniques for videography, editing, and analysis.

As I describe in my book, the process of recording, editing, and sharing vid-eos in late 2015 and early 2016 (featuring two white men and one Asian Amer-ican man who were at the time the focal participants in the study)—first with my dissertation committee, then for an article for *Kairos* that I wrote in 2016, and also for academic conferences presentations and job talks I gave in 2016 and 2017—helped me solidify my approach to narrating experiences and interactions in the dissertation and, eventually, the book. Specifically, the videos helped me identify and account for interactions that came to matter (in both a physical and a semiotic sense) over time and in evolving relations of bodies, understandings, technologies, and things. The videos also helped me explain the makerspace to academic audiences, many of whom were unfamiliar with makerspaces. For example, in my dissertation prospectus defense in early 2016, I shared a video I had recorded and edited in late 2015 of a white man makerspace cofounder operating the laser cutter and using his fingertips to flatten a warped piece of plywood on the cutting bed as the machine was cutting it. Most of my dissertation committee members had not visited a makerspace or interacted with a laser cutter, so the video was a way of inviting them into that experience and further contextualizing my written content. But it became much more than that in our conversation about what happened in that video and how and why I had recorded and selected that specific moment.

I realized that I was struck not only by the risky move itself (it is dangerous for human fingers to be near a laser beam), but also by the reactions to it, including my own, which the camera's positioning recorded. The fact that I knew enough about the laser cutter by that point to know the action was dangerous signified how my understanding of the technologies in the space had grown over that first year in the makerspace. And the fact that the camera, which was mounted on my forehead with a strap, follows my own gaze and stays trained on the laser cutter scene—rather than looking to the group of maker colleagues a few feet away in anticipation of an intervention—signified how my understanding of the people and relationships in the space had grown. I knew that this person's ethos in the space meant that no one would stop him from bending a safety protocol, and I simply carried on with the interview/observation (albeit with some awkward nervous laughter). That video recording—contextualized with my verbal and textual explanations—became an important way for me to situate both the makerspace and my relationship as a researcher for academic audiences. I shared that video in my *Kairos* article, in my research presentations on the academic job market, and eventually in the methods chapter of my book, because it paradoxically both mitigated and reinforced the "newness" and unfamiliarity of bodies, technologies, and relationships in the makerspace.

Navigating Technosolutionism in Research and Academic Processes

As I went on the 2016–2017 academic job market and then submitted a book prospectus and draft in 2018, the digital videos and photography in my project also took on another function: making me and my work marketable in digital rhetorics and technical communication spaces. As Amy Goodburn, Donna LeCourt, and Carrie Leverenz have observed, the rhetoric and composition academic job market is not exempt from the "narrowness and elitism" that often characterizes academic disciplines (xii), in that procuring an academic job in rhetoric and composition is often privileged over seeking work outside academia, and in that research-focused academic jobs are often privileged over teaching-focused jobs—despite the fact that there are fewer academic jobs than there are graduates, and that there are fewer research-focused jobs than teaching-focused jobs. In other words, capitalist market forces are at the heart of the academic job market. And as historian Ibram X. Kendi has argued, capitalism is inextricably bound up with and dependent on racism, from the foundational role of slavery to the continuing exploitation, criminalization, and disenfranchisement of Black, Indigenous, and people of color. While my use of digital photos and videos and my focus on digital fabrication technologies responded to demand in the areas of digital rhetorics and technical communication, my whiteness—my white body, my white English, my white habitus—afforded me entrée and ease, first in the academic job market, and then in the academic book publishing market.

At the time, I was more attuned to my sense of precarity first as a job seeker and then as a book contract seeker than I was to my privileges and advantages—much in the way that I was more attuned to my sense of discomfort from my gender and skills difference in the makerspace than I was to the ways my whiteness mitigated that discomfort. This allowed the two strands I introduced in the previous section to remain more separate in my conscience and practice than they should have been:

1. Privileging relatively recent digital technologies in the maker movement and in academic spaces, and
2. Using digital tools as a technique for storytelling and locating the embodied researcher gaze.

In academic job talks and later in my book prospectus, I would in one breath acknowledge the forces of neoliberal, fast capitalism in the maker movement (including technosolutionism, the view that relatively "new" technologies can bring about progress and equity), and in the next breath I would present digital techniques—and specifically "my" approach to interviewing with a body-worn or handheld camera—as a solution to the problem of researcher accountability. In pointing out this tension, I am not suggesting that digital technologies in the maker movement or in writing studies are inherently problematic, but I am acknowledging, as many scholars have before me (Banks *Race*, Haas "Race," Gonzales *Sites*, Selfe and Selfe, Sun) that technologies are culturally situated, and they must be accounted for as such both in the subjects and the means of my work.

From the early days of my project, I encountered and was instructed by critical engagements with technosolutionism and technological utopianism in the maker movement. Human-computer interaction scholars Silvia Lindtner, Shaowen Bardzell, and Jeffrey Bardzell observe that technosolutionism, which is the belief that "technology can unilaterally solve difficult social problems," is evident in "promotions of making that portray it as furthering sustainability, social justice for women, economic development for the Global South, and empowerment for all" (1390). Additionally, communication scholar Susan Currie Sivek, drawing on the work of Howard Segal and of David Nye, situates the discourses of technological access and empowerment in the contemporary maker movement (as manifested in *MAKE: Magazine*, a central publication of the movement) in a long history in the United States of technological utopianism, or the belief that technologies can bring about progress. Sivek notes that technologies refer to "not only the creation of specific devices and tools, but also their implementation within a society (re)structured 'on the model of a giant machine' (Segal, 2005, p. 103), under the control of rational, scientifically grounded (and, ultimately, elite) systems of governance" (189). Sivek connects this orientation to technologies with U.S. nationalism and manifest destiny, drawing on Nye's work: "people enter a new region, transform it using new technologies, and achieve prosperity, which attracts new settlers. This community builds wealth, and in the process, witnesses the disappearance of the original landscape and its replacement by a 'second creation shaped by the new technology' ([Nye] p. 13)" in continuing cycles of expansion (190). Sivek concludes that *MAKE: Magazine*'s creators

> likely have the best of intentions in crafting its content and are benefitting from the success of the branding strategies necessitated by today's capitalist media system. However, a critical perspective on the magazine and [Maker] Faire reveals the insufficiency of our culture's dominant narratives about technology [to meaningfully address social and ecological problems], and the need for journalism in magazines and elsewhere that provides alternative ways of thinking. (207)

While these articulations of technosolutionism in the maker movement were foundational to my orientation to the maker movement, I have also learned from former makerspace cofounder Clarissa San Diego to recognize that they are, to return to Suchman's words, located perspectives—specifically, they are located in academic perspectives. (This is not to suggest that people outside academia have not also described technosolutionism in the maker movement, but rather, to acknowledge that I sought and learned first from academic perspectives.) As I describe in my book and in our coauthored article, San Diego's praxis—as an original cofounder of the makerspace I studied and, later, as the founder and CEO of a technology agency that promoted the work of BIPOC, women, and LGBTQIA+ makers—profoundly transformed and nuanced my understanding of makers and technologies. My study began with a good/bad binary understanding of technosolutionism and capitalism in the maker movement, but one of the many things I learned from San Diego was to recognize the contributions of BIPOCs like her who dwell in the in-between (rather than the good/bad binary I brought to the project) by leveraging and redirecting corporate structures to benefit underrepresented communities and by actively and meaningfully working against the bifurcation of "business" and "community." As a result of learning from and working with San Diego, I changed the scope of my study in 2017 to include her maker technology agency alongside (and as a counter-narrative to) the makerspace she had founded (and left) that was the initial primary site of my study. In other words, while technosolutionism can be a useful frame for understanding the practices of a white male-dominated movement, it can also erase the work of BIPOC makers in and beyond the maker movement when it over-generalizes about the motives and backgrounds of makers. I needed to change both my orientation to and the scope of my study to enact a more careful approach.

And while technosolutionism is easy for academics like me to observe in the maker movement, it is certainly not unique to the maker movement. As CDA scholar Theo Van Leeuwen observes, "Contemporary corporate discourse is replete with positive self-affirmation, relentless optimism, and unquestioned belief in progress, and this kind of discourse increasingly infects other fields as well," including academic disciplines and the field of multimodality, which "tends toward a celebratory view of multimodality, as a tool for the design of effective communication" (5). In highlighting a critique of uncritical celebration of multimodality, I want to be careful to specify whose multimodality is in question here: I am referring to my own practice, as a white, abled-bodied researcher, of digital video and photo techniques situated in white-dominated conversations about video and ethnography and about 3D rhetorics.

The uncritical celebration of white practices of multimodality in my own work and in our field is also connected to the marginalization and erasure of the contributions and practices of BIPOC communities. As Victor Del Hierro points out, for example, Hip-Hop culture has been absent from technical and professional communication conversations, despite its global reach and use of "the same principles that technical and professional communication would identify as the user-localization (Sun, 2012) of digital and communicative technologies." Furthermore, I have learned from Laura Gonzales—both from her example and her scholarship—that celebrations of multimodality, and particularly the affordances of video, need to be accompanied by making the content accessible in ways that honor the relations of disability studies perspectives on interdependence and Critical Race Theory perspectives on Crenshaw's theory of intersectionality ("Designing").

Even as I continue to learn to engage more carefully, I have benefited materially from my engagement with digital technologies in the maker movement and from my engagement with digital technologies in writing studies research, even though (or perhaps especially because) those two strands were in tension. In 2017, I accepted a tenure-track job offer at a research-focused institution. My engagement with digital technologies had been central to my candidacy (including my job talk), and my white habitus and body undoubtedly made it easy for me—and my engagement with digital technologies—to be viewed as "competent" and "cutting edge" by white academic standards. That job came with a salary, research start-up funds, and yearly travel funds that enabled me to upgrade my digital tools (as I describe in my *enculturation* article, "Making Knowledge: A Kit for Researching 3D Rhetorics") and to continue my longitudinal project by making regular trips back to Seattle. One such trip, for the September 2017 Seattle Mini Maker Faire, served as the focal point of the *enculturation* article, in which I document how I use a variety of digital recording technologies, including the smartphone and GoPro that were staples from the beginning when I was a graduate student, as well as a 360 camera and an upgraded DSLR camera that I acquired with startup funds as an assistant professor.

In addition to material support for my research, dedicated research time, including a first-year course release in 2017, gave me time to expand my dissertation into a book and prepare it for submission. In 2018, I submitted a book prospectus and draft manuscript to the University of Michigan Press Sweetland Digital Rhetoric Collaborative Series' book prize competition, and while I was not selected for the prize, I was invited to use the editorial board's feedback to prepare a manuscript that the press would send out for peer review without an advance contract. Digital videos and photos, as well as visualizations, were (not surprisingly, given the nature of the series) central to my prospectus and my book's candidacy for the series.

But I was more attuned to my sense of precarity without a commitment from the press than I was to what I now recognize as the first of a series of privileged opportunities to get my foot in the door in the difficult process of publishing a first book, and then to stay in that process despite split peer reviews. I was again given the benefit of the doubt in early 2019, when split peer reviews led to a revise and resubmit decision, despite one reviewer's assessment that the book was not ready for publication and even though the series and press had no contractual obligations to me. My use of digital video and photo was not questioned by either reviewer, and upon reflection, I recognize that while including my voice and hands in the videos was an intentional methodological choice to locate my embodiment as a researcher, it also meant that during the review process, my embodied privileges were inextricably woven into the reviewers' experience of that content.

Later that year, when the reviews came back for my revised and resubmitted manuscript—one from the skeptical reviewer in the first round and one from a new, third reviewer—they were once again split (though, again, unanimously approving of the digital components), with the formerly skeptical reviewer now approving of the manuscript, and the third reviewer expressing concerns about my critique of new materialism and my use of narrative-driven, rather than thematic- and code-driven, analysis and data presentation. However, the third reviewer also acknowledged their positionality as a third reader in a second round of review and ultimately deferred to the editors to oversee revisions instead of insisting on another round of review. The editors, in turn, invited me to write a revision plan that they would forward, along with a recommendation from the series to the editorial board of the University of Michigan Press for consideration for a contract.

I was awarded a contract in January 2020, and after I completed revisions that incorporated reviewer, editor, and editorial board feedback and prepared my text and digital components for the press' specifications that spring, my book went into production that summer, with a scheduled release date in June 2021. And because this publishing timeline coincided with my third-year review, I was encouraged by my department to begin preparing for an early tenure bid, despite the economic uncertainties from COVID-19 that had by that point led to a near-universal pay cut program at my institution and the loss of many non-tenure-track and staff jobs. Again, my point in tracing the intersections of technosolutionism and my white privilege in my engagement with digital technologies is not to suggest that technologies cannot do useful work in the maker movement or in digital rhetorics research. Rather, my point is to attend to the ways my whiteness and multiply privileged identities are inextricably bound up with how I engage digital technologies and how, in turn, my work is received and rewarded.

Learning Relationality in Research and Publishing

In the previous two sections, I have described the ways I have benefitted from my engagement with digital technologies as both the subject and the means of a five-year project, even though I was not as critically aware of the interplay of those two strands as I should have been. In sharing and critically analyzing my experiences with digital research as a multiply privileged white person, I have attempted to locate and examine often-unacknowledged white supremacist discourses of meritocracy and of technosolutionism that circulate through and imbue early career research processes. By locating and examining privileged discourses, practices, and material effects in my experiences, I aim to create a little more space to resist and redress the ways I and others like me benefit from white, ableist, heterosexism in academia, to the exclusion and harm of others, in our engagement with research and technologies.

I also aim to participate in the work Natasha Jones and Miriam Williams have called us to do in imagining a more just future, which begins with naming and refusing racist systems:

> A just use of imagination recognizes that redress and remedy must follow behind a refusal to adhere to the confines and constraints of the status quo and this requires an acknowledgement that oppressive systems and institutions are indeed not broken or faulty, rather that they are working purposefully as designed—in support of white supremacist and racist ideas and ideals.

Crucially, Jones and Williams also emphasize that imagination is "not just conceptual" but must be enacted with a goal of transformation. Following are some example action takeaways from my experience:

- **In my ongoing engagement with digital technologies in research:** I must resist the temptation to invent or discover (read: to Columbus) a digital method or technology for the sake of having something to market myself and my work as "cutting edge." Following the wisdom of Angela Haas, whose words begin this chapter, I can orient myself to technology as the relations and interworkings of bodies and things, which reminds me to prioritize being accountable to and in responsible relationship with research participants, communities, and fellow researchers.

- **In my advising and evaluating others as a mentor and colleague:** I must resist the temptation to uncritically use my specific early career research experiences with digital technologies as a benchmark or model for others—such as people I mentor or, one day, make hiring or tenure and promotion decisions about—because without accounting for the ease and opportunity afforded to me by my positionality, privilege, and power, I perpetuate harmful assumptions that everyone experiences academic systems and digital technologies the way a white, cis, abled-bodied person (for whom those systems and technologies were designed) experiences them.

- **In my editorial roles:** I must acknowledge and redress bias in review processes, both in my work as a reviewer and in my work as an editor or associate editor. Specifically, I must resist the impulse to privilege technologies or techniques just because they are "new" or associated with dominant industry or academic practices. I must also recognize and intervene when the embodied privilege of a researcher and/or research topic affords them an opportunity or benefit of the doubt that is not extended to marginalized researchers and communities.

Furthermore, the critical analysis in this chapter must also function as part of continual, coalitional imagination and action in all aspects of my relationships and practices—not just in what I write for publication—to justly remake the way we relate, teach, and do research with digital methods. Therefore, in this final section, I acknowledge the labor and contributions of BIPOC women whose work, actions, and relationships have taught me to engage technologies more relationally and to dwell more carefully in the interplay of those two strands (the subject and the means) of my work. I do not mean to suggest that I have achieved any sort of pure state of insight or morality, but rather, that my critical journey is ongoing (and lifelong) and is indebted to the labor and patience of BIPOC women. Rather than relegate this recognition to an acknowledgments section or, worse, take individual credit for my journey, I take up Jones' call for coalitional work by concluding this chapter with the insights of the BIPOC women from whom I have learned.

From Jones' work and praxis, I have learned to situate myself more critically in relation to narrative traditions, including the ways I talk about and use digital technologies. Jones's decolonial approach to narrative inquiry, which she emphasizes is "concurrently a methodology, perspective, and practice" (520), has taught me to acknowledge and cite narrative traditions beyond relatively recent, white, Western approaches and to avoid an individualistic re-centering of my experiences (which also feeds myths of meritocracy) by instead contextualizing myself and my practices in relation to bodies, systems, traditions, and things. This includes not only the subjects of my research and teaching, but also the means of my work—including and especially how I navigate professional structures like writing a dissertation, going on the academic job market, preparing a book for publication, and preparing a tenure case. And I continue to learn from Angela Haas' words that begin this chapter, "technology is not just what does the work, it is the work—and that work relies on an ongoing relationship between bodies and things" ("Wampum" 291). At first, I applied my understanding of those words to the subject of my research, digital fabrication technologies in a makerspace, while allowing my own use of digital technologies in my research methods to stand as a neutral "accountability measure" for describing my researcher embodiment. I am still learning to apply her words more critically to my engagement with digital technologies, particularly in the ways I have benefitted professionally and materially from them.

Furthermore, as I have described above, Clarissa San Diego's praxis profoundly remediated my orientation to maker technologies by teaching me a more nuanced approach to critiquing technosolutionism in the practices of a white man-dominated movement, while also recognizing and amplifying the work of BIPOC makers. And as I describe in my book, her relational approach to making—building relationships among people, technologies, communities, and things—equally profoundly shaped how I came to theorize, teach, and practice making myself. Likewise, Laura Gonzales continues to teach me—in her scholarship, in her wise feedback on countless iterations of my work, and in her leadership—to honor and amplify the work of BIPOC makers and scholars not just in my research and publishing, but also in my mentoring and relationships. As I continue to learn from the coalition of BIPOC women she assembled for a Kapor Center-funded initiative, it is vitally important to build "technological innovation with (rather than just for or about) historically, structurally, and systematically marginalized and underrepresented communities," because "technological innovation, when it is made and developed through reciprocal mentorship networks, can disrupt a chain of signifiers of a privileged structure and create makerspaces for and with community knowledge and information" (Poudyal et al. 1–2). This is equally true for technological innovations in digital writing and rhetoric research. To imagine and enact a more just future for digital writing and rhetoric research, I can and must disrupt privileged structures—including my own participation in and benefitting from them—and center marginalized perspectives in coalitional work that, as Jones advocates, recognizes the collective over the individualistic.

Works Cited

Alvarez, Steven. "Rhetorical Autoethnography: Delinking English Language Learning in a Family Oral History." *Rhetorics Elsewhere and Otherwise: Contested Modernities, Decolonial Visions*, edited by Romeo Garcia and Damián Baca. National Council of Teachers of English, 2019, pp. 85–111.

Banks, Adam J. *Race, Rhetoric, and Technology: Searching for Higher Ground*. National Council of Teachers of English, 2006.

———. *Digital Griots: African American Rhetoric in a Multimedia Age*. Southern Illinois UP, 2011.

Banks-Wallace, JoAnne. "Talk that Talk: Storytelling and Analysis Rooted in African American Oral Tradition." *Qualitative Health Research*, vol. 12, no. 3, 2002, pp. 410–26.

Chachra, Debbie. "Why I Am Not A Maker." *The Atlantic*, 17 Oct. 2015, http://www.theatlantic.com/technology/archive/2015/01/why-i-am-not-a-maker/384767/.

Connelly, F. Michael, and Jean D. Clandinin. "Narrative Inquiry." *Handbook of Complementary Methods in Education Research*, edited by Judith L. Green, Gregory Camilli, and Patricia B. Elmore, Lawrence Erlbaum, 2006, pp. 375–85.

Crenshaw, Kimberlé. "Demarginalizing the Intersection of Race and Sex: A Black Feminist Critique of Antidiscrimination Doctrine, Feminist Theory and Antiracist Politics." *University of Chicago Legal Forum*, vol. 1, 1989, pp. 139–67.

———. "The Urgency of Intersectionality." *TEDWomen*, Oct. 2016, https://www.ted.com/talks/kimberle_crenshaw_the_urgency_of_intersectionality.

Del Hierro, Victor. "DJs, Playlists, and Community: Imagining Communication Design through Hip Hop." *Communication Design Quarterly*, vol. 7, no. 2, 2018, pp. 1–12, https://doi.org/10.1145/3358931.3358936.

Fox, Sarah, Rachel Rose Ulgado, and Daniela K. Rosner. "Hacking Culture, Not Devices: Access and Recognition in Feminist Hackerspaces." *Proc. of CSCW '15*. Association of Computing Machinery, Mar. 2015, pp. 56–68.

Goodburn, Amy, Donna LeCourt, and Carrie Leverenz, editors. *Rewriting Success in Rhetoric and Composition Careers*. Parlor Press, 2013.

Gonzales, Laura. "Multimodality, Translingualism, and Rhetorical Genre Studies." *Composition Forum*, vol. 31, 2015, https://compositionforum.com/issue/31/multimodality.php.

———. *Sites of Translation: What We Can Learn from Multilinguals about Writing, Rhetoric, and Technology*. University of Michigan Press, 2018.

———. "Designing for Intersectional, Interdependent Accessibility: A Case Study of Multilingual Technical Content." *Communication Design Quarterly*, vol. 6, no. 4, 2018, pp. 34–45.

Haas, Angela M. "Wampum as Hypertext: An American Indian Intellectual Tradition of Multimedia Theory and Practice." *Studies in American Indian Literatures*, vol. 19, no. 4, 2007, pp. 77–100.

———. "Race, Rhetoric, and Technology: A Case Study of Decolonial Technical Communication Theory, Methodology, and Pedagogy." *Journal of Business and Technical Communication*, vol. 26, no. 3, 2012, pp. 277–310.

Hackster.io. *Hackster.io Maker Survey*, 2016, https://www.hackster.io/survey.

Hatch, Mark. *The Maker Movement Manifesto: Rules for Innovation in the New World of Crafters, Hackers, and Tinkerers*. McGraw Hill, 2014.

Hawisher, Gail, Cynthia L. Selfe, Patrick Berry, and Synne Skjulstad. "Conclusion: Closing Thoughts on Research Methodology." *Transnational Literate Lives in Digital Times*, edited by Patrick Berry, Gail E. Hawisher, and Cynthia L. Selfe,

Computers and Composition Digital Press, 2012, https://ccdigitalpress.org/book/transnational/.

Jones, Natasha N. "Coalitional Learning in the Contact Zones: Inclusion and Narrative Inquiry in Technical Communication and Composition Studies." *College English*, vol. 82, no. 5, 2020, pp. 515–26.

Jones, Natasha N. and Miriam F. Williams. "The Just Use of Imagination: A Call to Action." *Association of Teachers of Technical Writing List Serv*, 10 June 2020, https://attw.org/blog/the-just-use-of-imagination-a-call-to-action/.

Jones, Natasha N., Kristen R. Moore, and Rebecca Walton. "Disrupting the Past to Disrupt the Future: An Antenarrative of Technical Communication." *Technical Communication Quarterly*, vol. 25, no. 4, 2016, pp. 211–29.

Kendi, Ibram X. *How to Be an Antiracist*. One World, 2019.

Lindtner, Silvia, Shaowen Bardzell, and Jeffrey Bardzell. "Reconstituting the Utopian Vision of Making: HCI after Technosolutionism." *Proceedings of the 2016 CHI Conference on Human Factors in Computing Systems*. Association of Computing Machinery, May 2016, pp. 1390–1402.

Maker Media. "Fact Sheet," *Maker Media*, 2015, http://makermedia.com/press/fact-sheet/ .

McKee, Heidi, and Dànielle DeVoss, editors. *Digital Writing Research: Technologies, Methodologies, and Ethical Issues*. Hampton Press, 2007.

Nye, David E. *America as Second Creation: Technology and Narratives of New Beginnings*. MIT Press, 2004.

Patel, Leigh. *Decolonizing Education Research: From Ownership to Answerability*. Routledge, 2015.

Pennington, Julie L., and Cynthia H. Brock. "Constructing Critical Autoethnographic Narratives with White Educators." *International Journal of Qualitative Studies in Education*, 2011, pp. 225–50, https://doi.org/10.1080/09518398.2010.529843.

Pink, Sarah. *Doing Sensory Ethnography*. Sage Publications, 2015.

Poudyal, Bibhushana, Tetyana Zhyvotovska, Estefania Castillo, Nora Rivera, Ann Shivers-McNair, Joy Robinson, and Laura Gonzales. "Interrogating What We Mean by 'Making': Stories from Women Who Make in Community." *Re-making the Library Makerspace: Critical Theories, Reflections, and Practices*, edited by Maggie Melo and Jennifer Nichols, Litwin Books, 2020.

Ríos, Gabriela Raquel. "Cultivating Land-Based Literacies and Rhetorics." *Literacy in Composition Studies*, vol. 3, no. 1, 2015, pp. 60–70.

Segal, Howard P. *Technological Utopianism in American Culture*. Syracuse UP, 2005.

Selfe, Cynthia L., and Richard Selfe. "The Politics of the Interface: Power and its Exercise in Electronic Contact Zones." *College Composition and Communication*, vol. 45, no. 4, 1994, pp. 480–504.

Sheridan, David. "Fabricating Consent: Three-Dimensional Objects as Rhetorical Compositions." *Computers and Composition*, vol. 27, 2010, pp. 249–65.

Shivers-McNair, Ann, and Clarissa San Diego. "Localizing Communities, Goals, Communication, and Inclusion: A Collaborative Approach." *Technical Communication*, vol. 64, no. 2, 2017, pp. 97–112.

Shivers-McNair, Ann. "3D Interviewing with Researcher POV Video: Bodies and Knowledge in the Making." *Kairos: A Journal of Rhetoric, Technology, and Pedagogy*, vol. 21, no. 2, 2017, http://praxis.technorhetoric.net/tiki-index.php?page=PraxisWiki%3A_%3A3D+Interviewing.

———. "Making Knowledge: A Kit for Researching 3D Rhetorics." *enculturation*, vol. 29, 2019, http://enculturation.net/3D_rhetorics.

———. *Beyond the Makerspace: Makers and Relational Rhetorics*. University of Michigan Press, 2021, https://www.fulcrum.org/concern/monographs/3197xn981.

Sivek, Susan Currie. "'We Need a Showing of All Hands': Technological Utopianism in MAKE Magazine." *Journal of Communication Inquiry*, vol. 35, no. 3, 2011, pp. 187–209.

Smith, Linda Tuhiwai. *Decolonizing Methodologies: Research and Indigenous Peoples*. Zed Books Ltd, 2013.

Somerville, Margaret. *Water in a Dry Land: Place-Learning through Art and Story*. Routledge, 2013.

Suchman, Lucy. "Located Accountabilities in Technology Production." *Scandinavian Journal of Information Systems*, vol. 14, no. 2, 2002, pp. 91–105.

Sun, Huatong. *Cross-Cultural Technology Design: Creating Culture-Sensitive Technology for Local Users*. Oxford UP, 2012.

van Dijk, Teun A. *Racism in the Press*. Arnold, 1989.

van Leeuwen, Theo. "Critical Analysis of Multimodal Discourse." *The Encyclopedia of Applied Linguistics*, edited by Carol A. Chapelle, Blackwell/Wiley, 2013, pp. 1–6.

Wilson, Shawn. *Research Is Ceremony: Indigenous Research Methods*. Fernwood Publishing, 2008.

Wodak, Ruth. "What CDA Is About—A Summary of Its History, Important Concepts and Its Development." *Methods of Critical Discourse Analysis*, edited by Ruth Wodak and Michael Meyer, Sage, 2001, pp. 1–13.

Chapter 2. Flipping the Table and Redefining the Dissertation Genre with a Digital Chapter

Temptaous Mckoy

BOWIE STATE UNIVERSITY

I remember the moment I decided to do a digital chapter. First of all, I was swamped trying to figure out how in the world would I complete my dissertation in time? I was having a meeting with my dissertation chair, at the time, at the local Starbucks about what I wanted the dissertation overall to focus on. I knew one of my chapters would focus on embodied rhetorical practices (Mckoy, 2019) at TRAP Karaoke, reviewing #Tees4TheTrap, and I knew simply writing about these practices would not be enough. We talked a bit about our best course of action, then it hit me, "What if I did a digital/video chapter instead of writing it?" I asked. My dissertation chair looked at me, turned their head, and shook it to affirm that we were indeed on to something. I knew I would need to produce a work that was far more visual as it would better showcase the rhetorical practices I would identify and found myself relying on in my analysis. I also knew I wanted to put my voice over and editing skills to use. Thus, birthing the idea to do a digital chapter as a part of my dissertation, and not as a supplemental piece to my completely written dissertation.

Now that I've finally completed my dissertation and two years on the tenure track as an Assistant Professor, I've been able to better reflect on and seek to answer the questions regarding my process and how I completed the chapter. What went into it? How did I complete it? What was the recipe used to create such sauce—the digital chapter? While I am grateful for these questions and the continued want by colleagues and other scholars to learn from my process, I've come to realize so much of the process was innate for me. Well, not necessarily innate, but more so a process that came from my various experiences inside and outside of my formal scholar training. Radio production, social media management, and establishing networks were some of the tools that were most pivotal to my chapter's production that I learned outside of the academy and long before I began my Ph.D. studies career. My life experiences and lessons were not and are not necessarily tied directly to my academic experience(s) and career. Yet, I learned to implement these tools when it came time to produce the digital chapter. However, I still see there exists a process that I used to complete the chapter, and it is important that I take the additional space to unpack some of those processes and what I've learned from them myself. In unpacking a bit of my methods, I also offer a bit of a personal assessment for other students to follow when taking on non-conventional methods of knowledge-making practices.

When I initially considered composing this chapter, I wanted to solely focus on what it is I did—action items. In a way, offer a step-by-step guide to my audience on how they too could finesse their way into curating a digital chapter. More specifically, I wanted to speak only to graduate students, as I always have an investment in how we support the work of graduate students. But in my planning stage, I realized can't nobody do what Temp does. I got my own set of skills that's been bestowed upon me and really, ain't no way I could provide a step-by-step manual of sorts on how I curated the digital chapter. I also realized that graduate student Temp had access to so many other resources (financial, emotional, social) at my reach, and it is critical I acknowledge my own set of privileges in that. However, what I can do is speak to how I used methods that included so much of myself that they felt all too naturelle. This is what I want to inspire other scholars to do. While I am speaking more to graduate students and/or early career scholars in this piece, I think there is space for everyone to learn here. Especially for those that hope to mentor scholars who plan to take on nontraditional forms of publications and scholarship. I want scholars to dig into their "tool kit" and think of the skills they already working with and what they can offer to those around them—including the academy.

In this chapter, I move to unpack three key areas of focus that went into the development of my digital chapter. First, I will provide a working definition for digital methods to offer a better contextual understanding of my approach to my dissertation project. Next, I will detail the importance of identifying one's current skill set and its limitations. As scholars move to produce non-traditional scholarship, understanding their own positionality in the grand scheme of things can offer a way of understanding how to move forward effectively and efficiently. I partner this area close to my working definition for digital methods because my definition is rooted so much more in the understanding of one's knowledge that may have been obtained outside of the academic space. Furthermore, this move of identification is also one of self-advocacy. One does not advocate for the use of non-traditional methods or going against the status quo without first understanding the barriers they gone run up against. Then, I will speak more specifically to my methods for completion of the digital chapter, which I earlier identified as innate. In doing so, I hope that scholars can see how their own experiences and life lessons can be made more apparent in their own studies and approaches.

In using my methods as a point for entry and analysis, I also somewhat offer a behind the scenes look into the existential labor that went into completing the digital chapter. This area will also offer examples of unforeseen circumstances that arose during my process which can arise for anyone. Also, to stay in line with digital scholarship, I will include a digital supplemental resource, my digital chapter's bloopers. Finally, I will move to conversations about general execution and how these methods can contribute to making our field more inclusive. As this chapter focuses more so on lived experiences and a fairly new style of scholarship, the citation practices may in fact be limited. However, I will ensure the chapter highlights some of the key pioneers (Carson; Ball; Smith; Banks) that have laid the foundation to produce digital and non-traditional scholarship. Furthermore, if you ain't picked up on it yet, I will rhetorically reject Standard American English throughout this piece. I use this rhetorical move, as I did in my dissertation and other scholarship, to highlight key areas for emphasis, but also to show my true self. Codemeshin' is one of the very astute ways I showcase who I am as a scholar and a Black woman. So yea, these forms of be, is, y'alls, and many others is damn intentional.

Ok, So What Is/Was This Digital Chapter?

So, you tellin' me that you don't know about the *#IssaTrapDissertation* digital chapter?! I mean if not, it's cool. I promise I ain't judging. First, my digital chapter is available via East Carolina University's dissertation database. They call it "The ScholarShip; East Carolina University's Institutional Repository." While I have considered placing the chapter on my professional site, I understand that there may be a time when I wish to change my site's name or something of that sort. So, I see it as best I leave the chapter hosted on the university's server—that I ain't gotta pay for. If you haven't seen the digital chapter, you are able to download the chapter from the repository and watch at your leisure. I promise it is mad entertaining and educational.

But check, the digital chapter was curated to showcase my theory, Amplification Rhetorics (AR) in action at a TRAP Karaoke. The event serves as a space for Black individuals to come together and celebrate all the greatness that is Black. On their social media sites, TRAP Karaoke describes their events as being like going to church and hearing "Back that Ass Up."[1] In the digital chapter, I highlight AR as identified in trap music, in addition to the showcasing of #Tees4TheTrap. I felt it was best that I produced a digital chapter for my dissertation because I did not think it would be possible to highlight the various Black rhetorical practices as seen and showcased at TRAP Karaoke with only traditional written composition.

I conducted interviews, captured audience interaction, and broke down the lyrics as heard in trap music. By simply writing these ideas and discoveries, I feel I would have dismissed the authenticity of the TRAP Karaoke space andddd, I wanted to be sure that the voices of those I interviewed were heard loud and clear. I ain't want to misinterpret what they said, nor attempt to identify the best practice to place their responses in SAE format. In other words, folks was talkin' how they wanted to talk and I wanted to be sure I captured that essence. 'Cause what we not fixin' to do is bad transcriptions of my people sharing their narratives, only for their areas of emphasis to be excluded and overlooked. This approach to dissertation publication, in the digital, is one of the many ways I hope we can enact change in not just the field of technical communication, but academia overall.

---

1. . . . Takin over for the 99 and the 2000 . . .

Why Digital Publishing?

Also, as you move forward in this chapter, you will see the primary focus here be on digital methods, yet I want to take a moment to focus specifically on digital publication. To begin, the term "publish" can be loaded and defined in several different ways. Due to the scope of this chapter, I wouldn't necessarily really be able to unpack such tangled terminology, however, I do think it important to discuss the distinction between digital methods and digital publication. I understand that there can be some overlap in the terminologies, but we must acknowledge digital publishing as a tool to change academia overall. I mean if we being all the way 100, digital publication is what has brought to light many of the injustices faced by Black individuals at the hands of police. How? 'Cause the evidence of reckless police behavior was captured and published across various social media sites, making the videos go viral. Now, I identify digital publishing as works produced with the intent of being shared through virtual sites and/or composed using technological tools. Digital publishing is not simply the taking of an article and placing it on a website, it is the interaction of digital processes and technologies, in tandem with traditional composition practices. Thus, leading to the publication of a work which we can identify as digital. In implementing digital publications into more of our academic composition practices, this can lead to the "creation of new formats made possible by digital technologies, ultimately allowing scholars to work in deeply integrated electronic research and publishing environments that will enable real-time dissemination, collaboration, dynamically-updated content, and usage of new media" (Brown et al. para. 6). This type of publishing is to include composition practices as showcased on social media websites, such as Twitter, all the way to multi-modal journal publications. Yet, before one can even jump to do some digital publishing, they gots to stop and understand digital methods.

Advocacy for Digital Methods and Assessing Your Skill Set

While assessing one's skill set, there is a reflective moment of what does it mean to really implement digital methods. So before we get too far, imma offer y'all my working understanding of digital methods. *Digital Methods* are processes, or a process, for moving to create knowledge and gain access to result(s) through a variation of two (or more) virtual communicative spaces. These means include, but are not limited to social media, technological software adaptations, virtual professional networks, virtual stores or commerce, and video and audio platforms. I came to create this definition based on my lived experiences and exposures. From being a member of the academy, but also navigating the world of radio production, I've learned that there are various ways to enact digital methods.

Look, I understand that my working definition is thick as hell, it is crucial to recognize its formation. So I wish to break down the definition a bit more.

Defining Digital Methods

First, digital methods *"are processes, or a process, for moving to create knowledge and gain access to result(s) . . ."* We think of research methods in a way that should only garner specific results or answers and not actually a way of *creating* insight. Just ask yourself, what if we considered the method the *result*? Much like Sarah J. Tracy, I believe that we enact research methods in our day-to-day life. As she mentions, "We ask questions, listen to stories, watch others, participate in meetings" (2) and much more. Given in her text she explicitly refers to qualitative research, I think her sentiments ring true for quantitative and mixed methods. Employing digital methods could also be considered one variation of a multimethod approach (Brewer and Hunter xiv) to research. This is where we see a combination of research methods working "in concert" (xiv), or jointly, with one another. This is different from mixed methods as the varying methods applied remain a part of their own category, per se. Furthermore, digital methods operate in a circle rather than linear in principle.

The choices we make while utilizing digital methods are often time reliant upon the feedback, as in additional digital interaction amongst other people, processes, and interfaces, or potential results that we may foresee. This constant digital interaction comes as a result of living in an update culture—a culture that requires the constant need to "reread, edit, and update texts in digital environment . . ." (Gallagher 32). Digital methods are taken up in virtual spaces that have various external influences that cannot always be mitigated. So we may plan for a+b=c, but as we utilize digital methods, "a+b/3- xy= c" can quickly become our equation. Digital methods must be adaptive and work alongside the other processes and variants as found in the virtual space. If we think of digital methods in their adaptive and ever-changing way, we can better analyze, not just the answers we gain from enacting various processes, but also what we learn while in the midst of doing them, aka, when things go wrong and we gotta change the approach or else we are stuck to be SOL. As the old saying goes, we don't take losses, only lessons. Digital methods, and their usage, are always a lesson. Hence, leading to the ability to create knowledge through our method process and gain access to the questions we seek to answer.

Next, these processes are enacted *"through a variation of two (or more) virtual communicative spaces."* This second potion comes out of the need for interaction between types of individuals/communities/automated systems in different types of virtual spaces. My primary thought for this definition was to suggest this communication would happen through means which were connected exclusively through technology, but then I realized paper and pencil are also a type of technology (Hertz; Wardle and Downs 694; Baron), but that's a conversation for another day. Point is, I am speaking specifically to virtual spaces to draw connections. I've also mentioned two spaces, at a minimum, because we need to recognize that in virtual spaces, we too become a part of the digital. Thus meaning, it is imperative we recognize our role in being a part of the virtual spaces' formation. You are the user of a digital interface, on a virtual platform. The real-life *you* ain't your virtual you (Koles and Nagy 5) or VID (virtual identity) (Kokswijk 5).

Our virtual identities are just as important to the use of digital methods because they alter the very way we communicate with other individuals in virtual spaces (Ribeiro 293) and/or utilize digital automated systems that are made available in virtual spaces. On the most basic level, someone that is not outgoing in a face-to-face environment may find themselves being more willing to engage on a broader level in a virtual space. Why does this matter? Because traditional research methods such as interviews and even observations require someone to place themselves, oftentimes physically, in a space to interact with other individuals on a more personal level. Removing the need to interact face to face, as mentioned in this example, in order to complete one variation of a research method can lead to an expansion of individuals and other data points to be included in one's research. In all, digital methods can allow research to take place and garner results for individuals that may be disabled, lacking institutional resources, and support.

While we as scholars and researchers may not peep it off rip, some traditional methods for conducting research can indeed act as barriers to knowledge access. As I will later discuss, conducting research requires resources, money, time, technology, etc. When you do not have the allocated resources to conduct efficient research, not only do you potentially lose the opportunity to broaden your understanding of a specific area, but your field of study also loses the chance to place your research in conversation with others. I'll use myself as an example here: one of the nontraditional methods I later discuss would be the way I used social media and my audio engineering background to develop a social media campaign. If I did not have access to the appropriate type of microphone and editing software, I would not have been able to create a piece of work that I am able to reflect on and be proud of today. From a more traditional standpoint, say you are to interview various participants for your study, which requires time and possibly travel. What happens when you are working full time, in addition to pursuing your Ph.D., and without a car? For many of us, our research methods are built out of our resource availability. This highlights the importance of digital methods serving as a key point for access and creation of knowledge. Advocating for digital methods is work that we still out here havin' to do. Why? I don't damn understand, but luckily, we see the field of TPC looking to nontraditional digital methods to move forward in broadening the way we make knowledge in different communities leading to better acceptance and understandings of new epistemologies.

Advocating for Digital Methods

Now that we done established this working definition, let's go into advocating for digital methods through self-assessment. Now I know it may make more sense for some for me to discuss this call for advocacy at the end, but I am instead bringing it to your attention early because it provides additional context for the research methods I used. Basically, advocacy here is used to understand where you comin' from, what's been done before you, and how you can move forward with the skillset(s) you've identified yourself to have. It's important here that I note I ain't trying to suggest that y'all get up here reinventing the wheel, yet, I am saying understand that there are various companies that specialize in the sale of tires and wheels. There is a foundational principle that is used, then each company works to make their wheel better based on their knowledge and skill set. This is how you should approach digital methods. Digital methods are not a one size fits all approach to scholarship and they require the usage and implementation of the knowledge as possessed by the scholar(s) that so choose to take up digital methods. Scholars such as A.D. Carson, Adam J. Banks, Sidone Smith, and Cheryl Ball have all used and/or made the call for digital methods in our scholarship. There is even the *Kairos* journal, that is dedicated to publishing digital and multimodal scholarship ("About *Kairos*"). The use of digital methods is the key way that we can see an expansion and decentering of university[2] acquired knowledge in academic scholarship.

This decentering leads to an assessment of one's skill set. The first step in assessing your skill set is to ask yourself how far are you willing to go? Completing any type of nontraditional scholarship requires a tenacity that is not always attributed to the same level of traditional scholarship. If that were the case, there would not be a debate concerning if the work completed is nontraditional or not.[3] So before even digging too deep into the tool kit, be reflective in what you 'bout to run up against. Next, it is important that a scholar takes a moment to reflect on what they feel is their most valuable set of knowledge that they can lean on when utilizing digital methods. And to be clear, I am speaking on, again, the knowledge that is not necessarily attached to an institutional or higher education place. The place is the physical, while space is what you curate that physical place to be. For myself, this meant leaning on my experience navigating social media, which I obtained through my lived experience as a Millennial attached to her phone, in an effort to connect with fellow researchers and members of the Black community that was most interested in trap music. This also meant utilizing the skills I obtained at my Historically Black College/University (HBCU), such as networking, relationship building, and marketing—which I did not learn in the classroom, but rather as I served a part of other organizations on campus.

---

2. To be clear, in this context I mean the institutional university. You know the formal higher education joint. We not talking about decentering the university of life. In fact, we are moving to center lived epistemologies.

3. I very well believe the work I am speaking to in this chapter, digital methods, should be much more widely received and accepted. However, I think it is important to acknowledge that utilizing digital methods does include additional labor that we may not find in traditional research methods, as will be discussed. To be clear, this is not me saying traditional research methods are not labor-intensive . . . just not on the same level as digital methods, in my opinion.

Understanding your own value and what you bring to your scholarship is one of the most powerful tools that I believe many early scholars overlook. We are trained to believe that things must go a certain way. Be completed a certain way. Yet, in the process of attempting to adopt practices that very well may not fit with our own identities, we also risk losing what makes us great as researchers, scholars, and teachers. This further amplifies why it is important that we see digital methods as a part of the conversation on research methods and not always one that is separate. Finally, assessing your toolkit means that you are able to identify what the hell you gon' need help with. It's easy to figure out what you gettin' at, it's even harder to figure out what you don't know. I use this same model when I discuss using one's Blackness to impact the future of higher education, but I believe the difference here is that identifying what you need help with may assist you in identifying the holes in your scholarship, but also where you can draw on outside resources and your fellow allies.

As mentioned, understanding your skill assessment can shift your methods from ordinary to extraordinary, especially when aiming to utilize digital methods in your scholarship. But another harsh reality, it can save you a shit ton of time. Ain't nothin like trying to learn something as you go wasting time, energy, and resources. I mean we all been there where we done tried to do something we knew we weren't familiar with, but we worked to learn how to do it. Yup, that's digital methods for many. Yet, the trick is negotiating when that approach is not worth the trade-off. I will give my own example of this happening below.

#IssaTrapDissertation Methods

While I think there may be a universal understanding of what a "traditional research method" is, I think it is worth slightly unpacking what makes a research method "traditional". In my research, I think of traditional methods as those that are rooted and derived in academic/scholarly practice. They are assumed to be theorized only by extensive frameworks and tend to assume the audience which will receive the information or take part in the methods are one dimensional. Traditional research methods do not always consider how different communities may not only read the results from a study but how other communities may seek to take up and implement said research practices. Now, this is not to say that I believe we should burn all the traditional research practices to the ground, no. Especially considering that I still implemented traditional research methods in my dissertation project, such as surveys, questionnaires, ethnography, archival, etc. (Mckoy 53). Instead, I am saying that it is important to take up nontraditional methods that are far more rhetorical and driven by new ways of learning and understanding the world around us—even when those ways are not our own.

So while the traditional methods all up in my diss were true in offering the insight and knowledge that I needed to complete my analysis, they were not the methods that I used which were based out of the definition I've provided for digital methods or considered non-traditional. The methods I will focus on in the sections comin' up will be 1) the use of social media to engage in a virtual campaign, 2) the implementation of an e-commerce store to forge research funding, and 3) overall network building and growth through the virtual space. While all three of these methods rely on or overlap with one another for their success, they each required different processes to provide and lead to suggested and needed outcomes. As well as offering new ways of understanding how each method can shift the way we conduct research and produce and transfer knowledge.

As you move through this next section, it is my hope and aims that you receive it as if you and I are having a conversation, outside, on the porch—or wherever you like to talk to folks. I offer this approach to sharing the methods I utilized as I wish to draw on the rhetorical power of narratives and storytelling as told by Black women (Baker-Bell; Richardson; Jones) as a means of epistemological practice for understanding digital methods.

#IssaTrapDissertation Virtual Campaign

Now since this chapter is on digital methods, I'm 'bout to jump over breaking down my dissertation and some of the specifics. Yet, if I was on an elevator and someone asked me what my diss was on I would give 'em two key points. First, the use of Amplification Rhetorics (Mckoy 28), a theory I developed, is important to ensure the field of technical and professional communication is more diverse and inclusive. Next, I developed a digital chapter to serve as a part of my dissertation and not as a supplemental text—which in some cases are overlooked and thought to not necessarily be needed in the grand scheme of things to highlight Black rhetorical practices in action. It's that second part there that *really really* matters to the digital methods and the social media campaign, fam.

The use of a social media campaign as a research method was beyond pivotal to not just the digital chapter's creation, but the overall dissertation. I knew using my social media was gone be important out the gate. Mainly 'cause my sites of study, TRAP Karaoke and HBCUs, were heavily on display all through social media, especially TRAP Karaoke. TRAP Karaoke is a user-generated concert experience that gives folks space to be unapologetically Black as fuck (Mckoy 24). They, TRAP Karaoke, came up on social media. It started in New York and became an international phenomenon. I attended a TRAP Karaoke event in Summer 2017, while I was preparing for my comps. I called myself goin' to the event to detach, I ain't think it would become my dissertation project. I decided to focus on the Black rhetorical practices that happen at TRAP Karaoke, such as, performing at TRAP Karaoke, being a crowd participant, and wearing what is referred to as a #Tee4TheTrap. I knew these were elements that would not be effective if only written about, so I was just like "I'm 'bout to do a digital chapter."

In planning for the digital chapter, I knew while it fit into the grand scheme of my dissertation project, it also needed to be able to stand on its own 'cause I made the argument that we need to start reconsidering just who our audience is for our dissertation. The digital chapter was more so #ForTheCulture and members outside of the academy than it was for my dissertation committee. With this in mind, I knew I would want various elements. I wanted the chapter to be entertaining yet informative. And since the chapter would focus on TRAP Karaoke, I had to also provide a lesson in trap music. Essentially, spittin a lil bit of history to help folks better understand why TRAP Karaoke and not Black Karaoke, which I later discussed in the digital chapter with TRAP Karaoke founder, Jason Mowatt. So I thought, "What better way to bridge the gap between my audiences than to reach out to prominent trap musicians T.I. and 2 Chainz." In hindsight, I believe I made this move 'cause I really wanted my digital chapter to be remarkable—initially. But as my project moved on, I realized that in interviewing and including T.I. and 2 Chainz in my project, I would be exemplifying my theory, Amplification Rhetoric, as I would offer the space for these artists to speak to their experiences in the trap music scene, which is heavily influenced by lived experiences, which impact the way people move about and enjoy(ed) TRAP Karaoke.

I completed a social media blitz, recorded a commercial, and did essentially a social media campaign to gain the attention of T.I. and 2 Chainz, all the while sharin' what my work was about to onlookers. T.I. Tuesdays and 2 Chainz Thursday. Every Tuesday and Thursday, we blitzed and bombarded the social media accounts of T.I. and 2 Chainz, in addition to, The Shade Room and TRAP Karaoke's social media pages and profiles. There was folks that were out there learnin' 'bout my work through my social media campaign. People would see threads of comments from my followers tagging my work on the feed of these artists and blog pages, leading people to want to investigate more about who I was. I turned my old blog Instagram account into my "academic" Instagram and used it to leverage my outreach. In addition, I made my personal Instagram account public, providing people the opportunity to see who I really was, away from the academic persona that many may have assumed me to have. Often, we fail to recognize that even as we move between our lives in academia and outside of it, people are only offered certain pieces of who we are and that's ok. Yet, in order to be most effective in my social media campaign, it was important that I displayed my authentic self on various levels. I also developed the hashtag #IssaTrapDissertation and #DrMckoy2019 to thread all my work together across all social media platforms. This resulted in not only my connecting with T.I., 2 Chainz's team said nah, but I was also able to identify research participants and spread additional knowledge about technical communication to those that may not have been most familiar prior to. Digital methods in practice is one way that we can disseminate information to various communities in a way that is quick and coherent. It allows onlookers to see the research process happen in real-time, offering new ways of understanding the context of research as it is presented at a later time.

Securing the Bag

While it may be something we may not generally consider when it comes time to knock out some research, funding can in fact play a major role in our ability to complete research. For my project, I needed to have funding to support travel and equipment needs. While I do not make claims to have a formal training in marketing, I do however know how to come up on a coin. I have had a job since I was 15. So securing the bag has never really been a problem, yet this project required I secured the bag in a different way.

While enrolled in my doctoral program, I decided to wear tee shirts that would display my speaking topic as I traveled for conferences. This way, folks could clearly identify who I was and if they wanted to follow me on to my talk. This was how I branded myself early in the game. Even if people ain't know my name, they would remember having seen a Black woman in an HBCUs Matters shirt. I decided to borrow this same idea of branding and open a store to sell T-shirts to offset the costs for my dissertation. Again, the goal was to mainly help find a way, so I was not having to take the major hit to my pockets in order to get the project done. While I am sure there were other funding opportunities available, I dead ass ain't have time to apply to them. I had less than a year to get my dissertation completed.

The external funding packages/fellowships take mad time to apply for and the money typically does not hit ya pocket immediately. I needed *right now* money to pay for right now expenses. Some of those items included additional camera equipment, travel funds, hotel stay, yes all that. However, what I learned was there are several ways I can support the funds needed for the project. So instead, I decided to go ahead and sell T-shirts. By selling the T-shirts I knew that people would learn what my project was about, but also be willing to spread additional awareness about the project by wearing the shirts. I had already established myself individually from wearing the T-shirts. So this was simply an extension of who I was to secure funding. I hit up my home girl that I met at my first TRAP Karaoke, DeElva Dash, and requested that she would make the shirt and I will place them on sale on my personal website. Very simple. The hashtag I established, #IssaTrapDissertation is what they said. I had people in other countries wearing the shirts, which would, by default, lead to those outside of the US to investigate the hashtag created and used on the T-shirts.

This model for securing funding is surely one that I will continue to use as I grow as a researcher. Yet, I think it is important that I acknowledge that selling T-shirts, or any kind of merchandise, is not as easy as it appears on the surface. Any attempts to obtain funding that does not match the traditional way of doing things requires so much more additional work. You see, it won't just 'bout what the shirts said. It was also about the quality of the shirts, the product availability, delivery time, pricing, etc. Not to mention, keeping up with all the coin so folks that were purchasing my items could see where their money went was just as important. As shown in Figure 2.1, all money was accounted for, and I still had to come out of pocket in some space. But I am still just as grateful for the people that helped me secure the funding needed for my project. While this approach was stressful, it also gave me better insight into how digital methods can be constructed and or built out of mad different approaches. 'Cause I was also able to learn where my outside audience was coming from by who was purchasing and rocking the T-shirts. In other words, I learned who else was in the room to hear what I had to say. As a result, I made sure to keep these audiences in mind when I edited by dissertation and continued to build my virtual network.

Item	Description	Cost
Equipment Rental	DJI Ronin	155.15
TRAP Karaoke Tickets	December Show/ Participant Interviews	60.00
Hotel	Raleigh, NC TRAP Karaoke	100.00
Hotel	Atlanta, GA / TRAP Music Museum (December)	75.00
Gas*	December (Greenville→ Atlanta GA) Roundtrip & City Travel	125.00
Gas*	Interview T.I. (Greenville → Durham)	$45.00
Gas*	Interview with Jason Mowatt (Greenville→ Raleigh)	$45.00
Caption Service	Captioning Service for Digital Chapter (Rev.com)	$73.00
Audio Recording Software	Adobe Audition Recording Software	$75.00
Travel Costs**	Travel Costs for D'Andra Drewitt (Food, Gas [Elizabeth City→ Greenville], Equipment Needed)	$165.00
	Item (s) Total	$918.00
	Shirt Purchases & Donations	**$770.00**
	Shirt Production Costs and Shipping	**-$390.00**
	Total Following Shirt Production Cost	**$380**
	Out of Pocket Costs (Total Following Shirt Production and Item Total)	**$538**

Figure 2.1. Financial report for dissertation. One asterisk (*) indicates items were rounded up to the next dollar. Two asterisks (**) indicate funds were used from money received via the Drewitt Donation Fund.

Network Building and Virtual Growth

Look, I ain't even gone hold yall, I really ain't think having and growing a solid virtual network mattered when it came to completing my research. Yet, I was shown to be wrong as hell. There ain't no way I could have completed my digital chapter without the backing and support of the people on social media. It wasn't just about these people connecting me with two artists that were in the trap music scene, it was also 'bout me finding other ways to produce and share my scholarship. When I got stuck on how to do something, like caption my digital chapter appropriately, I reached out to the people on social media. Whenever I was questioning if something would make sense or not, I'd send out snippets of the chapter to my people that I connected with online to get their feedback. That digital network made the chapter come to life.

Furthermore, establishing a solid network also led me to connect with other scholars that share the same research interest. Some that have even gone viral, such as Dr. Corey J. Miles (@CoreyMiles_), Dr. Frederick V. Engram Jr (@VanCarlito2003), Taylor Smith (@SmiffTaylor_), Jalisa Jones (@Jaesofamous) and many more. These individuals would interact with my tweets and offer insights for other ideas I hadn't even yet considered. Miles would oftentimes share scholarship that would point to conversations around Hip-Hop, trap music, and Black culture. Many times, he and I exchange ideas about the need for us to fill in the gap for scholarship we wish we had while we were dissertating or just in general as Black scholars, including his latest publication, "Black Rural Feminist Trap: Stylized and Gendered Performativity in Trap Music." Engram, whom I connected with through Smith and author of "An Act of Courage: Providing Space for African American Graduate Students to Express Their Feelings of Disconnectedness," engage in thoughtful conversations around Black student experiences and what it means to acknowledge these experiences in our scholarship and through our mentoring opportunities. Then there is Smith, an HBCU and College Access Advocate, has grown to become a wonderful friend and confidant that I am able to reach out to and express my moments of confusion in my scholarship. She has been a guest on many great Black podcasts, such as "Let's Talk Bruh" and continues to shine light on the ways we can shape and alter higher education for generations to come. Not to mention she always gasses me up. Finally, Jones, an unapologetic powerhouse and currently pursuing her own Ph.D.—fingers crossed she will be done by the time this chapter is published—always shows me and points to ways of being real and true about our words. She has gone viral many times for expressing the thoughts many of us have but may not have the ability to communicate to an outside audience. She has kept me on my toes and constantly reminds me to stay true to the work I produce. These connections that I've further elaborated on, along with many others, have helped push me to become a better researcher, scholar, and teacher.

While I know it may seem miniscule to have spent time elaborating on these four specific virtual connections, it is important that we look to the relationships we formulate while completing research as important to the research itself. The way I see it, research methods should be applicable in many different aspects of your academic career. Digital methods take shape in one space yet continue to blossom and live on even after you've completed your research. The ability to formulate strong and supportive relationships is important as they are the very relationships that will carry you on in your academic career

What Does This Mean for the Academy?

Well, I mean, hell it can mean a lot of things for the academy. Yet, I think I can sum it up in this way: Digital methods is/are the tools needed to dismantle traditional methods of data collection and research curation. Digital methods challenge just how we define methods, but they also challenge how many of us make understanding regarding the world around us. In my opinion, digital methods allow for a far more explicit embedding of the author in the actual research process. As a result, we get to have access to various ideas and ways of understanding the author as a person . . . and not . . . just . . . an . . . author. Yea, we sometimes read scholarship and forget that the author is an actual person too. This matters. Therefore, we have #CiteBlackWomen and #DecolonizeYourSyllabus as major talking points, because we cannot and should not separate the author from the work they produce. Whether the author is a graduate student or professor that's been in the game for decades, these types of insights matter to the way the author produces a text and interprets their own research. Utilizing digital methods is one way that we can see this happen. And to add a bonus for understanding Digital Methods behind the scenes, I've included a video of behind-the-scenes footage at https://www.dropbox.com/s/5fs5514hqfh5xoy/Trap%20Dissertation%20BTS.mov?dl=0

Works Cited

"About Kairos." *Kairos: A Journal of Rhetoric, Technology, and Pedagogy*, https://kairos.technorhetoric.net/about.html.

Baker-Bell, April. "For Loretta: A Black Woman Literacy Scholar's Journey to Prioritizing Self-preservation and Black Feminist–womanist Storytelling." *Journal of Literacy Research*, vol. 49, no. 4, 2017, pp. 526–43.

Ball, Cheryl E. "Show, Not Tell: The Value of New Media Scholarship." *Computers and Composition*, vol. 21, no. 4, 2004, pp. 403–25, https://doi.org/10.1016/s8755-4615(04)00038-6.

Banks, Adam J. "Dominant Genre Emeritus: Why It's Time to Retire the Essay." *CLA Journal*, vol. 60, no. 2, 2016, pp. 179–90, www.jstor.org/stable/26355916.

Baron, Dennis. "From Pencils to Pixels: The Stages of Literacy Technologies." *Passions, Pedagogies, and Twenty-first Century Technologies*, edited by Gail E. Hawisher and Cynthia L. Selfe, Utah State UP, 1999, pp. 15-33.

Brewer, John, and Albert Hunter. *Foundations of Multimethod Research: Synthesizing Styles*. Sage, 2006.

Brown, Laura, Rebecca Griffiths, and Matthew Rascoff. "University Publishing in a Digital Age." *Journal of Electronic Publishing*, vol. 10, no. 3, 2007, pp. 1–67.

Carson, A.D. *i used to love to dream*. U of Michigan P, 2020, https://doi.org/10.3998/mpub.11738372.

Engram Jr., Frederick V. "An Act of Courage: Providing Space for African American Graduate Students to Express Their Feelings of Disconnectedness." *The Vermont Connection*, vol. 41, no. 1, 2020, p. 4.

Gallagher, John R. *Update Culture and the Afterlife of Digital Writing*. Utah State UP, 2020.

Hertz, Mary Beth. "The Right Technology May Be a Pencil: Sometimes Paper and Pencil Are All You Need." *Edutopia*, George Lucas Educational Foundation, 29 Nov. 2011, www.edutopia.org/blog/technology-integration-classroom-mary-beth-hertz.

Jones, Natasha N. "Coalitional Learning in the Contact Zones: Inclusion and Narrative Inquiry in Technical Communication and Composition Studies." *College English*, vol. 82, no. 5, 2020, pp. 515–26.

Koles, Bernadett, and Peter Nagy. "Who is portrayed in Second Life: Dr. Jekyll or Mr. Hyde? The Extent of Congruence between Real Life and Virtual Identity." *Journal For Virtual Worlds Research*, vol. 5, no. 1, 2012, pp. 1–17, https://doi.org/10.4101/jvwr.v5i1.2150.

Mckoy, Temptaous T. "Y'all Call It Technical and Professional Communication, We Call It #ForTheCulture: The Use of Amplification Rhetorics in Black Communities and Their Implications for Technical and Professional Communication Studies." 2019, East Carolina University, dissertation.

Miles, Corey. "Black Rural Feminist Trap: Stylized and Gendered Performativity in Trap Music." *Journal of Hip Hop Studies*, vol. 7, no. 1, 2020, pp. 44–70, https://doi.org/10.34718/kx7h-0515.

Ribeiro, José Carlos. "The Increase of the Experiences of the Self through the Practice of Multiple Virtual Identities." *PsychNology Journal*, vol. 7, no. 3, Dec. 2009, pp. 291–302

Richardson, Elaine B. *African American literacies*. Psychology Press, 2003.

Smith, Sidonie. "Beyond the dissertation monograph." *MLA Newsletter*, vol. 42, no. 1, spring 2010, pp. 2–3, https://www.mla.org/content/download/31662/1498968/nl_421_web_no_links.pdf.

Tracy, Sarah J. *Qualitative Research Methods: Collecting Evidence, Crafting Analysis, Communicating Impact*. Wiley-Blackwell, 2013.

van Kokswijk, Jacob. *Digital Ego: Social and Legal Aspects of Virtual Identity*. Eburon Academic Publishers, 2007.

Wardle, Elizabeth Ann, and Douglas P. Downs. *Writing about Writing: A College Reader*. Bedford/St. Martins, 2011.

Chapter 3. Strategies for Accessing and Articulating Voices through Digital Writing Research Projects

Janine Butler
ROCHESTER INSTITUTE OF TECHNOLOGY

Land Acknowledgment. This chapter was written in the Rochester, New York area, the traditional territory of the Onöndowa'ga:' or "the people of the Great Hill." In English, they are known as Seneca people, "the keeper of the western door." They are one of the six nations that make up the sovereign Haudenosaunee Confederacy. Along with other members of the Rochester Institute of Technology (RIT) community, I honor the land on which RIT was built and recognize the unique relationship that the Indigenous stewards have with this land. That relationship is the core of their traditions, cultures, and histories. We recognize the history of genocide, colonization, and assimilation of Indigenous people that took place on this land. Mindful of these histories, we work towards understanding, acknowledging, and ultimately reconciliation.[1]

Interdependent Processes for Composing Audio and Video

The edited collection that houses this chapter is actively contributing to the knowledge of digital writing scholars who share innovative research to colleagues through *audio, video,* and other digital technologies. We digital writing researchers are experimenting with novel means of "speaking" to our audiences through sound, visuals, and other modes and media. While many of us are capitalizing on the affordances of digital modes and media, not every scholar might be familiar with the methodologies and methods that digital writing researchers can use to access sound and articulate our own and others' *voices* through digital writing research projects. In this chapter, I reflect on my interdependent methodology and methods for accessing and articulating voices through audio and video technologies in my research projects. By sharing my experiences, I encourage scholars to sense how experimenting with different methods for designing access to sound and visuals in our research practices is a fruitful process that positively connects researchers and audiences.

---

1. Light modifications have been made here to Rochester Institute of Technology's Native American Future Stewards Program's Land Acknowledgment. See *Native American Future Stewards Program—Land Acknowledgment* at https://www.rit.edu/diversity /futurestewards#land-acknowledgment.

DOI: https://doi.org/10.37514/PRA-B.2022.1541.2.03

In my line of research as a Deaf rhetoric and composition scholar who works to make videos and audio accessible for audiences with different hearing levels, I engage with *sound* in *visible* ways and with *visuals* in *sonic* ways so that meaning becomes accessible across modes (including in "Integral Captions and Subtitles," which was published in *Rhetoric Review*, and "Where Access Meets Multimodality," which was published in *Kairos*). Later in this chapter, I discuss the challenges and benefits of composing videos in which I communicate through my primary language of American Sign Language (ASL) to predominantly hearing colleagues in the field. I also reflect on the advantages and disadvantages of different methods that I have used to record and capture the signed and spoken statements of D/deaf and hard-of-hearing research participants in focus groups and interviews. These four context-specific examples, which are tied to the communication practices that participants and I use, can inform researchers about the constructiveness of continually reassessing our research methods and methodologies so that we can better access and articulate a variety of voices in our digital writing projects.

Before I share my methods, I first share my interdependent methodology, a methodology that is shaped by my values: *sound* in digital writing studies, *access* in digital publishing, *interdependency* in research, and the concepts of *articulation* and *voice*. As I discuss in the next section, designing manifold means of access to our own and our participants' spoken and signed meaning through visual, aural, and other modes diversifies and enhances the scholarly conversation that takes place in our field. If we have the goal of making our projects accessible to ourselves and others—and we should have that goal—then we should continually finetune strategies for merging sound and visuals in ways that capture the vision of our voices. With that in mind, I use the concept of "articulation" to represent how I work with technologies and other humans in an interrelated manner to give expression to my message—my voice—as a researcher and to the voices of the participants in my study. My interrelations with other tools and individuals—even in *in*dependent research projects in which I am the sole author and principal investigator—embodies the *inter*dependent aspects of digital writing and digital research.

My use of interdependency in this chapter builds on my collaborative work with Laura Gonzales. In an article published in *Composition Forum*, we argued for and shared "intersectional, *interdependent* approaches to accessibility in writing classrooms" that work toward social justice (Gonzales and Butler; emphasis added). Building on Julie Jung's exploration of interdependency in writing studies, we defined interdependency as the following: "In contrast to independence, interdependency is a product of the human condition in which we all rely on other human beings in various ways through different relationalities" (Gonzales and Butler). I extend our definition of interdependency in this chapter to reflect my interdependent methodology and the methods that I use in interaction with digital technologies and other human beings (including research participants and colleagues) to design and distribute digital writing projects that make voices, including my own, accessible.

The concepts of interdependency, access, voice, and articulation intertwine in my previous initiative with Joseph Cirio, Victor Del Hierro, Laura Gonzales, Joy Robinson, and Angela Haas. "With the goal of encouraging further representation and inclusion of minoritized scholars in computers and writing scholarship," we presented at a Town Hall session at Computers and Writing in 2017 and published video recordings of our presentations in a webtext in the Disputatio section of *Kairos* (Butler et al.). When each one of us captioned the video of our own presentation, I experienced the challenge of determining how to caption the rhetorical situation of a live interpreted professional presentation in which signs and speech are not temporally aligned. During this interdependent presentation, I signed my message and two professional sign language interpreters worked with me to voice my signs in spoken English. In real-time situations such as these, the audible words are not spoken until after the sign has been produced and perceived by an interpreter. While this is a natural process in live presentations, this poses a challenge for synchronizing captions.

As I worked to caption my video, I wanted to provide our audience with direct access to what I was saying through my signs, and I had to decide *when* to place the captions. I recursively went through every temporal-spatial moment in my recorded presentation and made choices that intended to temporally bridge the space between the signs and speech through the captions. Through this consolidated design, I aimed for our audience to stay with my embodied message; in other words, I *articulated* my message—my *voice*—as a scholar through the interdependent process of making my *aural* and *visual* composition *accessible* (as depicted in Figure 3.1).

In this chapter, I now ask my readers to stay with my embodied message as I present my reflections on and argument for an interdependent methodology and methods that commit to access in digital writing research.

Figure 3.1. Screen capture from Butler et al., "Janine Butler" (3:22)

Methodology: Access + Interdependency, Voice + Articulation

Sound and Digital Writing

The increasing prevalence of video and audio technologies in digital writing research demands an equivalent increase in attending to the accessibility of these technologies. Each new technological release and update improves the quality of video and audio recording devices that we use to *capture* participants, ourselves, and other moments; the capabilities of software programs that we use to *edit and create* our digital compositions; and the platforms through which we *disseminate* our message to our audiences. We can correspondingly design access into each step of our research process and show that there is space for diverse communication practices and abilities. This methodology section of this chapter establishes the intertwining values of *sound* in digital writing studies, *access* in digital publishing, access and *interdependency* in research, and the concept of *voice* in composition and publication. These commingling values illuminate the research methods for *accessing and articulating voices* that are detailed in the upcoming section of this chapter.

Scholars over the last few decades have enriched our understanding of the value of sonic composition in equipping composers with tools for communicating through sound and multimodal composition (notably Heidi McKee, Cynthia Selfe, and Jody Shipka, among others). Joining these scholars in further expanding the definition of writing to encompass sonic compositions, Bump Halbritter detailed the process of composing layers of audio-visual texts, including the technological tools that we use to record audio and visuals. In the digital space of *Kairos*, Tanya K. Rodrigue and eight co-authors shared and reflected on nine sonic compositions created by "a community of writers" and students involved in Rodrigue's digital writing graduate course; their webtext reveals various sonic composing processes that illuminate our understanding of sonic rhetoric. Even more recently, Courtney Danford, Kyle Stedman, and Michael Faris' digital edited collection, *Soundwriting Pedagogies*, established a space for nine chapters with "theories, examples, and lots of audio to encourage the use and value of soundwriting in composition, writing, rhetoric, and communications classrooms." The authors in this sonic-visual-textual collection share their messages through sound, with accompanying transcripts, to foreground the affordances of sonic composition. These scholars' enthusiasm motivates my research on and with audio and video when enacting my methodology for making sound accessible.

Digital Writing and Access

While sonic creators—particularly in recent years in our field—often include transcripts and captions to make sonic compositions accessible, it is crucial to ensure that every single composition is designed to be accessible to audiences. To borrow

Elizabeth Brewer, Cynthia Selfe, and M. Remi Yergeau's argument for creating a culture of transformative access in composition studies, we should "broaden our own and the profession's understanding of accessibility practices in ways that extend beyond simple standards to embrace, instead, the spirit and practices of both universal and participatory design. . . . [T]he aim is to transform texts as much as it is to transform readers, audiences, expectations, and composing practices" (152). Brewer, Selfe, and Yergeau show the value of a culture of access in which we all actively participate in the design and redesign of our composition practices. Through engaging in participatory design—a value that has been stimulated by Jay Dolmage as well as Yergeau et al. in "Multimodality in Motion"—we can transform all our practices and convey meaning to audiences across multiple modes.

Accessing communication via multiple modes enhances a researcher's ability to connect with participants in a research study, to analyze findings, and to compose publications for audiences. My discussion of my methods for accessing aural and visual modes in the next section can contribute to a culture of transformative access in digital writing research by highlighting accessible research practices that make sound accessible in visual form. Such accessible processes intersect with current catalysts in the field, particularly Douglas Eyman et al.'s webtext—the product of a collaboration of 27 members of a summer seminar on accessibility in digital publishing—which "aims to address the full range of barriers to access and suggest best practices for working toward the goal of full access/ibility for digital publications." The digital writing scholars and colleagues emphasize the "the importance of access in terms of usability for a wide range of users with varying abilities and disabilities." I want to spotlight the phrase, "usability for . . . varying abilities and disabilities," particularly as I proceed to discuss accessibility of research practices for researchers, participants, and audiences with varying hearing levels and communication preferences.

When I create videos in which I sign to hearing audiences, I create a rhetorical situation in which "standard" concepts of "accessibility" may be reversed. While sound scholars often add captions or transcripts to improve the accessibility of audio projects, I find myself including sound to make my spatial-visual message accessible to hearing audiences. Specifically, I enlist professional interpreters to record voice-overs for my videos. While I discuss this specific method later in this chapter, I first want to review the values that shape this method. The process of coordinating with interpreters to improve access and expand the reach of my digital compositions embodies the *interdependency* of research practices in disability studies (Price, "Disability Studies Methodology: Explaining"; Price, "Getting Specific"; Price and Kerschbaum) and in digital writing research (VanKooten).

Access and Interdependency

Margaret Price's commitment to disability studies methodological approaches can inform rhetoric and composition researchers who work to enact ethical and accessible research practices. Building on her review of disability study method-ological approaches ("Disability Studies Methodology: Explaining"), Price makes the following observation: "One interesting thing to note here is that DS [disabil-ity studies] researchers have been way out in front of most qualitative research-ers when considering the promises and pitfalls of digital methods" (2). She also argues that, "DS methodology has much to teach other disciplinary approaches about what 'access' really means. 'Accessible,' in DS methodology, should mean something akin to our emergent notions of participatory design" (3). To borrow and extend Price's argument, digital writing researchers can be informed by dis-ability studies researchers who encounter the limitations of inaccessible digital methods and participate in the redesign of digital research methods to make them more accessible.

Access emerges as a central theme in a methodology that acknowledges the *interdependency* of researchers and research practices. Julie Jung draws from disability studies' focus on the "fact of human *interdependency*" (104; empha-sis in original) to call on teachers and scholars in writing studies to "*choose to recognize* the interdependencies that enable our intellectual work [teaching, research, and service], and though this act of recognition identify unmet needs, invent possibilities for meeting them, and honor and then join those who are already doing both" (112; emphasis in original). Presenting the example of how our scholarship would not exist without others' scholarship, she espouses that our field's intellectual work "emerges and survives *interdependently*" (107; emphasis in original). Later in this chapter, I detail how I conduct indepen-dent research as the principal investigator while working interdependently with other members of the research team, colleagues, and other stakeholders to access and make my work accessible. When I discuss the interdependent process of coordinating with professional interpreters later in this chapter, I recognize how these connections enable me to design accessible intellectual work and reach my audiences.

Through sharing my interdependent methodology and methods, I extend the collaborative work of Laura Gonzales and myself. In our previously mentioned article, the two of us built on Jung to argue for teaching social justice in "writ-ing courses through intersectional, interdependent frameworks" that center on each individual's "overlapping and interlocking experiences of privilege, oppres-sion, and in/ability to access communication" (Gonzales and Butler). We cannot ignore our own intricate positionalities and our students' positionalities, as well as our research participants' and colleagues' positionalities, when conducting digital research with other human beings. Just as Gonzales and I wrote in our article that "theories of interdependency can help students and teachers engage in productive discussions about who is being privileged in a design decision and why," my chapter here shares my interdependent methodology and my methods for designing access in ways that do not privilege a single positionality, identity, or ability.

Interdependency and access dovetail in the work of writing scholars who conduct collaborative research. Stephanie Wheeler eloquently describes the relationship between interdependency and access when describing the innovative collaboration between faculty in her department and the university's access services program for students. She writes:

> having these conversations [among faculty and students] about access within a writing program prompted an engagement with writing studies and access in a productive way, necessitating an understanding of access as something that is networked, and relies on interdependent and symbiotic relationships in the department and beyond. (Wheeler, n.p.)

Such initiatives foreground *access and writing itself* as an interdependent process, a process that I sense in my own digital research methodology and the methods that I discuss later in this chapter.

The duality of interdependency and access is even more evident in Price and Stephanie Kerschbaum's collaborative description of their "interdependent disability-studies (DS) methodology" (20). Price and Kerschbaum describe a qualitative research project in which they worked closely with each other and their interview participants to ensure that each individual could access their interviews, the data, and other aspects of the research process. They explain: "Neither of us could have done this study alone, and what has become possible in the course of doing it has become so because of our interdependent collaboration" (27). Specifically, they write about the importance of access in an interdependent project: "our commitment to collective access—i.e., access not just for our participants alone, or for us alone, but for all of us together" (28). Through their interdependency, they designed a research project that included access throughout every single step—and this participatory design can be adopted by digital writing researchers.

Interdependency and Digital Writing

In addition to scholarship in the field of rhetoric and composition, interdependency in *digital* writing research has been meticulously detailed by Crystal VanKooten in her critical assessment of using video cameras in her research. In "A Research Methodology of Interdependence through Video as Method," VanKooten carefully details how she has now "reconceptualize[d] the research scene as *interdependent*: . . . [a] situation where participants, researcher, scene, and tools constantly influence and rely on one another" (3). Crucially, her methodology "takes the research scene as interdependent and does not ignore the role of the researcher; aspects that demand alternate methods" (5). Of especially particular relevance for this chapter is VanKooten's approach to interviewing participants in her research and her detailing of how she records interactions between herself as the researcher and her participants during the interviews (in addition to capturing participants from two angles).

The interdependent *digital* research scene described by VanKooten should remind qualitative researchers that we and our participants are actively responding to and informing each other. As such, recording all participants in a research scene—including ourselves in our role as interviewers and qualitative data collectors—foregrounds our connections and interactions. In VanKooten's persuasive words, "each element of the research scene is linked to another and has an active part in meaning-making—including the technologies used" (2). When selecting types, numbers, and placements of video cameras and other digital research methods, each one of us certainly shapes the creation of a scene in which participants (and we) express and capture each other's meaning. We furnish that scene with the technologies and tools that are available to us, that we choose to use, that are accessible or not accessible (to us, to participants, and/or to our audience). As I detail later in this chapter, we also shape the accessibility of our digital research scene and digital tools through our interdependent interactions with other individuals affiliated with our study.

Digital Writing and Articulation

Interdependency—which exists between me and D/deaf and hard-of-hearing participants in my research studies as well as between me and professional interpreters when composing my videos—is an asset that strengthens my articulation of my voice as a digital writing researcher who is committed to access to audio and video. Articulation can refer to the physical articulation of clear sounds as well as the physical articulation, or jointing, of the limbs. For this chapter, I borrow Merriam-Webster's definition of *articulation* as, among other points, "the act of giving utterance or expression" as well as "the state of being jointed or interrelated." Articulation fills out our concept of interdependency to reflect how I work with interpreters to merge aural and visual modes in a "jointed or interrelated" state so that we give "utterance or expression" to my voice as a digital researcher.

The interrelations of modes certainly play a central role in digital writing research. The 2007 edited collection *Digital Writing Research: Technologies, Methodologies, and Ethical Issues* includes a chapter in which Susan Hilligoss and Sean Williams delve into questions for digital research while building on the "interplay and interrelationships" between visual communication with "verbal expression" in digital spaces (238). I hope that my own chapter here contributes to the further jointing of aural and visual modes to show scholars how we can all embed access into our research practices.

Articulation and Voice

The term *articulation* includes the connotation of clearly expressing oneself through one's voice, a connotation that can be used to judge the quality of others' voices. I intentionally use the term *articulation* to complicate and expand the definition of voice in digital composition. In a crucial chapter in *Soundwriting Pedagogies*, Jennifer Buckner and Kirsten Daley described how they negotiated sound when Daley was the only deaf undergraduate student in Buckner's multimodal composition course. In their pedagogy-oriented chapter, they argue that our sound and composition theories cannot privilege speaking and hearing bodies and that we need to make sure that our theories are "informed by a multiplicity of voices, even those that do not audate."

To positively complicate our field's definition of voice, I begin with Michelle Comstock and Mary Hocks' 2006 description of voice: "In writing, voice acts as a metaphor for how a persona created in the text 'sounds,' with elements of diction, tone, and style informing this written voice. In multimedia, students use music, interviews, and voice-over narrations to create a tangible, not just metaphoric, voice." In their follow-up 2017 piece, Hocks and Comstock argued for embodied listening practices that move students "toward composing practices that integrate the human voice with other active sound producers and amplifiers in the environment, including rocks, water, air, bridges, buildings, mechanical engines, and non-human animals" (137). The digital writer's voice, then, is a metaphorical voice as well as a tangible voice that exists interdependently with the environment.

In addition to the metaphorical voice and tangible voice, the digital composer's own voice interacts with others' voices. This becomes especially evident in Erin Anderson's argument for teaching "voice-as-material" in sonic rhetoric; Anderson writes that composers "compose with the voices of others—and perhaps, in some sense, to speak through others' voices as if they were our own." Jean Bessette's own exploration of asking students to engage with gay liberation radio shows and compose digital projects argues that we can create "openness to difference" when we "speak with other voices" (74). By speaking with and through others' voices—including when speaking with and through interpreters—we foreground interdependency, interrelations, and the jointing of multiple modes of communication.

With a complicated definition of voice and articulation in mind, digital writing researchers access sound and articulate their own and others' voices through digital writing research projects. Bump Halbritter and Julie Lindquist's collaborative chapter in *Soundwriting Pedagogies* interrogates the nature of voice and how qualitative researchers disseminate recordings with participants' voices and their own voices. Halbritter and Lindquist open their chapter with a review of voice in writing studies that begins with Kathleen Blake Yancey's 1994 edited collection, *Voices on Voice: Perspectives, Definitions, Inquiry* and that suggests that interest in voice was "on the wane" since then (Halbritter and Lindquist n.p.). They argue that we can reconsider voice and its relationship with digital composition today and that, "when voices are made of other voices . . . then it becomes necessary to understand and approach voice as a shared, mediated, and negotiated thing." Most forcefully, they ask the following questions:

> What does it mean to have—that is, to be in possession of—
> an audible voice, one that is not your own but one with (and
> through which) you will speak? What does it mean to have a
> voice . . . in the sense that the audible voice in question truly
> belongs to someone else? What does it mean to have a voice—in
> the sense that the first voice your readers hear is neither their
> own nor your own? (Halbritter and Lindquist, n.p.)

Halbritter and Lindquist explore the ramifications of these questions when presenting data collected from research participants.

The intricate questions about voice are just as pertinent in other contexts, including when I work with interpreters to articulate my message as a researcher and when I utilize different technologies and tools to capture the statements of D/deaf and hard-of-hearing participants. This process is informed by the interdependent nature of situations in which we design and redesign access and articulate our interrelated voices in digital writing research.

Methods: Audio + Video, Sound + Visuals

With access, interdependency, and the complicated nature of **voice** in mind, readers can join me in reflecting on how I work independently and interdependently with others to articulate my voice as a researcher and the voices of research participants in accessible ways. The methods that I use across different projects are categorized into two sections so that each section centers on a single theme with two examples for each theme. The first section centers on coordinating with others to articulate the sound/vision of the researcher's voice; the second section centers on experimenting with digital technologies and tools for accessing participants' voices.

The methods that I discuss in the following sections complement and expand the principles for working with participants that I detail in my 2019 article in *Present Tense*, titled "Principles for Cultivating Rhetorics and Research Studies within Communities." In that article, I share the strategies that I used when conducting focus groups with D/deaf and hard-of-hearing participants to learn their perspectives on the current state of captions. I feature three research principles for research methodologies and methods in rhetoric and composition, including cultivating "the diversity that exists within groups, participants' knowledge, and the multiple modes of communication through which meaning may be transmitted." After reviewing the footage of each focus group, I independently transcribed the statements of all members of the signed group discussions into written English for my later analysis. With each participant signing in a different way—since not every individual signs in the same way—I had to determine how best to faithfully capture everyone's embodied, temporal-spatial-visual signs into the linear, static form of English so that individuals' perspectives would remain at the forefront of my research. However, attempting to capture every single linguistic marker and embodied message for every single project in the future would create an obstacle because the time-intensive process of transcribing three-dimensional and temporal signs into written words requires much energy and investment.

To explore more opportunities for articulating participants' messages, I use the following sections of this chapter to review several methods that I use to access and articulate voices throughout my research projects as well as the lessons that I have learned. While reviewing these experiences, I encourage readers to actively consider potential designs for different methods of accessing audio and video technologies in our field's research practices.

The Sound/Vision of the Researcher's Voice

In writing this chapter, I am making an assumption about my audience based on what I know about the makeup of the field of rhetoric and composition generally and digital writing more specifically: that the audience is largely composed of scholars who hear to some degree. I also make the assumption that a majority of these scholars are not fluent in American Sign Language (my primary language) and that they hear the audio in the podcasts, videos, and other sonic compositions that they create and listen to.

For some of these scholars, recording and disseminating their own speech as audio files might be an independent process that involves speaking directly into a microphone and hearing the resulting audio footage. My previous sentence intentionally compresses and oversimplifies the complex, rhetorical, creative, and inspiring processes that scholars in our field engage in to edit, amplify, and otherwise rework an astonishing wealth of insightful sonic compositions. My intention for sharing these assumptions is to underscore how the relatively straightforward practice of recording one's own voice can also be re-worked to amplify interdependent methods. I encourage digital writing researchers to join me in exploring the possibilities for articulating our own messages through the voices of others.

Accessing a "Professional Voice"

While working on different research projects over the past few years related to captions, sound, and access, I have created videos in which I disseminate my scholarship to colleagues in the field of rhetoric and composition. When recording these videos, I often face the camera and sign directly to the camera while reserving space around me for captions to be integrated into the screen during the editing process. I coordinate with a professional interpreter to incorporate voice-over in each video to articulate my multimodal message in accessible ways to my target audience of predominantly—but not exclusively—scholars who hear and are not fluent in my primary language. In many cases, challenges emerge when attempting to synchronize the audio-visual-textual-temporal layers of the audible voice, the signs on screen, and the captions. These challenges are not easily resolved but the interdependent nature of coordinating with others is another lesson that we learn as we work towards access in each project.

An early example of my methods for addressing my audience through a signed, captioned, and voiced-over video is a conference presentation in which I presented some of my findings from my dissertation research via prerecorded video at the Council of Writing Program Administration in July 2016. In this professional video, I addressed colleagues in the field and started with the following line: "In this presentation I integrated captions into the space around me so that you can follow my body language, my facial expressions, my meaning." At the time, I was a doctoral student at East Carolina University in North Carolina and this video presentation was part of my dissertation research on intentionally and thoughtfully designing a space for integral captions within our videos as opposed to treating captions as an afterthought to be automatically placed at the bottom of the screen (an argument that I have disseminated elsewhere, including in "Integral Captions and Subtitles," which was published in *Rhetoric Review*).

I intentionally planned for and integrated the captions into this video so that the captions would embody my multimodal message—and my professional voice as a signer (as depicted in Figure 3.2). When filming myself, I positioned myself so that the camera framed me from the waist up (a medium shot) and with space to my sides. Determining that black font would be the most readable color for my captions in this professional presentation, I stood in front of a light-colored wall and wore a black shirt that contrasted with my light-skinned hands and arms.

Figure 3.2. Screen capture from the author's dissertation video.

During the filming process, I had the eventual design of the captions in mind. As a right-handed person, I positioned myself mainly on the right side of the camera; that allowed me to use my dominant hand to interact with the captions that would appear in the space next to me. When I felt that it would be rhetorically effective to move myself and the captions, I moved to the center of the screen or the left side. For instance, several times in the video, I discussed conventional captions that appear at the bottom of the screen; in these instances, I moved myself to the center of the frame and placed the captions at the bottom of the screen. When editing those moments, I changed the color of the captions to white to embody the traditional color for captions *and* to make them readable when they appeared in front of my black shirt.

During the editing process, I used Windows Movie Maker to integrate captions into different places around the screen, depending on my meaning at any given moment. Nonetheless, the design of my captions was directly influenced by the affordances of the free version of Windows Movie Maker that I had as a doctoral student. For instance, while I could design the timing and pacing of my captions, I could not embolden, color, or italicize a single word or letter in a segment without also affecting the other words or letters in the same segment. In such ways, the potentials and limitations of my version of Windows Movie Maker influenced the final design of my video.

Knowing that it was important to articulate my voice as an emergent researcher, I enlisted one of my regular interpreters at the time who I trusted and who was comfortable voicing for me to provide the voice-over for this video. Although she normally spoke with a Southern accent, she informed me that she wanted to suppress her natural accent so that my identity as a non-Southerner would come through in the video. I told her that she did not have to make that change, but we then decided together that she would do so, and this decision has remained with me over the years as I recognize that we worked together to maintain our metaphorical *vision* of what my *audible* "professional voice" should sound like to colleagues in the field.

In digital writing, the concept of "professional voice" can be problematic if we hold on to a limited vision of what our own and others' voices should "sound" like and whether these sounds should be audible. Yet, just as cooperating with an interpreter enabled me to improve access to my professional voice, the professional relationships and digital tools that all digital researchers draw upon, including tools for transforming captions, can help us concretize our messages in living color—rhetorically and literally.

Accessing Sonic Conversations

With the ongoing creation of additional programs and platforms, professional opportunities to converse with colleagues in digital spaces frequently materialize and it is crucial that all members of our online communities can access these conversations. As an example, after the 2018 publication of *Soundwriting Pedago-gies*, I was asked to contribute to a podcast series that extended the work of the edited collection. For this podcast series, scholars in our field submitted questions for the authors of each chapter to respond to, and the resulting episodes were circulated on the Computers and Composition Digital Press platforms (Hope). I developed a few questions about the theories and practices for Jennifer Buckner and Kirsten Daley about their chapter in the edited collection, "Do You Hear What I Hear? A Hearing Teacher and a Deaf Student Negotiate Sound." My video-recorded questions and Jennifer Buckner's audio responses to my questions were merged into a visual podcast episode for the series.

When I was first asked to contribute to the series, I was eager to engage in a conversation about negotiating and accessing sound in visual *and* aural form. I reflected on and created a list of the most compelling questions about the chapter that I wanted to ask Buckner. As I drafted my plan for my component of the episode, I anticipated that my video would be merged with Buckner's audio responses. By this point in my career as an assistant professor with additional resources, I had been using Adobe Premiere Pro to create and edit videos with sound and captions. With Adobe Premiere Pro, I could now finetune the design of my captions to embody my message even more emphatically. This program gave me greater control over the size, typography, placement, and other nuances that I wanted to design in my captions. Most relevantly for this podcast series, I could amplify the size of specific words in the way that one would raise their pitch in speech for emphasis.

With my final composition *and* the eventual podcast in mind, I recorded myself signing with space for traditional lines of captions below me and I integrated amplified captions for key terms in the space next to me. Through this preparation, the captions appear at the same time as my signs (as depicted in Figure 3.3). For instance, I explained that Buckner and Daly's use of "'audate' jumped out at me as a term that could help scholars formulate our understanding of how each body experiences sounds." To embody the impact of that term on me, I used Adobe Premiere Pro to place that term in my line of sight next to my eyes and signs.

I enlisted a professional interpreter to read the captions in the video so that the voice-over would align with the signs and the captions. I then included the audio file in my video project in Adobe Premiere Pro, synchronized the modes, and finalized the video. This interdependent process with an interpreter and Adobe Premiere Pro led to a final composition in which signs, captions, and speech simultaneously present shared meaning. Based on my unique and interdependent sonic experiences, I strongly encourage digital writing scholars who engage in professional conversations and other shared sonic events online, including podcasts, to experiment with innovative methods for making such dialogue multimodal and accessible through collaborating with and learning from other voices.

Figure 3.3. Screen capture of the author from Lacy Hope (1:10).

The Sound/Vision of the Researcher's Voice: Conclusion

These two examples may serve as a reminder that the methods that can be used in each research situation are not identical and that there is no single template to follow when working independently and interdependently to access and articulate voices. Rather, each new research project presents a distinct opportunity—with its corresponding affordances—for actively considering different methods of capturing the sound/vision of our professional voice through the interrelations of speech, captions, and other modes.

Recording, Transcribing, and Accessing Participants' Voices

In addition to dialoguing with colleagues, I use my research projects to improve access to sonic and multimodal compositions and I strongly value involving the perspectives of users of these compositions. As a result, a major component of my qualitative research processes entails collecting information from D/deaf and hard-of-hearing individuals about their experiences with and preferences for accessible technologies. Over the past few years, I have used and revised several methods for recording and transcribing the statements of research participants in different focus groups and interviews. Each recording and transcribing method creates benefits and limitations when working with participants with different communication practices, including participants with different preferences for signing and speaking. Evaluating the best technology to use and procedure to follow for recording and transcribing participants' statements begins anew with the start of each new research project (and with the release of each new technology). This self-evaluation is necessary because we are essentially asking ourselves to complete an important mission: to always improve access to and articulation of our participants' voices.

Transcribing Sound and Visuals: A Relatively Low-Tech Method

While I have often worked independently as the principal investigator with an interdependent methodology, one collaborative project was an especially interdependent process in which I worked closely with a colleague and other individuals to access and articulate participants' voices. In this project, Stacy Bick, a visual communications senior lecturer who teaches filmmaking and related courses, and I interviewed D/deaf and hard-of-hearing students who had taken at least one filmmaking course at our institution about their experiences creating films with sound and captions; some of these participants spoke in their interviews, some signed, and some spoke *and* signed. Stacy Bick and I hired a deaf graduate student assistant who was comfortable communicating in spoken English and sign language to review our video recordings and transcribe the entirety of these interviews.

I share this example here to acknowledge that an interdependent methodology and methods are context-specific while ever-evolving with technology—yet always drawing on traditional methods, tools, and technologies. The graduate student assistant had to take the time to recursively review each video recording to capture each participant's spoken and/or signed message and place all the aural and visual voices in written English in the transcripts. This relatively low-tech method relied on digital tools and affordances—including the ability to slow down video recordings and replay the same moments over and over to capture all signs—and provided us with what we needed to accomplish our research goals: versions in written English of each participant's statements.

After the graduate student assistant completed each transcript, I reviewed the videos and transcripts. I likewise had to slowly view and read the two texts—the written and the multimodal—side-by-side to ensure that I did not miss a moment in either version. Reading the choices that the graduate student assistant made in transcribing particular signs or sentences was an edifying experience for me as a rhetorical scholar because I experienced firsthand the slightly different ways in which she and I might have transcribed a signed statement into written English. Notably, the choices she made in determining where a participant's signed sentences began and where they ended were at times different than my choices would have been. While reminding the editor side of me to resist the desire to move punctuation marks in the transcripts that did not need to be moved, I had to acknowledge that some of our transcription choices may have differed in relatively minor ways, but that both approaches articulated the signer's original intentions. In the end, reading transcripts created through another mindset productively compelled me to recognize expanded possibilities for transcribing visual statements in written English—and that will benefit me in the future.

After finalizing the transcripts, I used a qualitative data analysis program (MAXQDA), proceeded with the next steps in the research process, and disseminated our findings (Butler and Bick). While scholars certainly use such digital programs to analyze content in videos and delve deeper into digital and multimodal research methods—including methods reviewed elsewhere in this edited collection—the relatively traditional process of articulating multimodal messages in written English persists as an interdependent and digital method in our toolkit that we can use to improve how each one of us accesses and represents one mode in another mode.

Transcribing with 360-Degree Cameras: A Relatively Novel Method

My confidence in traditional methods for transcription parallels my professional enthusiasm for new digital methods of collecting data that can enrich our access to participants' voices. I used a relatively exciting method when I conducted a qualitative research study that I designed as part of a larger team project with colleagues in engineering departments who aimed to develop voice assistant interfaces (such as those for Alexa, Siri, and Google Assistant) that would be more accessible for D/deaf and hard-of-hearing individuals. To inform the team about voice assistant users' current needs and preferences, my qualitative study began with two small focus group discussions so that I could first collect information from D/deaf and hard-of-hearing individuals about their experiences giving voice commands to voice assistants.

Since participants in this study used spoken communication, I decided to reassess my methods for recording participants' statements. First, I wanted participants to be comfortable deciding whether they wanted to speak or sign their responses in their focus group discussions. I arranged for sign language interpreters to voice in real-time during the focus groups for the participants who preferred to sign while other participants chose to speak. I obtained two separate recording devices: a digital voice recorder and a 360-degree video camera that I would use to capture panoramic visual footage of all individuals in our shared space during the discussions.

Prior to the focus groups and in accordance with the team project's timeline, I contracted a captioning agency who would create a transcript of the focus group discussions based on the audio file. I anticipated that the captioning agency might not catch every audible statement made by participants who spoke; thus, the footage captured by the 360-degree video camera and the audio captured by the digital voice recorder could provide me with access to participants' signed and spoken statements when verifying the initial transcripts and analyzing the data. As it happened, having a recording of the panoramic visual-temporal scene made it possible for me to fully access participants' *voices* within the context of our discussion. For instance, one participant sat next to me and looked directly at me while speaking without signing; I in turn looked directly at him and regularly nodded to indicate my understanding. At times, including when reaching the end of thoughts, he would lower the volume of his voice and whisper a few words or sign these final words. These moments were not captured by the captioning agency, which left these moments incomplete in the transcripts—and I was able to fill in these gaps with my access to the panoramic video. In other words, through this interdependency with the transcription service and the 360-degree camera, I was able to access and articulate this participant's voice.

Regardless of the size of a research study, digital writing researchers should embrace the concurrent use of multiple digital tools and interrelations since these combinations will increase our chances of making voices accessible to ourselves and ultimately to our audiences.

Recording and Accessing Participants' Voices: Conclusion

In each one of these qualitative research studies, my role as researcher has seen me coordinate interdependently with other human beings and various technologies to access and articulate participants' voices. No single method is infallible, but each technology and collaboration can bring forth novel possibilities. As another example of a collaborative project (Butler, Trager, and Behm), two colleagues and I used a custom automatic speech recognition program to automatically generate a rough transcript of our interviews with participants. We then cleaned up the transcripts to correct the errors and prepare the transcripts for analysis. Automatic speech recognition programs may become more reliable in the years to come—but it is crucial to always triple-check all transcripts for accuracy so that we can trust the subsequent analysis and findings. The malleable nature of digital writing research, especially in the face of technological advancements, means that we all will always have to continue to evaluate the affordances of each method for accessing and articulating participants' voices.

Implications: Accessing + Articulating Voices

The intertwining of interdependency, access, and jointing of multiple modes of communication productively enables the articulation of voices in digital writing research. The methodology and methods detailed in this chapter can be redesigned by other scholars in the continual process of improving how we all capture and disseminate our research findings with each other. I encourage such redesigns, which would—as I mentioned earlier—embody Jung's insistence that our field's intellectual work is interdependent, and that each individual's scholarship would not exist without the scholarship of colleagues in our field (107). We design each new project within the current context of scholarship in our field; with consideration to the affordances of traditional tools; with attention to the ever-evolving technologies that may have emerged since our previous research project; and with recognition of the need for different methods. Through being flexible and innovative with our methods, we can respond to Halbritter and Lindquist's forceful questions about speaking with and through "an audible voice, one that is not your own."

My experiences visualizing sounds and sounding visuals underscore that voice is not a singular property owned by a person who utters audible sound— sound that is heard by those who hear and not heard by those who do not hear. Voices—a researcher's voice, participants' voices, interpreters' voices, and others' voices—are shared entities through which our visual, aural, and other modes of communication are jointed and interrelated. Our interdependency and our continual commitment to designing access will enable us all to reassess and improve every project that we work on. Through this commitment to each other and to ourselves, we create novel possibilities for different individuals to articulate their own voices in rhetoric and composition. We show the value of making sound visible, of making visuals sonic, of sharing multiple voices with those who hear, see, feel, and communicate in different ways.

By always assessing our current research methods and methodologies, we can make rhetoric and composition even more inclusive and unveil new ways of articulating voices that can further expand the reach of audio and video to new audiences—and new researchers—in our field. I conclude this chapter by encouraging readers to actively engage with sound in visible ways, with visuals in sonic ways, and with other interrelated modes to enable as many people as possible to access and articulate our voices as writers, researchers, and fellow contributors to digital spaces.

Works Cited

Anderson, Erin. "Toward a Resonant Material Vocality for Digital Composition." *enculturation*, vol. 18, 2014, http://enculturation.net/materialvocality.

"Articulation." *The Merriam-Webster.com Dictionary*, https://www.merriam-webster.com/dictionary/articulation. Accessed 9 May 2022.

Bessette, Jean. "Audio, Archives, and the Affordance of Listening in a Pedagogy of 'Difference.'" *Computers and Composition*, vol. 39, 2016, pp. 71–82.

Brewer, Elizabeth, Cynthia L. Selfe, and M. Remi Yergeau. "Creating a Culture of Access in Composition Studies." *Composition Studies*, vol. 42, no. 2, 2014, pp. 151–54.

Buckner, Jennifer J., and Kirsten Daley. "Do You Hear What I Hear? A Hearing Teacher and a Deaf Student Negotiate Sound." Danforth, Stedman, and Faris, https://ccdigitalpress.org/book/soundwriting/buckner-daley/index.html.

Butler, Janine. "Integral Captions and Subtitles: Designing a Space for Embodied Rhetorics and Visual Access." 2017. East Carolina University, dissertation.

———. "Integral Captions and Subtitles: Designing a Space for Embodied Rhetorics and Visual Access." *Rhetoric Review*, vol. 37, no. 3, 2018, pp. 286–99.

———. "Principles for Cultivating Rhetorics and Research Studies within Communities." *Present Tense: A Journal of Rhetoric in Society*, vol. 8, no. 1, 2019, http://www.presenttensejournal.org/editorial/principles-for-cultivating-rhetorics-and-research-studies-within-communities/.

———. "Where Access Meets Multimodality: The Case of ASL Music Videos." *Kairos: A Journal of Rhetoric, Technology, and Pedagogy*, vol. 21, no. 1, 2016, http://kairos.technorhetoric.net/21.1/topoi/butler/index.html.

Butler, Janine, and Stacy Bick. "Sound, Captions, Action: Voices in Video Composition Projects." *Computers and Composition*, vol. 62, 2021, pp. 1–15.

Butler, Janine, Joseph Cirio, Victor Del Hierro, Laura Gonzales, Joy Robinson, and Angela Haas. "Caring for the Future: Initiatives for Further Inclusion in Computers and Writing." *Kairos: A Journal of Rhetoric, Technology, and Pedagogy*, vol. 22, no. 1, fall 2017, http://kairos.technorhetoric.net/22.1/disputatio/butler-et-al/index.html.

Butler, Janine, Brian Trager, and Byron Behm. "Exploration of Automatic Speech Recognition for Deaf and Hard of Hearing Students in Higher Education Classes." *Proceedings of the 21st International ACM SIGACCESS Conference on Computers and Accessibility* (ASSETS '19). Association for Computing Machinery (ACM), Oct. 2019, pp. 32–42, https://doi.org/10.1145/3308561.3353772.

Comstock, Michelle, and Mary E. Hocks. "Voice in the Cultural Soundscape: Sonic Literacy in Composition Studies." *Computers and Composition Online*, 2006, http://www.cconlinejournal.org/comstock_hocks/index.htm.

Danford, Courtney S., Kyle D. Stedman, and Michael J. Faris, editors. *Soundwriting Pedagogies*. Computers and Composition Digital Press, 2018, https://ccdigitalpress.org/book/soundwriting/.

Dolmage, Jay. "Disability, Usability, Universal Design." *Rhetorically Rethinking Usability*, edited by Susan Miller Cochran and Rochelle L. Rodrigo, Hampton Press, 2009, pp. 167–90.

Eyman, Douglas, et al. "Access/ibility: Access and Usability for Digital Publishing." *Kairos: A Journal of Rhetoric, Technology, and Pedagogy*, vol. 20, no. 2, 2016, http://kairos.technorhetoric.net/20.2/topoi/eyman-et-al/index.html.

Gonzales, Laura, and Janine Butler. "Working Toward Social Justice through Multilingualism, Multimodality, and Accessibility in Writing Classrooms." *Composition Forum*, vol. 44, 2020, https://compositionforum.com/issue/44/multilingualism.php.

Halbritter, Bump. *Mics, Cameras, Symbolic Action: Audio–Visual Rhetoric for Writing Teachers*. Parlor Press, 2012.

Halbritter, Bump, and Julie Lindquist. "Sleight of Ear: Voice, Voices, and Ethics of Voicing." Danforth, Stedman, and Faris, https://ccdigitalpress.org/book/soundwriting/halbritter-lindquist/index.html.

Hilligoss, Susan, and Sean Williams. "Composition Meets Visual Communication: New Research Questions." *Digital Writing Research: Technologies, Methodologies, and Ethical Issues*, edited by Heidi A. McKee and Dánielle Nicole DeVoss, Hampton Press, 2007, pp. 229–48.

Hocks, Mary E., and Michelle Comstock. "Composing for Sound: Sonic Rhetoric as Resonance." *Computers and Composition*, vol. 43, 2017, pp. 135–46.

Hope, Lacy. "Soundwriting Conversation: Introducing Soundwriting Pedagogies' Podcast Project." *Computers and Composition Digital Press*, 7 June 2019, https://ccdigitalpress.org/blog/2019/06/07/soundwriting-conversation.

Jung, Julie. "Interdependency as an Ethic for Accessible Intellectual Publics." *Reflections: Public Rhetoric Civic Writing and Service Learning*, vol. 14, no. 1, 2014, pp. 101–20.

McKee, Heidi. "Sound Matters: Notes Toward the Analysis and Design of Sound in Multimodal Webtexts." *Computers and Composition*, vol. 23, 2006, pp. 335–54.

Price, Margaret. "Disability Studies Methodology: Explaining Ourselves to Ourselves." *Practicing Research in Writing Studies: Reflexive and Ethically Responsible Research*, edited by Katrina M. Powell and Pamela Takayoshi, Hampton Press, 2012, pp. 159–86.

———. "Getting Specific about Disability Studies Methodology: Negotiating Reciprocity, Vulnerability and Validity (and a bunch of other stuff)." *Society for Disability Studies Conference*, Orlando, FL, 27 June 2013.

Price, Margaret, and Stephanie L. Kerschbaum. "Stories of Methodology: Interviewing Sideways, Crooked and Crip." *Canadian Journal of Disability Studies*, vol. 5, no. 3, 2016, pp. 18–56.

Rodrigue, Tanya K., et al. "Navigating the Soundscape, Composing with Audio." *Kairos: A Journal of Rhetoric, Technology, and Pedagogy*, vol. 21, no. 1, 2016, http://kairos.technorhetoric.net/21.1/praxis/rodrigue/index.html.

Selfe, Cynthia L. "The Movement of Air, The Breath of Meaning: Aurality and Multimodal Composing." *College Composition and Communication*, vol. 60, no. 4, 2009, pp. 611–63.

Shipka, Jody. "Sound Engineering: Toward a Theory of Multimodal Soundness." *Computers and Composition*, vol. 23, 2006, pp. 355–73.

VanKooten, Crystal. "A Research Methodology of Interdependence through Video as Method." *Computers and Composition*, vol. 54, 2019, pp. 1–17.

Wheeler, Stephanie K. "Communities of Access: A Program Profile of the University of Central Florida's Faculty Liaison Program in the Department of Writing and Rhetoric." *Composition Forum*, vol. 39, 2018, https://www.compositionforum.com/issue/39/ucf.php.

Yancey, Kathleen Blake. "Introduction: Definition, Intersection, and Difference—Mapping the Landscape of Voice." *Voices on Voice: Perspectives, Definitions, Inquiry*, edited by Kathleen Blake Yancey, National Council of Teachers of English, 1994, pp. vii–xxiv.

Yergeau, M. Remi, et al. "Multimodality in Motion: Disability and Kairotic Spaces." *Kairos: A Journal of Rhetoric, Technology, and Pedagogy*, vol. 18, no. 1, 2013, http://kairos.technorhetoric.net/18.1/coverweb/yergeau-et-al/pages/index.html.

Chapter 4. "Tell Virgil Write BRICK on my brick": Doctoral Bashments, (Re)Visiting Hiphopography and the Digital Discursivity of the DJ: A Mixed Down Methods Movement

Todd Craig

The Graduate Center of the City University of
New York and Medgar Evers College (CUNY)

Tracklist

Track 1:
"Lemme Start from the Beginning at the Top of the List":
The Needed Introduction Before We Get Started . . .

Track 2:
"Everyone, Meet King Johnson":
How Do I Envision and Imagine Teaching in the 21st Century?

Track 3:
"Everyone, Meet Griselda":
The Fashion Rebels of Cloth and Linguistic Textures in 2020

Track 4:
"A Quick Pause for the Cause . . . " aka
"I Might Just Listen to This While I Transcend"

Track 5:
"Ayo, you ever ate burgers on a Wednesday? You ever ate chicken on a Thursday?":
The Doctoral Bashment is in Full Effect in the Galaxy of Queens

Track 6:
The DJ Rhetoric Juggle:
How the Culture and Academia Mix on Two 12s

Track 7:
"Everyone, Meet Flores and Rosa":
So Get Down, Get Down with The Raciolinguistic Foundation

DOI: https://doi.org/10.37514/PRA-B.2022.1541.2.04

"Lemme Start from the Beginning at the Top of the List": The Needed Introduction Before We Get Started . . .

In true Hip-Hop DJ fashion, it's important to start with shout outs.
These words were originally birthed in locations
that should be recognized.
With that, I would like to give a respectful shout out,
acknowledgment and offer of deep gratitude to
the Onondaga Nation, firekeepers of the Haudenosaunee,
as well as the Lenape people,
the original custodians of the land and water
that supported these words.
When engaging in equity and social justice work,
I feel it's always critical to discuss historical aspects of land
and the shift of people in any given space's demographics.
At the time this piece was first conceived,
it was birthed sonically on
Onondaga Nation ground, then continued to grow on
Lenape ground–thus, this shout out is mandatory . . .
Not to be footnoted, endnoted or sidebarred.

In thinking about culturally relevant and equitable teaching and research practices, I always find it useful to identify the intermingling of these ideas in my own groove. My research constantly informs my teaching and vice versa; because I rarely see a distinction between strong research and pedagogical practices, "'Tell Virgil Write BRICK on my brick': Doctoral Bashments, (Re)Visiting Hiphopography and the Digital Discursivity of the DJ," reflects on research methodologies that emanate from my personal classroom praxis. In envisioning the vital nexus of contemporary research theories and methodologies in my own teacher-researcher processes, this chapter (re)views the idea of hiphopography alongside raciolinguistics as a way to both interrogate the presence of Hip-Hop pedagogy specifically within my teaching, as well as (re)envision and (re)illuminate hiphopography and raciolinguistics as an avenue by which to spotlight Hip-Hop participants and practitioners in order to avoid the stereotypical "NatGeo" perspective of Hip-Hop research and scholarship as wax poetic motions. And to be clear, I define "the NatGeo perspective" as the feeling I still get when I happen to be skimming through TV channels and land on an episode of National Geographic. You know the feeling: there's video of an animal landscape, that's usually accompanied by a voice, typically of the British or Aussie-sounding persuasion. Said voice functions in semi-golf-announcer whisper and serves as the "silent observer" aka "the innocent bystander" aka the "videographic voyeur" who "reports" on the "climate" of a subject's "life and culture" from a distance that makes these real lives and real lived experiences feel implicitly and blatantly judged by the referential of the speaker/viewer/voyeur.

Be clear—we ain't about that NatGeo life here . . .

During this journey, we will think about a young boy named King Johnson and his connection to my students, and Hip-Hop artists Jay-Z and the Notorious B.I.G. This will bring us to the importance of hiphopography in research via DJ Rhetoric. We will then make a turn towards hiphopography in scholarship creation via DJ dissertations, bouncing to Griselda and embracing aspects of raciolinguistics through the lens of Hip-Hop aesthetics. This chapter also intends to demonstrate how all these research and pedagogical methodologies are aligned with culturally relevant and culturally sustaining approaches in their best ways.

Moreover, because my work is rooted in DJ Rhetoric (Craig), I approach this chapter as DJing on the page. Like any good DJ set, it requires that the listener has enough faith in the DJ to embark on a sonic journey. The listener never truly knows where the DJ will go but has the faith and trust to know that, by the end, the DJ will have served as a tour guide on a fantastic voyage that'll always be Coolio (Big Pun intended, and intended). Note that part of the theory here unfolds in the praxis encompassing not only *what* words are on the page, but *how* they are placed, sequenced, and programmed. Thus, I ask you to embark on a digital-rhetoric research-methods journey with me, DJ style. If you can hold fast and follow along, I promise you'll pick up some jewels along the way—by the end, you'll be happy you took this trip with me, word.

"Everyone, Meet King Johnson": How Do I Envision and Imagine Teaching in the 21st Century?

We start this chapter with an introduction to the young homie named King. King Johnson is a Chicago public school student. He was around eight years old when he wrote this journal entry in January of 2018, which probably puts him in third grade. I came across King when I first saw an image of his writing. A picture of his journal entry was posted on Facebook by King's mother, but quickly went viral. I found it shared as "The 10 Blackest Things About This Kid's Journal Entry

Roasting His Teacher for Lying About Christopher Columbus" in a blog written by Damian Young days before the semester started; I immediately included it into the second-day fabric of my Intermediate Composition course. I projected it onto the board, and upon first glance, most students simply recognized it as a funny meme. If you have never seen it, I will quote it below so you can follow along:

> Today was not a good learning day. Blah blah blah I only wanted to hear you not talking. You said something wrong and I can't listen when I hear lies. My mom said that the only Christofer we actnokledj is Wallace. Because Columbus didn't find our country the Indians did. I like to have Columbus day off but I want you to not teach me lies. That is all. My question for the day is how can white people teach black history?

The reader, who we mostly assume is King's teacher, responds in red ink writing: "King I am very disappointed in your journal today." The final response is written by King . . . one word: "Ok."

King is an example I use in my writing classes when I want to introduce the concept of research. I have a student read the entry aloud, then I give everyone a chance to write quietly on what they see, think, and feel about the text. Then, students are paired and given about ten minutes or so to discuss what they've written based on three questions:

1. Tally up the similar points you and your partner made.
2. What would you and your partner tell King?
3. What might you and your partner tell King's teacher?

Afterwards, we engage in a longer class talkback session, where I ask pairs to share their take on King Johnson, on the teacher's response, on King's final response, and other issues they might deem relevant to the conversation.

Over the past few semesters, I've used this text and I have accumulated what I will label here as a very unscientific poll consisting of responses students give from their experience and initial reactions to King's writing. The responses have emanated from courses I teach in first-year writing, intermediate composition, and Hip-Hop worldview. And depending on the student demographic, the responses vary. It's also important to recognize that I see these students as the future scholars in the field, so they hold such value in this moment. Many of them will be the practitioners who will inevitably be teaching the K-16 versions of King Johnson.

These moments become paramount in how perspectives can be interrupted, disrupted and even altered for the sake of the students who are being engaged, and the future Kings that these student-scholars-as-educators will engage. For example, in my intermediate composition class (which is a mix of both English and education majors), students describe how they felt King was "disrespectful," "kids say unfiltered things," "you can tell he doesn't care about his teacher (and thereby, authority)." In other discussions, I've heard students say that King situating his mother as the source of knowledge seems to be the way he can validate his connection to and the cultural relevance of Hip-Hop. While we address these comments as a class, I use this journal entry to shift students to my overarching argument about King: he's an extraordinary researcher and writer. I'd love to take King under my wing and explore some of his thoughts and ideas. Here's why . . .

Most of my students do not understand the reference that King makes when he states in his journal that the "Only Christofer we actnokledj is Wallace." This is a quote from Shawn Carter, who we all probably know as Beyonce's husband . . . but sometimes we know him as Jay-Z. It is a quote from his song "Oceans" featuring Frank Ocean. In this discussion, I walk students through the song, which is an interesting take on the waters that serve as a puzzle piece in what we consider to be a luxurious lifestyle, while those same waters serve as part of the vehicle that brought Africans to the Americas as slaves, in addition to the environmental contexts of exploitation for big business' sake ("the oil spill at BP ain't clean up"). When Jay-Z describes it, he states:

> It's like, me now, no matter where I go in life, and the things I accomplished, right? You walk in that room and your past still come in with you. You know, people talk, like "that guy who used to be the dealer from the projects and" do-do-do-do-do-do! Then back again to that duality, the sound of like a celebration of where we are now, you know, on some big yacht and throwing champagne in the water, but the undertow of the thing is like this same water is the water that brought us here, you know, originally as slaves. So it has this whole duality, and how we write history. You know, even the stories we were told about the history of America. "I'm anti-Santa Maria" —talking about these stories. "Only Christopher we acknowledge is Wallace" —Biggie Smalls. "Silk and fleeces, lay on my Jesus, oh my God I hope y'all don't get seasick" —You know, playing with the theme now: being seasick, or seeing these things and being jealous of it.

After walking through Jay-Z's commentary, the rich and deep context that emerges from Jay-Z's lyrics can truly be helpful in getting students to (re)envision and (re)imagine what "text" and "writing" look like in the 21st century. Furthermore, it demonstrates how Hip-Hop permeates a younger generation and can be harnessed as a teaching tool when educators are willing to be open and receptive to the cultural capital students bring with them into the classroom on a daily basis.

In addition, this pedagogical wrinkle in time marries both methodology and digital practices. This teaching technique is a method that, in and of itself, involves culturally relevant and culturally sustaining pedagogical sentiments. The conversation around "research" is on my students' terms. It meets them where they are in a contemporary fashion, while it simultaneously models approaches they can employ and deploy as rising educators. Just look at the lesson materials: a meme, a video, a song and potentially a digital article (if you want to take the next step and review how King's mother assessed and analyzed this situation). In fact, all these tools are digital. There is not a print-based textbook to be found, not a single white page with black alphanumeric symbols in hand. This lesson is virtual, as every material interfaces with either the digital or sonic world.

I hope students walk away from this conversation with a sense of how we see aspects of research, student language, literacy, citizenship and participation, and composing strategies, especially when thinking about Hip-Hop culture as the lens through which our students speak, write and interact with us in formal and informal settings. And when I think about Hip-Hop language and literacy in our current times, I'm immediately drawn to Griselda.

"Everyone, Meet Griselda": The Fashion Rebels of Cloth and Linguistic Textures in 2020

When I think about freedom from the formulaics of linguistic conventions, the first contemporary example that comes to mind is Griselda. I can clearly recall the day I was in the Classic Material store when the homie Carlos said to me, "Oh, you don't know Griselda? Nah, you gotta sit down and listen . . . " For those who are not familiar with Griselda, they are a Hip-Hop family (literally). The best ways to describe Griselda—which is the trio of Conway the Machine, Westside Gunn and Benny the Butcher—is to think about the first time you heard "Protect Your Neck" by Wu-Tang Clan. Couple that feeling with the feeling you get when you hear the song "Shook Ones Part II" by Mobb Deep. For those that don't know the song, think about the movie 8 Mile with Eminem: listen to the opening credits and then the instrumental that comes on during the culminating battle scenes. The impact of those two feelings will bring you to the sonic experience presented by Griselda.

I invoke Griselda because they are one of the next Hip-Hop landmarks. If you let them tell it, Westside Gunn will declare "we didn't switch up and go South Paw." Their main concern was not to chase financial wellness by bending their musical and artistic vision to that of the Hip-Hop money-makin' status quo. Let Conway tell it, and he gives it to you in rhyme: "I ain't bring New York back / I put Buffalo in the front!"—highlighting how other artists began to rhyme like they were from a southern state in the past ten years or so, even when they are from Brooklyn, or Manhattan, or one of the other five boroughs of New York City. What is most exciting about Griselda is they have not compromised their music or sound at all. Convention for Griselda is predicated on unconventional attitudes and approaches that don't just bump back against, but instead bumrush and bodyslam the expected norms and calculations. There are a few tradition-ally formatted songs, but for the most part, they rhyme until they're finished, shattering the whole "sixteen-bar-verse-eight-bar-chorus" blueprint we're used to . . . and a brilliant shattering, it is. Their music is very gritty, grimy—ask Benny the Butcher and he'll say, "you know Conway likes them spooky beats." Whenever you're listening to Griselda, you feel as if you are walking down a dark alley—the streetlights are flickering, you can't see the end of the path. It's that part of the movie when you scream at the screen, "Noooooo . . . don't go that way!!!"

So, in summoning Griselda, I'd like to take us to "DR BIRDS"—the first single off their debut album *WWCD* (What Would Chine Gun Do) with the video produced by Hype Williams. Hype Williams is the video director of Hip-Hop's golden era of big-budget three-to-five-minute blockbuster visuals. Imagine the lush color palettes of *The Great Gatsby*, the intricate on-screen complexities of *Inception*—then, wrap those cinematic stylings into classic storylines like *Casino*, *Goodfellas*, *Titanic*, and *Bad Boys*. To help establish a particular context, Hype served as Hip-Hop's Baz Luhrmann ("The Get Down"), Chris Nolan, Martin Scorsese, James Cameron and Michael Bay all in one, as he has directed videos for artists including Busta Rhymes, Kanye West, Missy Elliot, Beyonce, LL Cool J, Puff Daddy, Mobb Deep, Nas, Tupac, Jay-Z, TLC, Jessica Simpson, Nelly Furtado, Boyz II Men, Pharrell Williams, Travis Scott, Ke$ha, Jennifer Lopez, Janet Jackson, John Legend, Jamie Foxx and Drake. Finally, Williams directed the cult Hip-Hop classic film *Belly*, starring Nas, DMX and T-Boz of TLC.

Another notable distinction for Griselda is their ability to navigate language that runs the gambit. Westside Gunn's alias is "Flygod"—he'll basically tell you about the high-brow fashion pieces he has purchased right off the runway in Milan or Paris in one line, but then tell you the crack just finished cooking and needs a little more time to dry in the next line. The epitome of this moment in "DR. BIRDS" is the thread that loops the needle of the song between Westside Gunn, Conway the Machine and Benny the Butcher . . .

That moment: "Tell Virgil write BRICK on my brick."

With those lyrics, Flygod is essentially telling Virgil Abloh (RIP), the Creative Director of Louis Vuitton, and one of the most brilliant minds behind the fashion line we all know as Off-White (which we've seen touch down on everything from Nike Sneakers to Ikea bags, rugs and other home decor,) to write the word "BRICK" on a brick (which is slang for a pound, or a kilo, of cocaine). On the surface, this juncture is a very clear marriage of street-corner politics and high-fashion couture. The best visuals to describe this intersection come from legendary fashion designer Dapper Dan: take a second and think back to Jam Master Jay in the custom-made Louis Vuitton tracksuit, Eric B. and Rakim in the custom Gucci sweatsuits for the *Follow the Leader* album cover, or Bobby Brown in the head-to-toe bright-red Gucci suit (Day; Mahon). The Dapper Dan aesthetics of the early-1980s to mid-1990s is simply unmatched in Hip-Hop fashion culture. Dap would take your favorite high-end luxury brand (Louis Vuitton, Gucci, MCM) and remix it (although we could argue that Dapper Dan was the Original Hip Hop Repurposing Fashionista) for anything from clothing to car interiors . . . sound familiar?

So, when Westside Gunn hits that lick with this lyric, he is evoking a historic Hip-Hop fashion flashpoint, but also invoking a long-standing Hip-Hop sentiment, merging multiple worlds to weave a snapshot of the times we live and breathe in; be very clear, if the new "War on Drugs" was aimed at crack, this line simply wouldn't exist in 2021, when crack has been the scourge of the urban inner-cities since the 1980s. Thus, Westside would have nothing for Virgil to write on! It makes me think that maybe Big Meech should've *been* asking for organic soul food . . . but alas, I digress. . . .

But the importance of that phrase, "Tell Virgil write BRICK on my brick," has more levels to it. Let's leave it here for a second. But fear not, I'll be right back to address it . . .

"A Quick Pause for the Cause . . . " aka "I Might Just Listen to This While I Transcend"

At this point, it is important to recognize that neither Dr. Craig, The Graduate Center of the City University of New York, Medgar Evers College, the City University of New York at large, nor the editors of this collection, condone or promote the usage, distribution, or sale of crack cocaine or any other illegal narcotic. The analysis of the line, "BRICK on my brick," however, is important for educational purposes.

I'm finished what I had to say, now we can continue on (Prodigy).

And now, back to the regularly scheduled program . . .

"Ayo, you ever ate burgers on a Wednesday? You ever ate chicken on a Thursday?": The Doctoral Bashment is in Full Effect in the Galaxy of Queens

In April 2020, Hip-Hop media personality Peter Rosenberg interviewed Westside Gunn for the release of his album *Pray for Paris*. During their discussion, they talk about the importance and the background behind Westside Gunn's song with iconic DJ/Producer, the legendary DJ Premier, entitled "Shawn vs. Flair." As they listen to the beginning of the song, and the opening chorus, Rosenberg stops and asks Westside the importance of the line: "you ever ate burgers on a Wednesday? You ever ate chicken on a Thursday?" (Gunn). In this moment, Westside Gunn chuckles and then explains how this language is a frequency geared specifically towards his Griselda fans that have been incarcerated in a federal penitentiary. Westside details those lyrics as:

> . . . well, when you in the Feds, they feed you burgers on Wednesday and chicken on Thursdays. So when I was in prison, you

know what I'm saying, that was the line that if you was locked
up in the Feds, you get this automatically, you know what I'm
saying? It's like I was talking to them . . . that was just for the
homies that was locked up behind the wall, in case they hear it.
And just people that's fresh home or did a bid, they can relate to
it automatically.

This moment in conversation continues to push forth the range within which
Westside Gunn and Griselda have been able to oscillate when it comes to language
and literacy practices. Moments like this contribute to my analysis of Griselda,
which builds upon my ruminations around DJ Rhetoric and literacy.

The idea of DJ Rhetoric began to really percolate with me on March 5, 2013:
the day I defended my dissertation. After writing three hundred pages, I honestly
had nothing else to say. So, what made the most sense was connecting all the
songs from the first chapter of my dissertation, so my committee could see and
hear the discursive elements I spent all that time writing about. And yes—the
majority of my doctoral defense was a DJ set that would've been a great party if
we did it later in the day! To imagine what my work means and represents in real-
time, it *must* start with the DJ. I've been a DJ longer than I haven't been a DJ, and
my work has consistently focused on the rhetoric and literacy of the DJ. As well,
the common mantra I learned in my creative writing experiences has always been
"show, don't tell." So, I've been fine with telling by simply showing people about
the telling. This has been my normal modus operandi; I've attended many a Conference on College Composition and Communication (CCCC), many a National
Council of Teachers of English Assembly on Research (NCTEAR), many a Wat-
son conference with two portable turntables and a mixer—and shown the room
as the telling. I did do some talking, but I mainly let the sonics of the songs show
my telling. It is also critical to note that digital methodologies were present in
my DJ work. At the time of these conferences, Serato Scratch Live was a software
that allowed a DJ to interface with any iTunes playlist with two digital control
records. With a small convertor box, the outcome was the ability to transform a
mp3 in your iTunes catalog into a record on a turntable, manipulated by the control vinyl. This showing has always been forward-thinking, in conversation and
interaction with digital interfaces. Know that "DR BIRDS" is the latest song in my
DJ set, which stems from an intellectual research roadmap. It's also important to
note that this chapter, in fact, started *solely* as a DJ set.

The thinking around my research on DJ Rhetoric and literacy (Craig) ema-
nates from the space of not being able to find enough Hip-Hop DJ scholarship that
not only adds onto, but also simultaneously includes experts and practitioners of
the culture. I have been a DJ for over twenty years; my research interests come
from having knowledge of the discursive forms and operations of DJs, and stem
from a love of Hip-Hop culture and a genuine desire to represent Hip-Hop DJ
culture thoroughly. Specifically, my knowledge of DJ discursive modes serves as

the construct of Hip-Hop aesthetics introduced by Emery Petchauer. In his article, "Starting with Style: Toward a Second Wave of Hip-Hop Education Research and Practice," he labels "the word *aesthetic* to signal that one would find these 'ways of doing and being' in the sonic, kinesthetic, linguistic, and visual practices/expressions of hip-hop" (Petchauer 79).

Throughout the landscape of academia, many academics have been placed at the forefront of conversations around Hip-Hop culture, yet these same people were never able to dictate what Hip-Hop is in any circle beyond limited academic ones. By allowing this alternate spotlighting, two critical issues become apparent. First, the alternate spotlight shifts the focus away from the cultural practitioners and organic intellectuals who have truly contributed to the historic narrative of Hip-Hop culture. Second, it diminishes the cultural capital and felt senses of students who enter our classrooms with innate and, many times, inherent knowledge of the music and culture. Thus, educators who engage in this practice are in effect rejecting the students they claim to love working with so much via "Hip-Hop in the classroom." This is not to say that only an elite few can participate in meaning making; it *is* to say we should be thoughtful and deliberate about who is "chosen" to tell the story or speak for the culture, so that knowledgeable voices are not marginalized or ostracized from academic conversations around Hip-Hop.

The DJ Rhetoric Juggle: How the Culture and Academia Mix on Two 12s

In order to define and identify DJ Rhetoric, I use English scholar Carmen Kynard's work as a springboard. When discussing African American student protest history, she recognizes rhetoric as a concept that stretches beyond stylized speech and language. Instead, she envisions rhetoric as a culmination of cultural and historical knowledge, and ways of knowing that are perpetually communicated in the written and spoken word, as well as visuals, physical movement, banter, and other aspects of social and cultural community participatory activities (Kynard). In pushing towards a DJ Rhetoric, it is here where I add onto Kynard's definition; part of a DJ's language extends beyond just the "language, oral and written." It is also about what gets said "sonically" by a DJ as well. The ways in which a DJ decides to express herself and communicate that expression amongst members within and outside of DJ culture via turntables and the sounds she creates with her highly researched archive and collection of music has everything to do with the sonic quality and kinesthetic actions of the choices she makes.

Because DJ Rhetoric centers the DJ in both definition and practice, I contend we must do this work in a way that responds to how Hip-Hop scholarship within English studies has excluded community members of the culture in that scholarly conversation. This approach will require a change in the typical "Nat-Geo ethnography" perspective that runs throughout English studies, and instead needs to privilege a different set of voices in this integral cultural conversation. Even though I am a researcher and English scholar, my DJ peers know, understand, and trust my commitment to the DJ community, to Hip-Hop culture and to ensuring DJ Rhetoric, pedagogy, literacy, and culture is presented in a way that is objective, while still serving as an honest portrait of the cultural, communicative, and discursive principles of the Hip-Hop DJ.

I place the DJ and DJ Rhetoric squarely in the midst and the tradition of Hip-Hop literacy, Hip-Hop rhetoric, and Hip-Hop pedagogy. While Hip-Hop may currently serve as global popular culture, it was birthed, nursed, and raised by African American culture. There's also an argument to be made that since the DJ is the ultimate creator of Hip-Hop culture, that Hip-Hop literacy sits underneath the umbrella of the DJ, which sits within the umbrella of African American rhetoric and discourse.

Since the inception of Hip-Hop, DJs have always done work that is rooted in the Black feminist tradition. Ask any of the founding fathers or first-generation Hip-Hop DJs, they will tell you they borrowed from their mothers' multi-genre record collections; in fact, it most oftentimes is the feminine figure in their lives who have cultivated their sonic sensibilities and curation skills. For example, in "Crate Digging Begins at Home," Jennifer Stoever outlines how pioneering DJs such as Afrika Bambaataa, Grandmaster Flash, Grandwizzard Theodore and Larry Levan pulled their first tunes from their mothers' record collections. In exploring and highlighting the details of a "feminist listening praxis," Stoever identifies the concept:

> Particularly when understood as a method of critically listening to the past, feminist historiography bears striking resemblance to record collecting and selecting as innovated by Bronx mothers. Black and Latinx women collecting and selecting records manifested new forms of listening—to themselves, to history, and to their present surroundings—what I am calling a feminist listening praxis . . . Bronx mothers freed these sounds to create new contexts, audiences, and meters, particularly when changed up, back spun, and cut by their DJ-ing sons and daughters. (11)

Pushing back against the dominant narrative that all things Hip-Hop flowed from a male-dominated perspective, Stoever pinpoints the connection with each of these foundational DJs and how they have learned to listen, apprehend, and manipulate music from their mothers, sisters, aunties, and the likes; this connects the origins of the Hip-Hop DJ directly to the Black feminist tradition, as

> there is something specifically feminine and radically black/brown about hip hop's sonic labor—DJing in particular—and such work often begins with a woman's hand dropping the needle, spinning another-worldly soundscapes of radical love, politics, affirmation and care. Both record collecting and hip

hop are more gender diverse and multigenerational than previously understood, and women's living room selecting func-
tioned as an important practice in its own right, congruent with
and intimately related to public DJing. (Stoever 9–10)

This Black feminist labor culminates in Grandmaster Flash's understanding of
the power of music to viscerally change the human emotion, Bambaataa's acknowledgement of sonic and visual influences, or Larry Levan's technical ritual of placing
a needle on a record at age three. All of these skill sets were birthed and taught by
women and feminist praxis, thus influencing the ways that the progenitors of Hip-
Hop would bring the sound, the visuals and the technical sentiments to the forefront.

Ultimate Breaks and Beats (UBB) co-founder Louis "Breakbeat Lou" Flores also
discusses the importance of both his mother's records and his sister bringing him
to his first Hip-Hop jams. Hip-Hop's foundational DJs will tell you they learned
music from the various records their mothers and grandmothers and aunts and
sisters would play on Saturdays and Sundays, or would play at times when certain
emotions needed to be induced, maintained or soothed; these tunes were not the
background or the backdrop—they were the soundtrack to life, the score to child-
hoods, and the planted seeds that would grow the sonic roots of what we now know
as Hip-Hop culture. This concept is keenly documented by Stoever. In the spirit of
UBB and as a homage to the work Breakbeat Lou and Breakbeat Lenny did, take
this moment as me pointing you to one of the numbered compilations in citing
Stoever—she hits a series of critical tracks integral to this conversation (including Tricia Rose, Elaine Richardson, Toni Blackman, Joan Morgan and Gwendolyn
Pough). This is where I'm sampling from the volume with all the funky joints on it.

So now, as we think about DJ Rhetoric and literacy, and situate it in African
American rhetoric and literacy, why mention King Johnson and Griselda? King's
ability to cite references that help us to understand his innate cultural capital, or
Griselda's deft maneuverings between elite class fashion talk and straight gutter
crime slang reflects the ideas presented by Nelson Flores and Jonathan Rosa. In
their article "Undoing Appropriateness: Raciolinguistic Ideologies and Language
Diversity in Education," they highlight the idea of raciolinguistic ideologies,
"that conflate certain racialized bodies with linguistic deficiency unrelated to any
objective linguistic practices" (150).

"Everyone, Meet Flores and Rosa": So Get Down, Get Down with The Raciolinguistic Foundation

What's particularly interesting about Flores and Rosa, is when they describe
the effect of raciolinguistic ideologies on Heritage language learners, long-
term English learners and standard English learners, and when they mention
Tamara—a long-term English learner who fluidly adjusts her language based on
her listening public—they state the following:

> We find that these so-called long-term English learners are adept
> at using their bilingualism in strategic and innovative ways-in-
> deed, in ways that might be considered quite appropriate and
> desirable were they animated by a privileged white student . . .
> were Tamara a privileged white student engaging in English
> linguistic practices in the ways that she did in this interview,
> her linguistic practices would likely be perceived differently. In
> fact, were she a privileged white student who was able to engage
> in the bilingual language practice that she described, she might
> even be perceived as linguistically gifted (Flores and Rosa 158).

There is a leap here that I am making, where I am clearly putting Latinx theories around bilingualism in solidarity with theories around both Hip-Hop literacies and African American Vernacular English (AAVE)—which is work that
Flores and Rosa also do in their article. Where this moment resonates with me,
is where we might think about both King and Griselda. Let's return to my very
unscientific study about student responses to King from the start of this chapter. Many students felt King's dialogue with his teacher was inappropriate, even
though no one realized the research-filled savvy in his youthful assertion that
the "only Christofer we actnokledj is Wallace" (Johnson). And very few students
would even acknowledge what King said is actually truthful from a historical perspective. Let's use a different lens to approach this idea: some might be appalled to
hear any Griselda member talking about cooked crack cocaine drying, yet somehow, we feel a little bit better when our good friend Marshall Mathers used to talk
about poppin' pills and committing violent acts against his daughter's mother,
while his daughter served as his accomplice. In no way is this an attack against
Eminem, who is an extraordinary lyricist. But this is a commentary that hope-
fully helps us to look at the double standard that exists around language usage,
linguistic dexterity, and who is privileged as "savvy" (aka "worthy") versus "ele-
mentary" (aka "indictable") users and communicators.

Subsequently, what about the potential implications of the raciolinguistic ideologies that label DJ Rhetoric inadequate to stand alone (as this chapter stemmed
from a DJ set that could speak to all these issues with two turntables and a mixer),
and required me to type these very words to you in a privileged academic alphanumeric type of font? At this point, the methodological approach that serves to
(re)introduce and center cultural participants and practitioners is hiphopography.

"What We Gon' Do in Ninety-Two, Even Though We Had Fun in Ninety-One . . ." aka "Everyone, Meet Spady": The Importance of Hiphopography in Research Methodology

In order to have a clear view of the importance of a contemporary spotlighting of hiphopography, it makes sense to push towards its definition, into its past

appearances, and then towards its timeliness in 2021 and beyond. The initial introduction to the methodological approach known as "hiphopography" comes from scholar and independent researcher James G. Spady. In *Nation Conscious Rap*, the first of Spady's three-book exploration of Hip-Hop, he and Joseph D. Eure are clear on their approach in thinking about the cultural and scholarly importance of Hip-Hop participants and practitioners; in talking with those "Hip-Hop visionaries" who are responsible for making various aspects of Hip-Hop music and culture grow and thrive, Spady and Eure identified the connection with these early Hip-Hop tastemakers as

> necessary to realize that the interviewers/editors were as interested in the rap artists' narrative discourse as its historical context. An interview is a speech event. You should have been physically on location as these visionaries/knowers rapped . . . that is why we decided to do a HipHopography of the Bronx rather than an Ethnography of the Bronx. The crucial difference is the fact that in our case, we shared the cultural, philosophical values embedded in Black life stylings. HipHopography provides unique means of assessing and accessing the word/world realities found therein . . . as Hip Hop investigators we saw it as crucial to render the subject's cultural realities as accurately as possible. (Spady and Eure vii)

This methodological approach is picked up most notably by H. Samy Alim throughout a series of texts worth mentioning here. In his early educational teacher-researcher experiences with middle and high school students, Alim came to a critical conclusion, one that brings us full circle back to my good friend King. In "'The Whig Party Don't Exist in My Hood': Knowledge, Reality, and Education in the Hip Hop Nation," Alim states that

> I have frequently drawn upon Hip Hop Culture in educational practice, but I have also developed ways of using Hip Hop Culture itself as educational practice. It is one thing to view the culture of our students as a resource for teaching about other subjects, and it is quite another to see our students as the sources, investigators, and archivers of varied and rich bodies of knowledge rooted in their cultural-linguistic reality. (17)

Alim's desire to extend value to his students' cultural capital and ways of knowing, richly vast and deeply steeped in the knowledge frameworks lent to them via Hip-Hop culture, is the same line of thinking that informs his research when thinking about his approach to understanding his concept of Hip Hop Nation Language (HHNL) and Hip Hop Linguistics (HHLx). This approach is highlighted in Alim's seminal text *Roc the Mic Right: The Language of Hip Hop Culture*. In this book, Alim describes the importance of Hiphopography to his own research, and its overarching relevance to making sense of the importance of communicative practices when thinking about ethical research with Hip-Hop practitioners:

> The hiphopography paradigm integrates the varied approaches of ethnography, biography, and social, cultural, and oral history to arrive at an emic view of Hip Hop Culture. It is hiphopography that obligates [Hip Hop Linguistics] to directly engage with the cultural agents of the Hip Hop Culture-World, revealing rappers as critical interpreters of their own culture. We view "rappers" and "cultural critics" and "cultural theorists" whose thoughts and ideas help us to make sense of one of the most important cultural movements of the late twentieth and early twenty-first centuries. (Alim 11)

It is here where Alim connects the idea of hiphopography as a research methodology that not only centers the cultural practices of Hip-Hop, but also the cultural participants and practitioners. In an effort to capture those conversations as accurately as possible, both Alim and Spady argue that it requires understanding the context of the language used by Hip-Hop cultural practitioners, and presenting those moments in conversation, from a researcher perspective, as raw and uncut as possible. This research methodology allows for a humanizing effect similar to that purported by other research methodologies so readily accepted in the academy:

> Hiphopography began as the study of Hip Hop cultural practice, a Hip Hop Cultural Studies, if you will—not as a subparadigm within cultural studies, but as a movement lying somewhere between cultural studies and cultural anthropology. My own studies seek to reinvigorate cultural studies' commitment to the people and put into practice what cultural anthropology espouses, that is, a nonhierarchical, anticolonial approach that humanizes its subject . . . hiphopography humanizes Hip Hop. (Alim 12)

Thus, hiphopography becomes a research-based methodology aimed at preserving the Hip-Hop aesthetics (Petchauer) as they are created, engaged in, and described by members of Hip-Hop culture.

Alim continues to dig into defining hiphopography in his article "'The Natti Ain't No Punk City': Emic Views of Hip Hop Cultures" when he states:

> Hiphopography can be described as an approach to the study of Hip Hop culture that combines the methods of ethnography, biography, and social and oral history. Importantly, hiphopography is not traditional ethnography . . . hiphopography assumes that the culture creators of Hip Hop are quite capable of telling their own story. (Alim 969–70)

It is here where Alim addresses the multi-faceted approach that is needed with hiphopography; this same approach requires that the weight of the research, the storytelling and meaning-making lies with the members of Hip-Hop culture, and not necessarily with the researcher's preconceived notions of what Hip-Hop "might" be, as "in hiphopography, the values, aesthetics, thoughts, narratives, and interpretations of the culture creators are our starting point" (Alim 970). This approach is far from another episode of NatGeo—feel me . . . ?

Years later, Spady would return to his definition of hiphopography. In his 2013 article "Mapping and Re-Membering Hip Hop History, Hiphopography and African Diasporic History," he reflects on his two-decade old methodology. In reflecting on the "insider-outsider" debate in field research, Spady revisits his methodology by stating:

> What we do as Hiphopography, a paradigmatic shift away from 'insider/outsider' language and practice. We purposely embraced a non-hierarchal method that enabled interlocutors engaged in the old philosophical practice of conversation to be mutually present. Conversation presupposes that interactants are mutually present to one another. There is equanimity within discourse ciphas; or, at the very least, that is the goal. (130)

At its best, hiphopography serves as a mixed-methods formulated approach that neutralizes the categories of insider and outsider, and lends itself more to the sense of focused conversational happenstance. The knowledge of doing and being comes primarily from the Hip-Hop practitioner, who serves on an equal footing to that of the researcher, who aims to gain understanding of said cultural phenomena.

We see this idea germane to scholarship that identifies new and innovative approaches to understanding a second wave of Hip-Hop education and research (Petchauer). We also see this research methodology used by recent scholarship that addresses Hip-Hop communities around practitioners of Hip-Hop elements; most notable are scholarly pieces that submerge themselves in the conversation of knowledge and meaning-making from Hip-Hop participants (Craig; Baez and Craig; Castillo and Craig; Lacey and Craig; Craig and Kynard) as well as from Hip-Hop based communities and communicators (Del Hierro; Duthely; Stoever; Mckoy). These are just a few sources that not only align with the practices that emanate from hiphopography, but also research that makes both conscious and subconscious choices towards centering the voices of Hip-Hop community members in a way that reflects the importance of culturally relevant and culturally sustaining research and pedagogy. Think back for a second to the teaching conversation around King Johnson, who evoked Jay-Z through the life lessons given to him by his mom (who is clearly an avid Hip-Hop listener, evidenced by her ability to quote a lesser-known Jay-Z album cut, as opposed to the larger-than-life singles that Jay has used to permeate radio, satellite, and popular culture airwaves). Both King and his mother are participants and not just observers. This is the type of connectivity that hiphopography can provide to classroom settings. Finally, the act of a dissertation defense that centers around two Technic 1200s fully displays my work as a DJ as methodological praxis from a Hip-Hop cultural participant; this cultural inclusivity is presented to us early by Spady via hiphopography. At this nexus, where King Johnson, DJ dissertation defenses, Griselda, raciolinguistics and hiphopography meet, we can find the heuristic for ethical and inclusive research that centers the participants and the intrinsic elements of the culture. To put it plainly, it's like Sy Sperling used to say in that old Hair Club for Men commercial: "I'm not only the Hair Club president, but I'm also a client."

The Chapter's Cipha: When All the Ingredients in the Pot Come Together

As we come to the close of this mix, it's important to spend some time recapping the journey. Marley Marl used to do it with Mr. Magic, as did Pete Rock with Marley, as did Prince Messiah with KOOL DJ Red Alert and, of course, as did Bobbito with Stretch Armstrong. Where Spady and the (re)introduction of hiphopography become paramount is in thinking about our young friend King Johnson, and the moment that his teacher has missed out on. Instead of being able to elevate King's cultural capital around Hip-Hop culture and use it as the basis by which they can have a student-centered conversation around historical fact-checking and meaning-making via research and referencing, King is simply diminished and not taken seriously for the researcher and scholar that he is. This is a conversation I pushed my students to (re)think; as English and education majors, how are we missing the "teachable moment" that has presented itself? Consequently, what message are we sending to faculty and students of racialized and marginalized communities when we don't examine, interrogate, and address these missed moments right when they appear? Flores and Rosa offer the following remedy to confront these ideologies:

> The question of whether members of racialized communities are accepted as appropriately engaging in these linguistic practices continues to be determined by the white listening subject, not by the speakers' actual practices. Therefore, antiracist social transformation cannot be based solely on supporting language-minoritized students in engaging in the linguistic practices of the white speaking subject but must also work actively to dismantle the hierarchies that produce the white listening subject. (167)

So how does this work for us in this moment? I think what Flores and Rosa are calling for is, similar to Spady and Alim, a (re)examination as well as a restructuring of these oppressive and exclusionary hierarchies. So there is something quite disruptive in knowing that Griselda initially signed to a distribution deal with Shady Records. Interestingly enough, Eminem had a sense of disrupting the status quo when he signed Curtis Jackson at the turn of the century in 2002. He has followed the same disruptive strategy by signing Griselda, and letting them not go Southpaw.

While this chapter starts from a lesson that focuses on King Johnson, it also comes to life from a doctoral dissertation DJ set. While I am not able to share that set with you as the offering of this chapter in and of itself, I was fortunate enough to have a mentor and a diss committee who could see that my discursive practices as a DJ were more than enough in defending the theoretical framework I had created in writing around DJ Rhetoric and literacy. Not only was it disruptive, but it was also rhetorically savvy and communicative in a visceral way that cannot always be conveyed or even transferred onto the page. And often, the work required of or transmuted by digital tools cannot always make that leap. However, digital resources can become extraordinarily helpful in the ways they allow us to engage in timely and on-time, contemporary inquiry, while they also align with the Hip-Hop mantra of "making something out of nothing." What started off as a very Hip-Hop meme-inspired comedic moment was flipped and remixed into a culturally relevant teaching tool that speaks to research sensibilities in a tangible and digestible conversation.

Furthermore, hiphopography is invaluable in showing educators, researchers, and students a path of inclusion that overtly rejects the NatGeo posturing of older research positionalities. For example, look at how Temptaous Mckoy and her clever construction of Amplification Rhetorics led her social media charge to connect and engage with Hip-Hop artists with her hashtag #IssaTrapDissertation. Her weekly IG postings led to fruitful discussions with Trap rappers because her intention was to engage with members of the culture; not pontificate about it from a distance (Mckoy). I see this cultural acumen as much more aligned with hiphopography as opposed to other scholars in the field who show up to conference presentations talking about various Hip-Hop artist's work from afar, but when asked, they reveal that they didn't even try to send a DM, a tweet, or a homer pigeon to said rapper they're analyzing (in this particular moment, I was able to contact said rapper before the person finished reading their conference paper *talking* about said rapper). By nature, digital ecologies allow us to reject various NatGeo moments at all costs, as the world has now become infinitely more connected and connective. Incorporating this type of cultural inclusion philosophy is a valuable lesson to be learned, and digital resources can sit at the forefront of this methodological blueprint.

Similarly, a look at A.D. Carson's most recent academic project with the University of Michigan Press entitled *I Used to Love to Dream*, finds Carson fully immersed in Hip-Hop aesthetics and cultural rituals, deftly rhyming his way through an album that serves as the primary sonic scholarly text that spawns an accompanied textual writing to make sense of the sonics. Carson, a long-standing lyricist, enacts that ethical heuristic of hiphopography in word, rhyme and deed; his engagement with the culture as a participant and practitioner marries his theoretical musings with his participatory embodiment of the culture. Both Carson and Mckoy are exemplars for the roadmaps one might use in deploying digital resources to intermesh ethical practices rooted in cultural communities, where the community members become the stakeholders who dialogue in the assessment of cultural production.

Spady very clearly rejected the NatGeo move, which in 2021, serves as a problematic power dynamic clearly erected by white hegemonic academic structures to privilege certain "research voices" and diminish others. Hiphopography by nature functions as an anti-racist methodology in that it invites, invokes, involves, and invests first and foremost in the participants of Hip-Hop culture. It does not stand off at a distance and then later wax poetic about what the culture "might be." Hiphopography serves as the roadmap by which a heuristic for ethical research is illuminated in that it only functions properly with the culture and its participants both in mind and in the forefront of conversations; to stand back and talk "of" or "about" without direct engagement most often leaves that vocal twinge that might come with that British or Aussie-sounding announcer's voice. And no disrespect to my Brit and Aussie sisdren and bredren, I'm just saying . . . or as the youth say, "I ain't even gon' hold you!"

I hope this chapter helps you and (re)invigorates you to push back against the oppressive ideologies of the status quo, to embrace those students whose work and linguistic practices you may not get just quite yet: allow them the space to grow, the space to share, the space to learn and the space to teach. I hope it allows you to really (re)think how your teacher-researcher praxis might lend itself to not only including, but also embracing and fostering the brilliant mind we know named King Johnson.

And I hope it allows you the space to ask your students to tell Virgil to write BRICK on their bricks, in their own ways.

. . . Rest in Power to James G. Spady and Virgil Abloh—thanks for the paths you've left for us . . .

The Sights and Sounds of This Mix-Down (Works Cited)

8 Mile. Directed by Curtis Hanson, Universal Pictures, 2002.

A Tribe Called Quest. "Scenario (remix)." Jive Records, 1992.

Alim, H. Samy. *Roc the Mic Right: The Language of Hip Hop Culture*. Routledge, 2006.

———. "'The Natti Ain't No Punk City': Emic Views of Hip Hop Cultures." *Callaloo* vol. 29, no. 3, 2006, pp. 969–90.

———. "'The Whig Party Don't Exist in My Hood': Knowledge, Reality, and Education in the Hip Hop Nation." *Talkin Black Talk: Language, Education, and Social Change*, edited by H. Samy Alim and John Baugh, Teachers College Press, 2006.

Baez, Krystal "DJ Shorty Wop" and Todd Craig. "'Let the Records Spin . . .': A Conversation with DJ Shorty Wop." *Changing English*, vol. 24, no. 2, 2017, pp. 213–15.

Breakbeat Lou. Personal Interview. 19 Sept. 2017.

Carson, A.D. *i used to love to dream*. University of Michigan Press, 2020, https://doi.org/10.3998/mpub.11738372.

Carter, Shawn. "*Genius Jay-Z Breaks Down 'Oceans' and Leaves Timbaland Looking Confused As Sh*t!*" *YouTube*, 19 July 2013, https://www.youtube.com/watch?v=nEH2cApjNhI.

Castillo, Maria "TOOFLY" and Todd Craig. "'Let the Writers Write . . .': A Conversation with TOOFLY." *Changing English*, vol. 24, no. 2, 2017, pp. 159–61.

Conway the Machine. "Hawks." *Look What I Became*. Griselda Records, 2019.

Coolio. "Fantastic Voyage." *It Takes a Thief*. Tommy Boy/Warner Bros. Records, 1994.

Craig, Todd. "'Makin' Somethin' Outta Little-to-Nufin": Racism, Revision and Rotating Records—The Hip-Hop DJ in Composition Praxis." *Changing English*, vol. 22, no. 4, 2015, pp. 349–64.

Craig, Todd, and Carmen Kynard. "Sista Girl Rock: Women of Colour and Hip-Hop Deejaying as Raced/Gendered Knowledge and Language." *Changing English*, vol. 24, no. 2, 2017, pp. 143–58.

Day, Daniel. *Dapper Dan: Made in Harlem: A Memoir*. Random House, 2019.

Duthely, Regina. "Black Feminist Hip-Hop Rhetorics and the Digital Public Sphere." *Changing English*, vol. 24, no. 2, 2017, pp. 202–12.

Flores, Nelson, and Jonathan Rosa. "Undoing Appropriateness: Raciolinguistic Ideologies and Language Diversity in Education." *Harvard Educational Review*, vol. 85, no. 2, 2015, pp. 149–71.

Gangstarr featuring Lil Dap and Jeru The Damaja. "Speak Ya Clout." *Hard to Earn*. Chrysalis/EMI Records, 1994.

Griselda. "DR BIRDS." *WWCD*. Griselda/Shady Records, 2019.

Hierro, Victor Del. "DJs, Playlists, and Community: Imagining Communication Design through Hip Hop." *Communication Design Quarterly Review*, vol. 7, no. 2, 2019, pp. 28–39.

Homeboy Sandman. "Shorty Heights." *Don't Feed the Monster*. Mello Music Group, 2020.

Jay-Z featuring Frank Ocean. "Oceans." *Magna Carta Holy Grail*. Roc-A-Fella Records, 2013.

Kynard, Carmen. "'The Blues Playingest Dog You Ever Heard Of': (Re) Positioning Literacy Through African American Blues Rhetoric." *Reading Research Quarterly*, vol. 43, no. 4, 2008, pp. 356–73.

Lacey, Sharif "Reef the Lost Cauze," and Todd Craig. "'My Pen is Mightier Than Your Sword . . .': A Conversation with Reef the Lost Cauze." *Changing English*, vol. 24, no. 2, 2017, pp. 186–89.

Mahon, Fiona. "Ten Classic Designs by Dapper Dan." *Hunger*, 12 Sept. 2017, https://www.hungertv.com/feature/ten-classic-designs-by-dapper-dan/.

Mckoy, Temptaous T. "Y'all Call It Technical and Professional Communication, We Call It #ForTheCulture: The Use of Amplification Rhetorics in Black Communities and Their Implications for Technical and Professional Communication Studies." 2019. East Carolina University, dissertation.

Mobb Deep. "Shook Ones Part II." *The Infamous*. Loud/RCA Records, 1995.

———. "The Infamous Prelude." *The Infamous*. Loud/RCA Records, 1995.

Mobb Deep featuring Nas and Raekwon the Chef. "Eye for an Eye." *The Infamous*. Loud/RCA Records, 1995.

Petchauer, Emery. "Starting with Style: Toward a Second Wave of Hip-Hop Education Research and Practice." *Urban Education*, vol. 50, no. 1, 2015, pp. 78–105.

Spady, James G. "Mapping and Re-Membering Hip Hop History, Hiphopography and African Diasporic History." *Western Journal of Black Studies*, vol. 37, no. 2, 2013, pp. 126–57.

Spady, James A., and Joseph D. Eure. *Nation Conscious Rap*, vol. 3, PC International Press, 1991.

Sperling, Sy. "Sy Sperling President of Hair Club for Men." *YouTube*, 19 May 2016, https://www.youtube.com/watch?v=lXkOo7grE5A.

Stoever, Jennifer Lynn. "Crate Digging Begins at Home: Black and Latinx Women Collecting and Selecting Records in the 1960s and 1970s Bronx." *The Oxford Handbook of Hip Hop Music*, edited by Justin D. Burton and Jason Lee Oakes, Oxford UP, 2018, pp. 1–21.

Westside Gunn. "Shawn vs. Flair." *Pray for Paris*. Griselda Records, 2020.

Westside Gunn, and Peter Rosenberg. "Westside Gunn Opens Up on COVID-19 Experience: 'I Thought I Was Going to Die.'" *YouTube*, uploaded by Hot 97, 21 Apr. 2020, https://www.youtube.com/watch?v=-oxXpxsqG8E&ref=1vibe.

Wilson, Elliot, and Brian "BDot" Miller. "Rap Radar: A Griselda New Year." *Rap Radar*, episode 85, https://tidal.com. Accessed 10 January 2020.

Wu-Tang Clan. "Protect Your Neck." *Enter the 36 Chambers*. Loud Records. 1993.

Young, Damon. "The 10 Blackest Things About This Kids Journal Entry Roasting His Teacher for Lying About Christopher Columbus." *The Root*, 23 Jan. 2018, https://verysmartbrothas.theroot.com/the-10-blackest-things-about-this-kids-journal-entry-ro-1822337363.

Section 2. Memory and Documentation: Digital Archives and Multimodal Methods of Preservation

Chapter 5. Digital Story-Mapping

Eda Özyeşilpınar
ILLINOIS STATE UNIVERSITY

Diane Quaglia Beltran
PROVIDENCE COLLEGE

Land Acknowledgment: We acknowledge that the state of Israel is built on the lands that have been home to the Palestinian people for centuries. As a settler-colonial-nation state, Israel has been displacing Palestinian people with military force and violence and has been actively trying to erase the presence of Palestinian history, culture, language, and bodies from the land by demonizing the Palestinian identity.

In the absence of a formal land acknowledgment by Clemson University, we acknowledge that Clemson University, a Land-Grant Public Institution, is located on what was formerly Cherokee Land and that the Cherokee were forcibly displaced. We also acknowledge that enslaved, and imprisoned labor helped to enrich the families who lived at the Fort Hill Plantation, and which ultimately enabled the university's founding.

This chapter works towards a methodology of digital story-mapping (DSM). We see DSM as both a method and means for discovery and invention of meaning and knowledge, one that relies on the importance of the embodied experiences of space and place, and the mapping of that experience. This methodology recognizes the digitality of story-mapping, and its inherent multimodality, as foundational concepts. Our methodology is framed by what we consider to be the key components of DSM: space and place, embodied storytelling, and multimodal writing. These key components are derived from our reflections on individual cases of practicing DSM, using ArcGIS StoryMaps® software, both in research and teaching. Through these reflections, we can determine that DSM is a method of discovery and of writing that, overall, provides a methodology which benefits from rhetoric's spatiality and materiality.

We introduce our methodology of DSM drawing from concepts of space and place, mapping, and storytelling in rhetoric and writing studies to the computers and writing community. We suggest that the method is useful for teachers and scholars who are interested in exploring spatially oriented and culturally responsive ways to be attentive to the discursive-material relations between bodies, spaces and places, objects and memory, and the technologies used that support investigation and interpretation. We find that, when using DSM as a method, possibilities emerge for map makers and storytellers to change their awareness

DOI: https://doi.org/10.37514/PRA-B.2022.1541.2.05

of the spatial landscape and its multiplicity of meaning by revealing and sharing uncharted counter-stories, and stories that are too often silenced. In essence, hegemonic, and colonial systems prevent these stories from being revealed, through their use of cartographic and scientific legitimacy of mapmaking as a moral and ethical basis. We promote the idea that digital story makers should bear the ethical responsibility for inverting this morality and ethical bases of colonial logic, and DSM helps to achieve that.

We first unpack each key component of DSM which is followed by our individual research-teaching stories of DSM. First, Eda will discuss her project, "Mapping Cartographic Discourse: Reading the Israel-Palestine Conflict Across In/Visible Borders of the Middle East," in which she uses digital story-mapping to uncover the colonial logic that dominates the cartographic narrative of the *Israel in Pictorial Maps* atlas, how that narrative continues to practice power and inflict violence over the current space of occupied Palestine, and finally, the ways in which the embodied stories of Palestinian people have been writing counter-stories in and across the bordered spaces of Palestinian resistance. Then, Diane will review her use of DSM in an Advanced Writing course, to demonstrate how DSM is both a practice and a product that has the potential to reveal influences and messaging of objects of historical memory and legacy on a university campus. Using examples of student projects created with ArcGIS Survey123, and StoryMaps, Diane shares student examples of story maps that interrogate and analyze the presence and influence of a narrative of legacy. Those story maps perform resistance to hegemonic representation of whiteness—one that elides the reality of the campus' history as a plantation, and its relationship with ardent segregationists.

Our aim is to provide a methodological frame for DSM that emphasizes accessibility and a wide array of applicability which can inform researchers and teachers about the innovative and creative ways of using different digital writing technologies as part of the practice of DSM.

A Digital Story-Mapping Methodology

While the term "digital story-mapping" echoes current terms like digital storytelling, digital maps, and mapped stories in digital-spatial humanities, we approach DSM as more than a generic Geographic Information System (GIS) and a web-based story-mapping technology. GIS industry leaders like Esri or Google have capitalized on these terms as they launched their web-based mapping applications (ESRI's ArcGIS StoryMaps and Google's Tour Builder) for telling digital stories *with* maps. GIS is a powerful software that provides users with tools and opportunities to "discover relationships that make a complex world more immediately understandable by visually detecting spatial patterns that remain hidden in texts and tables" (Bodenhamer, Corrigan, and Harris vii). However, the way that Esri/ArcGIS marketed their StoryMaps applications appears to capitalize on "enhancing digital storytelling with the power of maps," which in turn, "tend[s] to relate to simple, linear storytelling via web maps with ancillary content, such as text and images" (Field 99). As a result, for many, StoryMaps applications seem to appear as "just an alternative way of telling a story through the use of maps" (Field 100). Approaching DSM to tell digital stories with maps as ancillary visual information, situates space as a static, empty void to be filled, as if space is always-already waiting to be discovered, which truly centralizes and reproduces the colonial logic of Western onto-epistemology. Our methodology does not view space as static, but as one of possibility made manifest through embodied experiences, and one that has relation to the body experiencing it—be that viewing a map, or mapping as an action across space—and that is the focal point of understanding the difference between storytelling with maps, and DSM.

While DSM takes advantage of Esri /ArcGIS StoryMaps' powerful digital and spatial affordances—e.g., spatial juxtaposition, clustering, layering of maps and spatial data, using pictures and text—as a digital research and writing methodology, DSM treats and engages space and place, and maps and mapping not as secondary elements of and to storytelling. Thus, we again introduce DSM as a three-part methodology: 1) space and place, 2) embodied storytelling, and 2) multimodal writing. We consider space and place both as our main departure and the key that links the storytelling qualities and the digital and multimodal affordances of DSM, and introduce the following key premises that shape DSM as a digital, multimodal, and spatially situated digital research and writing methodology:

1. *Space is a product of social and cultural relations of the human practice of place. It is a social, political, and ideological construct and used in the transaction of power.* Henri Lefebvre contends that all space is based in human construction, and subject to social, political and ideological forces. Space is a social set of relations (116) between persons, their actions, interactions, and their environment. "Everything that is produced either by nature or by society" including "living beings, things, objects, works, signs and symbols" (101) is part of that socially constructed space.

2. *Space is fluid, open, dynamic, and always emergent . . . it produces and is produced by the stories we tell.* As Doreen Massey explicates, space is a product of interrelations that represent a sphere of coexisting possibilities, multiplicities, and heterogeneity, which is why space "is always in the process of being made" that could be imagined "as a simultaneity of stories-so-far" (9).

3. *Space, place, and storytelling are connected through lived, embodied experiences.* Malea Powell elucidates this connection for us: "By 'space' I mean a place that has been practiced into being through the acts of storied making, where the past is brought into conscious conversation with the present and where—through those practices of making—a future can be imagined. Spaces, then, are made recursively through specific, material practices rooted in specific land bases, through the cultural practices

linked to that place, and through the accompanying theoretical practices that arise from that place—like imagining community 'away' from but related to that space" (388).

Building on these three premises, our DSM methodology defines the act of mapping as an inherently digital, multimodal form of writing that shares stories of, and about, space and place; and it engages with maps as digital and multimodal text representing and communicating spatial stories.

At its simplest, multimodal writing is any mode of communication that avails itself of multiple modalities: "visual, audio, gestural, spatial, or linguistic means of creating meaning" (Selfe 195). What informs our understanding of the value of multimodality aligns with the cross-disciplinary perception of how human beings perceive and engage with the world that surrounds us through "our multiple senses, our emotions, our actions, and our reflections" (Boyd 155). According to Gunther Kress, our wide range of engagement with the world is what "from the beginning, guarantees the multimodality of our semiotics world" (181), which echoes the New London Group's perception of "all meaning making [as] Multimodal" (29). Jason Palmeri considers these approaches to multimodality "as a fundamental aspect of embodied human communication [that] opens up space for digital writing scholars to explore how our approaches to contemporary digital writing might be informed by the much longer history of multimodal composing practices" (28). Megan Fulwiler and Kim Middleton write that, with new media technologies, the epistemological shift from page to screen has "opened up new ways of reading, writing, representing, and understanding that will, by necessity, be grounded in the ontological actions of the new media era" (40). It is this importance of multimodality that we embrace as an inherent component of DSM.

Our understanding of DSM stems from its inherent digitality that is not limited to computerized environments. Ways of knowing, afforded by multiple modalities that limit the term "digital" to computer applications and programs in turn limit what is meant by digital. Angela Haas writes that "'digital' refers to our fingers, our digits, one of the primary ways (along with our ears and eyes) through which we make sense of the world and with which we write into the world. All writing is digital—*digitalis* in Latin—which typically denotes 'of relating to the fingers or toes' or 'a coding of information'" (Haas "Wampum as Hypertext" 84; emphasis in original). Adding digital elements to multimodality adds a layer of complexity which enhances any modality's "inter-animation" of components and yields a whole text that means more than its constituent elements (Blakesley 112). It is that digitality, afforded by mapping, that is used when we connect the embodied actions in space as the material for DSM as a method. Additionally, we employ Ellen Cushman's conceptualization of digital story that is grounded in "social practices of storytelling as epistemological activities" (116) and that centralizes "the notion of story as epistemological center of knowledge making" (128). We understand that ways of expressions opened by computerized technologies are enhanced and "interanimated" when embodiment is included as the way of knowing and responding via multimodal writing.

Finally, we recognize that mapping is an inventional method which "extends beyond the map maker or even the map itself" and that "while the map maker's choices provide constraints and affordances to users, [the choices] do not control the user's reading [of the map] . . . understanding mapping as an inventional method means appreciating how the map maker, the map, and the user influence one another" (Unger and Sánchez 103). So, through the purposeful use of embodied subjectivity of mapping encounters, experience with digital affordances, and storytelling, DSM offers possibilities for uncovering counter-stories, as well as the silenced experiences of under-represented groups.

DSM Projects

While we both used ESRI's ArcGIS StoryMaps applications in our DSM projects, we do not advocate specifically for these applications; we merely use the apps as representative examples of DSM as a practice. Even though there are differences between our projects, our approach to digitality and multimodality is inherent in the ways we used that digitality.

Eda's Project

My digital story map project "Mapping Cartographic Discourse: Reading the Israel-Palestine Conflict Across In/Visible Borders of the Middle East," analyzes how various pictorial and iconographic representations in the 1957 Israeli National Atlas, *Israel in Pictorial Maps* (Stern), produced borders that constructed the memory-place of the Israeli-Palestinian conflict around victim and enemy images. I practiced Brian Harley's cartographic deconstruction to unpack how the colonial logic and memory of this atlas's cartographic story represents the material and violent consequences of the decades long Israeli occupation over the social, cultural, and everyday reality of occupied Palestine today. In my rhetorical examination of this atlas, I deconstructed the cartographic narrative of each map to uncover the settler-colonial logic that continues to displace, erase, and silence the Palestinian people today. The settler-colonial logic that informs the cartographic discourse of this atlas is central to the contemporary national narrative of the state of Israel which dehumanizes and demonizes the Palestinian people as the enemies while positioning the Israeli nation as the victim. I challenge and disrupt this narrative and its settler-colonial logic with the Palestinian activist Ahed Tamimi's story. Ahed's story represents the border-culture of the Palestinian resistance which produced a new heroine image that disrupted the enemy and victim images of the Israeli-Palestinian conflict.

I used the conceptual framework of the map journal application, one of the Esri /ArcGIS StoryMaps' applications, to produce this project as a digital story map.

Map journal provided me with the digital and multimodal affordances to represent dynamic movements, and how this atlas's overall cartographic story of enemy and victim images extends itself into the physical geography of the spaces of occupation and resistance, which offers a way into unpacking the Israeli-Palestinian conflict.

I practice DSM methodology as an embodied mapping performance that focuses on the relations between spaces, borders, body/bodies, and materiality. What accounts for the digitality of DSM in my practice is heavily influenced by Angela Haas's articulation of digitality as introduced previously in this chapter and her explication of how digital rhetoric is perceived by "digital cultural rhetoricians ... [as] a negotiation—an interfacing—between bodies, identities, rhetoric, and technology" ("Toward a Digital Cultural Rhetorics" 412). Drawing from the considerations in digital-cultural rhetorics that emphasize materiality, bodies, and embodiment (Eyman; Gonzales; Haas "Wampum as Hypertext"), Ann Shivers-Mc-Nair introduces her framing of 3D rhetorics, which "focuses on fabricated objects ... [and] necessarily includes the digital—both in the sense of fingers-as-digits and in the sense of the code and interfaces that connect humans to fabrication machines" (np). While I do not consider DSM methodology as 3D rhetorics in the way that Shivers-McNair explicates it, what inspires me is how her framing accounts for digitality as an extension of the body and embodied experiences. This is how I see the connection between DSM and digital rhetoric in my practice. The DSM project I focus on in this chapter is a product of my embodied mapping performance, which is a practice of rhetorical cartography and border rhetorics. I explain my articulation of DSM as an embodied mapping performance to demonstrate my practice of DSM through specific examples from my DSM project.

DSM as an Embodied Mapping Performance

What informs my practice of rhetorical cartography is Amy Propen's "visual-material rhetorical approach, one that not only accounts for the multimodal, spatially-situated artifact but is also mindful of its impact on the embodied subject" (36). Following Propen, I engage with maps as visual-material artifacts and pay attention to the consequences a map's story has over communities who share the experience of the colonial wound. In this context, I examine cartography's colonial logic, which, as Karen Piper delineates, is invested in establishing whiteness, producing spatial realities orientated around a world order that unfolds from the West to the rest of the world, while erasing, silencing, and covering over the lived experiences of non-Western, non-white, and Indigenous bodies. This reading engages Walter Mignolo's decolonial theory of epistemic disobedience to problematize and lay bare cartography's colonial past-present and logic. Therefore, my focus is on what a map's story strategically covers over and how this strategic covering over is accomplished by using bordering practices to produce space as an extension of the colonizing body.

DSM is more than simply reading and analyzing the stories that maps tell; it is a mapping performance. I articulate this mapping performance in relation to the recent turn in cartographic theory from a representational to a processual understanding of maps and mapping. This processual turn recognizes a map's subjective-ideologically loaded story as a product of its maker's positionality, which is informed by a map-maker's socio-cultural context. In addition, this turn advocates for recognizing the "multiple, reiterative production and reproduction of maps as they are engaged in multiple times and spaces" (Harris and Hazen 51). This processual shift understands maps and their stories not merely as rhetorical and intertextual (Harley), but also always emergent and fluid in meaning. This emergence and fluidity are relational to different contexts of map engagements, interactions, and makings performed by mapmakers and map-users (Kitchin, Gleeson, and Dodge). Thus, I consider my own engagement with the *Israel in Pictorial Maps* atlas and its cartographic narrative as an embodied mapping performance, which is an extension of and relational to my own experiences as a Turkish-Muslim woman living in the US.

While there are no short cuts to demonstrating what it means to live in the US as a Turkish-Muslim woman, the many encounters that I had with different people on various occasions for the last ten years showed me that people always already have preconceived perceptions about Turkey and how a Muslim woman should look/act like. Once, after telling an Uber driver that I am from Turkey and Muslim (both responses to his questions), he told me not to worry because, as I quote, "You do not look like the rest of them so you will fit just right in." What's so disturbing about this sentence is not necessarily about me, a non-Hijabi Muslim woman not looking like the "other" Muslim women who freely choose to wear their Hijabs, but it is the immediate xenophobic, Islamophobic, and racialized representation of how Hijabi Muslim women are perceived as subjects who do not and cannot fit into the so-called modern-civilized Western society.

What I experienced with this Uber driver is just one example, and a simple one, that speaks to the material-violent effects of borders as devices of and bordering as "a mobile technology of colonial [and imperial] control" of spatial knowledge production (Lechuga 38). Thus, I understand and practice border rhetorics through Queer Chicanx feminist Gloria Anzaldúa's theorizing of borders and borderland spaces as embodied. Anzaldúa explains a borderland space as "*una herida abierta* where the Third World grates against the first and bleeds . . . the lifeblood of two worlds merging to form a third country, a border culture" (*Borderlands* 25; emphasis in original). As Gabriela Raquel Ríos articulates, "Anzaldúa means this [una herida abierta] quite literally. The borderlands as physical spaces bleed . . . Borderland culture emerges out of particular embodied relationships to particular histories of particular land bases" (82). Through Anzaldua's theorizing of borders and borderland spaces as embodied, I perform mapping to tell embodied border-stories of resistance that disrupt the stories enforced on the land and the people by the colonizing body.

I came to understand my engagement with the larger cartographic narrative of *Israel in Pictorial Maps* atlas as an embodied mapping performance; that engagement led me to Ahed Tamimi's story. In December 2017, young Palestinian activist Ahed Tamimi slapped one of the heavily armed Israeli soldiers who were right outside of her family home. After Ahed's mother posted a video of the incident online, Ahed was arrested, put on trial by the Israeli government, sentenced to eight months in prison, and released in July 2018. Ahed gained global recognition and support, while the Israeli government did everything to portray her as an evil terrorist out there to ruin Israel.

For me, the most striking thing was when the Israeli government questioned Ahed's 'Palestinian-ness' as a way to attack her credibility, and, in turn, to prevent her from gaining international support for the Palestinian resistance to the Israeli occupation. The Israeli government directed attention to Ahed's blonde hair, blue eyes, and light skin and raised the question *how could she possibly be Palestinian?* The Israeli government even made the argument that Ahed's parents were probably not her real parents since, again, she looked nothing like them. As a non-hijabi Muslim woman, I am almost never considered as Muslim-enough by non-Muslim Westerners and many Muslims (not all though) with diverse backgrounds living in the West or back home, in Turkey. In other words, my 'Muslim-ness' is almost always in question because, apparently, I do not look Muslim without a hijab on. This was probably the reason I was so drawn to Ahed and her story. As a result, Ahed's story became central to my mapping performance since it represented a border culture that emerged out of the Palestinian resistance and the decades long struggle of the Palestinian people living under oppression of the Israeli settler-colonial state.

DSM In Practice

Through my embodied mapping performance, I engaged with the larger cartographic narrative of *Israel in Pictorial Maps* atlas with a focus on cartography's colonial logic. This cartographic narrative tells the story of Israeli people returning to their so-called promised historic homeland. The great return home narrative is a strong part of the current Israeli national identity as well, which was built on the assumption that their historic homeland was empty, waiting for Israeli people to return and claim it (Özyeşilpınar). The reality of Palestinian people's presence in the land was a deviation from this storyline and if the land was going to be made the national homeland of the Israeli people, then "Palestine had been characterized as *'A land with no people for a people with no land'*" (James 404). To re-invent this land as an empty space waiting to be reclaimed, each map-story in the atlas was narrated by taking advantage of cartography's colonial logic.

What I consider to be the most strategic colonial practice in each map is the salient demarcation of the border that clearly marks and signifies the land of the Israeli nation-state while removing and pushing the Palestinian people out to the other, empty, grey side of the border. For example, the pictorial map of Tel Aviv from the atlas offers a clear demonstration of the border line through coloring and usage of signs that direct the attention of the map-users to 'Israel,' which effectively designates 'Palestine' as the other, empty side of the border (see Figure

5.1). I read the storyline of each pictorial map through this strategic bordering, while paying close attention to the ways in which the bordering practice continues to inflict violence over Palestinian bodies.

My goal was to capture and illustrate how the colonial logic of this atlas's cartographic narrative marks the early stages of the decades long and still ongoing Israeli occupation of Palestine, as well as the violent consequences of the settler-colonial logic over the social, cultural, and everyday life and reality of the Palestinian people. I used the interface of the map journal application for this project. The structure of the map journal application offers its users two lay-out options: 1) Side Panel and 2) Floating Panel (see Figure 5.2). I chose the side panel layout for my project because this layout is specifically designed for text-intensive stories. Further, this layout gave me the opportunity to form a spatial juxtaposition that presented maps in Israel in Pictorial Maps atlas and their map-stories in geolocational connection to the contemporary cartographic visualizations of the land. The side panel layout has a side panel and a main stage (see Figure 5.3). Side panel is designed to present text and other visuals and multimedia, and the main stage is mainly for featuring maps, charts, and other visuals and multimedia.

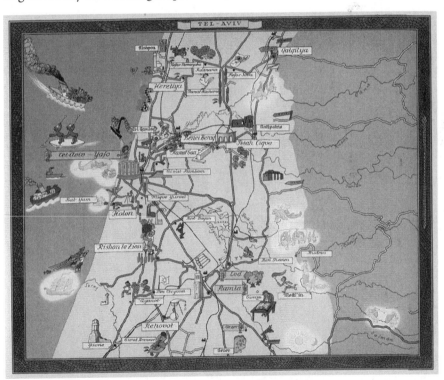

Figure 5.1. Pictorial Map of Tel Aviv in Israel in Pictorial Maps Atlas. Used by permission of the David Rumsey Map Collection, David Rumsey Map Center, Stanford Libraries

Figure 5.2. Screenshot of Esri StoryMaps Map Journal Application Layout Options

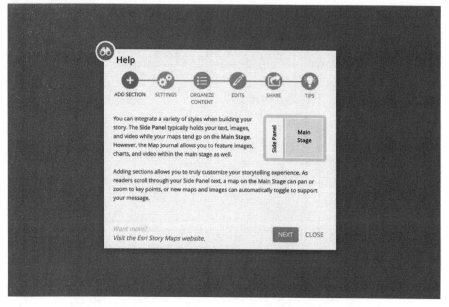

Figure 5.3. Screenshot of Esri StoryMaps Map Journal

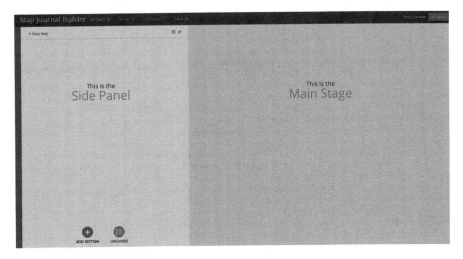

Figure 5.4. Screenshot of Esri StoryMaps Map Journal Application's empty interface of the side panel layout

Application Side Panel-Main Stage Descriptions

The empty interface of the map journal's side panel layout offers possibilities for users to make creative decisions and customize the map journal for their own purposes and audience (see Figure 5.4). While customizing the side panel layout of the map journal application, I made a conscious decision to deconstruct the colonial logic of this atlas's cartographic narrative. However, using this application could easily open re-colonizing opportunities if I were not cognizant of the atlas's colonial logic. In the context of my project, one such instance would be using the main stage to present each map of the atlas, while using the side panel to provide textual descriptions. This organization would result in centralizing the colonial logic of this atlas. Even if the textual descriptions in the side panel were to address the colonial logic that informs the cartographic narrative of the atlas, centralizing the maps and their stories through the main stage would privilege the colonial logic.

I produced my map journal around the satellite map images of the cities represented in the *Israel in Pictorial Maps* atlas. This allowed me to use the maps in the atlas to demonstrate the cartographic past of the Israeli occupation and then show how this cartographic past continues to operate as the ongoing setter-colonial logic of the Israeli nation-state today. This past-present connection offered me a visual-spatial perception to show how maps in the atlas extend their narrative scene onto the physical space of the land, while covering over and pushing the Palestinian experiences and stories out onto the other side of the constantly shifting and expanding borders of the state of Israel (see Figure 5.5).

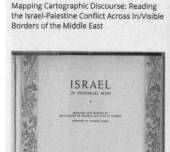

Mapping Cartographic Discourse: Reading
the Israel-Palestine Conflict Across In/Visible
Borders of the Middle East

*Figure 5.5. Screenshot of the introductory panel to the "Mapping
Cartographic Discourse" map journal story map*

*Figure 5.6. Screenshot of the "Mapping Cartographic
Discourse" map journal story map design*

The rest of the map journal (see Figure 5.6) is designed to maintain this past-present connection. The side panel includes the pictorial maps from the atlas (left) and the main stage is where the satellite map images are presented (right). I created sections in the side panel and assigned each section to a pictorial map from the atlas. Since each map offers a visualization of different cities, these sections are paired with the satellite maps of the cities that each pictorial map visualizes. This side-by-side juxtaposition was a way for me to visualize the spatial extension from the pictorial maps to the physical space of the Israel-Palestine conflict, demonstrating how the colonial logic of the Israeli government's cartographic narrative replaces the spaces of resistance and occupation with the victim and enemy images, while silencing and covering over the counter-stories of resistance.

The satellite map image on the right moves from one city to the another as the reader scrolls through one section to the next. This dynamic movement contributes to the past-present connection and the visual representation of the pictorial maps writing on the physical space while alluding to a sense of change, openness, and interconnectedness (Massey 107). Through the design layout and features of the map journal application, I enacted this sense of movement perhaps not in a direct manner of breaking away from the limits of cartographic visualization of space, but more so in an indirect way that created the opportunity to start interrupting the immobility and stillness of this atlas's cartographic space. This interruption was critical because understanding space as an open happening means that there are ongoing stories being experienced and written on spaces (Massey 107) and the flat surface of a map does not tell these stories.

I used the side panel to introduce Ahed's counter-story, which I divided into parts and paired each part with the map sections in the side panel (see Figures 5.7 and 5.8). By adding this third layer into the map-section, I carved a space for Ahed's story to be told through the story map's dynamic movement and past-present connection. In this way, I was able to connect Ahed's counter-story and her image as a heroine to the spaces of resistance and occupation. This layer produced a dynamic spatial storytelling that disrupts the dominant colonial narrative of the atlas through the victim and enemy images.

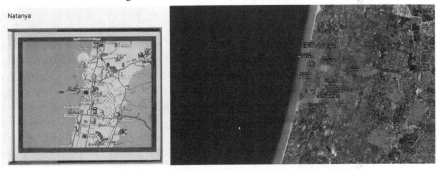

Figure 5.7. Screenshot of Ahed's Story Side Panel Introduction in "Mapping Cartographic Discourse" map journal story map

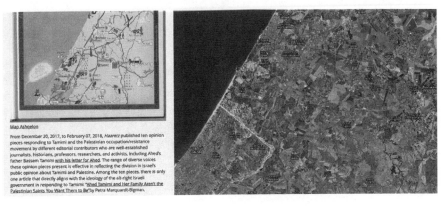

Figure 5.8. Screenshot of Ahed's Story Side Panel

Diane's Project

"Reading and Writing Memory" was an advanced writing course that employed Digital Story-Mapping as a method of inquiry and interpretation. By reading representations of memory on the Clemson University campus, students learned about the descriptive operation of maps (Corner), students found that the 3D area maps of the campus they viewed were not neutral. The location for Diane's project using DSM was the main campus of Clemson University, a public Land-Grant institution. Built on Cherokee land, home to the Fort Hill house of slave-owner and segregationist John C. Calhoun, the land for Clemson University was deeded to a board of trustees for the construction of a "high seminary of learning" by Calhoun's son in law, Thomas Green Clemson. Home to buildings named after ardent segregationists Benjamin Tillman, and most notably, Strom Thurmond, the campus has a tense, ethnocentric history that only recently is beginning to be addressed by the university.

My positionality informed the approach to the course. I'm a non-traditional aged graduate student instructor whose cultural experiences of living in New England before moving to South Carolina to pursue a Ph.D. informed how I saw memory texts operating on the campus. Because my research on kairotic emplacement and memory texts formed the course content, I sought to introduce the concept of opportunity (to read what is emplaced) as a readable event. What I wanted was a method and affordances that students could easily use to defamiliarize themselves with the every-day experience of being on campus: Did they realize that the university was built on the backs of enslaved persons, and later by prison labor? What would either mean to their embodied experiences, and their own positionality as students from different ethnicities and backgrounds?

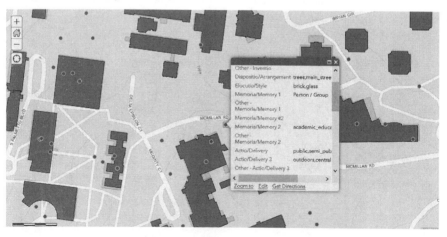

Figure 5.9 Example of Survey 123 responses as part of DSM. Image used with Permission.

I wanted students to use what Jaqueline Jones Royster calls "critical imagination" as part of their rhetorically "grounded process of discovery, analysis, and interpretation" (83) and to "clarify the contexts and considerations of [their] interpretations" as means to exercise their "commitment making connections and seeing possibility" (83). Other than what they accepted as the truth of who and what memory texts presented, I wanted them to make connections and imagine that those connections and conclusions had value in being articulated, to uncover what memory was being presented and perpetuated on campus. We sought to challenge the silence of historically oppressed persons, as well as the repression of those persons' stories, while also understanding that a dominant memory was always at work in ways they might not have considered.

The Course: Preparatory Work

The purpose of the course was to have students understand that architectural memory spaces and places (like historical homes) and architectural memory texts (like monuments, memorials, and their associated signage and placards) work to influence opinions and thoughts. The first part of the semester was spent understanding how space is created socially, materially, architecturally, and institutionally. We unraveled the conflated terms "memory," "history," "tradition," "heritage," and "nostalgia," as we worked to understand what was being presented and re-produced in "historic homes"—homes that were former houses of plantation owners who used enslaved labor. From there, we were able to address what I thought was the most obvious "historic building on campus:" Fort Hill, the original home to John C. Calhoun Home, and later home to the founder of the university.

Despite the prominence of the home (multiple signs directing visitors to it, signs that proclaimed Calhoun as a man of national importance, its visibility from no less than four dormitories, one of the campus' bus routes, and directly across the street from the campus' main dining hall) I was surprised to learn that several of my students in each of the 19 person sections did not realize that Fort Hill was a plantation manor; nor did these students know that Fort Hill's original owner Calhoun was an ardent racist, or that the university's founder deeded the building and its surrounding lands to a board of trustees with the intention that the building remain part of the campus. The campus has a racist history, and a racist present if one considers buildings named after noted white supremacists Tillman and Thurmond. The university still struggles with its ability to tell the whole story of its past, despite the 2014–2017 efforts of student A.D. Carson's academic work on revealing the university's past, his "See The Stripes" organization, or his protest that sought to change the name of Tillman Hall back to its original name, Old Main. After Carson's (now Dr. Carson) graduation from the university, the university engaged a Clemson professor, Dr. Rhonda Thomas, in creating a history of Clemson's vexing legacy—the result of which was a work in progress when I taught the "Reading and Writing Memory" course.

The aim of the course is to let students know that monuments, memorials, signs, building names, and street signs are legible texts of memory, or "memory texts" (Young xiii–ix). As texts, they are readable, understandable, communicative objects that require a different kind of reading approach beyond simple perception and description. To that end, a dual heuristic method with user-created maps as tools of invention was used. Using participatory mapping, each student used the ArcGIS Survey123 program loaded to their smartphones. A survey presented questions about the rhetorical, architectural, and spatial attributes of memory texts according to a modified version of the rhetorical canon (the survey is extensive and can be viewed at http://bit.ly/Survey123Form). As students traversed the campus looking for memory texts, they completed their surveys on their smartphones. The geographic locations and images of the memory texts were also input into the Survey123 questionnaire that automatically populated an unlabeled map of campus, based on their on-the-ground, embodied encounters with memory texts. The initially unpopulated map eventually contained pop-up information for each student's Survey123 responses to memory texts that students would later use to analyze the location, and characteristics (rhetorical, spatial, and physical) to understand how the memory texts conveyed meaning about who and what is remembered on campus.

The decisions students made to include and describe a geo-located memory object in the ArcGIS Survey123 program, reveal what the map maker decides. Because an entire class is responding to these objects by completing a questionnaire about spatial, rhetorical, and memorial significance, students have to look more intently at objects of memory that their peers have described and look more intently at what has not been identified as a memorial text. This in turn opens more possibilities for what can be considered a memory text. Further, the decision they make to include or exclude these objects as part of their understanding of spatial relations (similarity, grouping, juxtaposition, manner of approach) when they view a populated map, gives the map maker choices that illuminate some discoveries, while minimizing others. This was the story they read, mapped, and shared.

Digital Mapping as Practice

The use of DSM enabled students to compose and tell a story of their embodied experience reading emplaced memory texts across space, calling into operation Deborah Hawhee's understanding of Wayne C. Booth's definition of rhetoric as the opportunity to engage and respond to "the entire range of resources that human beings share for producing effects on one another" (Hawhee 158; Booth xi). Envisioning students as the authors of their own individual embodied experiences, the method recognizes that that mapping is another resource that can be used to create and respond to those effects.

Figure 5.10. An example of a map being populated by students, based on their individual Survey123 field results.

The Strom Thurmond Institute is specially placed on a side of campus that does gain a lot of foot traffic. Current students take buses to the bus stop in the area, and potential students take tours of the campus and stop in the area.

However, is it ever thought about why the building is essentially underneath the ground? If they are so prideful of Strom Thurmond, why would they keep the building hidden?

Clemson is relatively trying to keep their memorial of Strom Thurmond under wraps. They don't want these potential students to dig into his history too much, so his name is not plastered all over it.

The Placement

Figure 5.11. The map with student's memory texts located. Students could expand and zoom in on the map, allowing them a more defined view of the memory texts in each area. Image used with permission.

The digitality of map making is tied to the embodied experience of mapping objects of memory in the field—on the university campus—and then using digital mapping to analyze and interpret what is conveyed as a preferred memory, versus their experience of reading those memory objects. The digitality of populating and explaining the map made for a richer descriptive expression. The experience of digitally responding to survey questions was done spatially, and temporally; the students sought, read, and responded to objects of memory while encountering them. Their digitality was both embodied as reading, and as writing by way of their responses that were their StoryMaps. Using digital tools to populate a collaborative map that was shared by each class was a way for them to apply their reading of memory objects in a way that could be shared and accessed by their class peers.

From DSM as Practice to DSM as Product

As the small groups discussed the story the populated map was telling, students made decisions to include or exclude memory texts that they viewed on the collaborative map, as part of their understanding of spatial relations (similarity, grouping, juxtaposition, manner of approach). They were able to make connections between how the memory texts are arranged on campus. Student groups as mapmakers would invariably choose some memory texts as more important than others, based on their experience and positionality as college students. The interpretation of what students saw both on the ground and on the map was theirs to make, and theirs to voice in a digital story map. What matters was not the story map, per se, but which memory texts students chose to highlight as part of their reading of memory on campus. By including signage like banners and historical markers as memory texts, one group of students found a cluster of activity about Clemson's historical past and legacy that marginalized the enslaved persons who made the Fort Hill property possible. Another group chose to focus on building names as memory texts, avoiding typical monuments and placards to reveal their experience of being Black students on a campus with two buildings named after notable racists, set on a north-south axis. Figures 5.12 and 5.14 represent examples of the memory they read, mapped, and the story they shared. The resultant small group story maps demonstrated the students' newly acquired way of applying Royster's "creative imagination," interpreting what, in most cases, was the public display of a memory that the institution perpetuated, and what their understanding of that meant to them as students.

In the case in Figure 5.12, a group of students, using the concept of axial progression and organization, determined that the memory texts worked together and across space to project a memory of whiteness, in what they called, the "Axis of whiteness." Buildings named after white supremacists were located at the north and south vertical axis. The campus library in Figure 5.13 was interpreted to be a larger, more prominent and modernized version of a plantation home, located at the intersection of the east to west axis. In their digital story map, they were able to support their interpretation that the university was reminding students of its whiteness. When sharing their digital story maps with their course peers, the Black students who came up with the interpretation were just as surprised as their course peers in discovering the tacit racist message being perpetuated as memory. Their digital story map recounted, location by location, what was being presented on the "Axis of whiteness." The digital story map is lengthy and students who collaborated did so by inserting links at the bottom of each section of the story map to move from section to section. The digital story map, used with permission, is at https://bit.ly/33Lamw9.

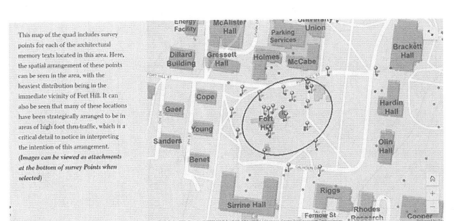

This map of the quad includes survey points for each of the architectural memory texts located in this area. Here, the spatial arrangement of these points can be seen in the area, with the heaviest distribution being in the immediate vicinity of Fort Hill. It can also be seen that many of these locations have been strategically arranged to be in areas of high foot thru-traffic, which is a critical detail to notice in interpreting the intention of this arrangement. *(Images can be viewed as attachments at the bottom of survey Points when selected)*

Figure 5.12. One group's interpretation of campus memory texts were buildings themselves, and their placement on what they called "the Axis of whiteness."

Figure 5.13 The university's main library with white columns, and deep porch reminded some students of a modernized version of a plantation house. Cooper Library. Clemson University Libraries. 2020. https://libraries.clemson.edu/clemson_libraries_zoom_16/

Another group found that the cluster of signs on the campus' small, but well-traversed quad (adjacent to Fort Hill) contained an over-abundance of historical signs and banners touting the historical significance of Fort Hill, its owner, and family. Most of the large banners had images of John C. Calhoun, his wife Anna Calhoun, and the university's founder. Only two banners contained an image of the formerly enslaved persons who worked at Fort Hill: one a groomsman, the other, a nanny. The interpretation by the student group was that, based on the clustering of memory texts, it appeared that the university was perpetuating a memory of the white owners of Fort Hill as a legacy that could be shared with members of the university community, as seen in Figure 5.14. Based on that interpretation, they concluded that the university was using historical figures to represent a partially true memory in public places, and one that conflated memory, history, heritage, and nostalgia about pre-Civil War southern life. Their digital story map, used with permission, can be found at https://bit.ly/3kAoFJQ.

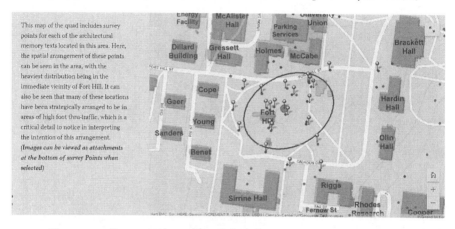

Figure 5.14. Some students found that there was a density of objects in a relatively small area, so they used spatial analysis tools in ArcGIS to give visual description to what they saw when they reviewed the collaboratively populated map of campus. Image used with permission

The digital story maps that I've included in this chapter were selected because they contained evidence of DSM to facilitate readings of space, place, and objects to make an argument about the way that memory is presented. The dual heuristics and creation of their digital story maps connected the application of digital mapping, with the process of multimodal storytelling. The resultant digital story maps were the product of several stages in the long process of seeing and responding to memory texts on their campus. It took several weeks for students to create their story maps, develop their ideas, and discover what and how they needed to say about what they encountered while reading the memory texts across the spaces of the place called their university. The process was lengthy, taking several weeks to complete, but was made easier using digital tools and affordances. DSM as both practice and product is worthy of continued application and study.

Conclusion

DSM as a practice and product of composition does not necessarily require the use of proprietary applications, or heavy programs. We understand that GIS software is expensive, and that it is a resource which may not be available to every student, teacher, or researcher in every institution of higher education. Even though basic mapping and digital story-mapping programs are available on a non-subscription basis through ArcGIS StoryMaps, we do not advocate for any specific program or platform, preferring to offer a digital methodology that uses mapping. There are different Geographic Information Science (GIS) software programs that can be used in combination with digital storytelling affordances, as simple as MS Powerpoint, or Adobe Spark to accommodate story-mapping. We encourage the use of powerful practice, one that enables a richer multimodal composition, based on embodied readings and experiences.

Minor limitations of GIS programs are typically the reduced ability to share and collaboratively create maps. Widely accessible and modifiable web-based programs include open-source QGIS.org, openstreetmap.org, and Google Tour Builder (https://tourbuilder.withgoogle.com), which are effective alternatives to Esri/ArcGIS StoryMaps. Freemium programs like mapbox.com can also offer the opportunity to use DSM.

We also recognize that there is a learning curve associated with any program and application—mapping, or otherwise. In this regard we encourage scholars/teachers to consider the everyday affordances available to nearly every scholar/teacher and students: physical maps that can be modified, aerial photography, or images that convey spatial visualization to capture spatial stories and stories embedded into specific places. Examples include newspaper images that show persons in place, and people across space. Additionally, scholars/teachers can encourage students to use their smartphones to capture instances of people in place, and acting in space, and then combine them with other students' images to create a visual map.

We think that DSM, with its focus on embodied digital storytelling through analysis and interpretation using maps, could be productive across a variety of topics, issues, and writing situations.

Note

Earlier, I noted that I do not look Muslim without a hijab on. I find it critical to address that not wearing a hijab grants me many privileges and advantages that many hijabi-Muslim women do not get. I do not intend to position my experiences as more challenging than the hyper-visible experiences of the hijabi-Muslim women. These hyper-visible experiences demonstrate that hijabi-Muslim women are the subjects of direct and violent racialized attacks. My goal here is to show how my positionality and experiences were the reasons I am so drawn to Ahed and her story.

Works Cited

Anzaldúa, Gloria. *Borderlands/La Frontera: The New Mestiza*. Aunt Lute, 1987.
Blakesley, David. "Defining Film Rhetoric: The Case of Hitchcock's Vertigo." *Defining Visual Rhetorics*, edited by Charles A. Hill and Marguerite Helmers, Lawrence Erlbaum Associates, 2004, pp. 111–33.

Bodenhamer, David J., et al. *The Spatial Humanities: GIS and The Future of Humanities Scholarship*. Indiana UP, 2010.

Booth, Wayne C. *The Rhetoric of Rhetoric: The Quest for Effective Communication*. Blackwell Publishing, 2004.

Boyd, Brian. *On the Origin of Stories: Evolution, Cognition, and Fiction*. Harvard UP, 2009.

Corner, James. "The Agency of Mapping: Speculation, Critique, and Invention." *Mappings*, edited by Denis Cosgrove and Reaktion Books, 2002, pp. 213–52.

Cushman, Ellen. "Wampum, Sequoyan, and Story: Decolonizing the Digital Archive." *College English*, vol. 76, no. 2, 2013, pp. 115–35.

Erll, Astrid and Ansgar Nunning, editors. *Cultural Memory Studies: An International and Interdisciplinary Handbook*. Walter de Gruyter, 2008.

Eyman, Douglas. *Digital Rhetoric: Theory, Method, Practice*. University of Michigan Press, 2018.

Field, Kenneth. "The Stories Maps Tell." *Cartography and Narratives*, special issue of *The Cartographic Journal*, vol. 51, no. 2, 2014, pp. 99–100.

Fulwiler, Megan, and Kim Middleton. "After Digital Storytelling: Video Composing in the New Media Age." *Computers and Composition*, vol. 29, 2012, pp. 29–50.

Gonzales, Laura. *Sites of Translation: What Multilinguals Can Teach Us about Digital Writing and Rhetoric*. University of Michigan Press, 2018, https://www.press.umich.edu/9952377/sites_of_translation.

Haas, Angela M. "Wampum as Hypertext: An American Indian Intellectual Tradition of Multimedia Theory and Practice." *Studies in American Indian Literatures*, vol. 19, no. 4, 2007, pp. 77–100.

———. "Toward A Digital Cultural Rhetoric." *Routledge Handbook of Digital Writing and Rhetoric*, edited by Jonathan Alexander and Jacqueline Rhodes, Routledge, 2018, pp. 412–21.

Harley, Brian J. "Deconstructing the Map." *The New Nature of Maps: Essays in the History of Cartography*, edited by Paul Laxton, The John Hopkins UP, 2001, pp. 49–169.

Harris, Leila, and Helen Hazen. "Rethinking Maps from a More-Than-Human Perspective: Nature-Society, Mapping and Conversation Territories." *Rethinking Maps: New Frontiers in Cartographic Territory*, edited by Martin Dodge, Rob Kitchin, and Chris Perkins, Routledge Studies in Human Geography, 2009, pp. 50–67.

Hawhee, Debra. "Rhetorics, Bodies, and Everyday Life." *Rhetoric Society Quarterly*, vol. 36, no. 2, 2006, pp. 155–64.

James, Oliver. *Middle East Realities: A Guide to Understanding*. 2nd ed., America Star Books, 2016.

Kitchin, Rob, Justin Gleeson, and Martin Dodge. "Unfolding Mapping Practices: A New Epistemology for Cartography." *Transactions of the Institute of British Geographers*, vol. 38, no. 3, 2013, pp. 480–96.

Kress, Gunther. "Multimodality." *Multiliteracies: Literacy Learning and the Design of Social Futures*, edited by Bill Cope and Mary Kalantzis, Routledge, 1999, pp. 179–200.

Lechuga, Michael, and Antonio Tomas De La Garza, "Forum: Border Rhetorics." *Communication and Critical/Cultural Studies*, vol. 18, no. 1, 2021, pp. 37–40.

Lefebvre, Henri. *The Production of Space*. Blackwell, 2016.

Massey, Doreen. *For Space*. Sage Publications, 2005.

Mignolo, Walter D. "Epistemic Disobedience, Independent Thought and Decolonial Freedom." *Theory, Culture, and Society*, vol. 26, no. 7–8, 2009, pp. 159–81.

New London Group. "A Pedagogy of Multiliteracies: Designing Social Futures." *Multiliteracies: Literacy Learning and the Design of Social Futures*, edited by Bill Cope and Mary Kalantzis, Routledge, 1999, pp. 9–38.

Özyeşilpınar, Eda. "Mapping Cartographic Discourse: Reading the Israel-Palestine Conflict Across In/Visible Borders of the Middle East." *Regarding Borders, special issue of Immediacy: An Online Media Journal*, 2018, http://immediacy.newschool.edu/previous/?p=1028

Palmeri, Jason. "Multimodality Before and Beyond the Computer." *The Routledge Handbook of Digital Writing and Rhetoric*, edited by Jonathan Alexander and Jacqueline Rhodes, Routledge, 2018, pp. 27–37.

Piper, Karen. *Cartographic Fictions: Maps, Race, and Identity*. Rutgers UP, 2002.

Powell, Malea. "Stories Take Place: A Performance in One Act." *College Composition and Communication*, vol. 64, no. 2, 2012, pp. 383–406.

Propen, Amy D. *Locating Visual-material Rhetorics: The Map, the Mill, and the GPS*. Parlor Press, 2012.

Ríos, Gabriela Raquel. "Performing Nahua Rhetorics for Civic Engagement." *Survivance, Sovereignty, and Story: Teaching American Indian Rhetorics*, edited by Lisa King, Rose Gubele, and Joyce Rain Anderson, Utah State UP, 2015, pp. 79–95.

Royster, Jacqueline J. *Traces of a Stream: Literacy and Social Change among African American Women*. University of Pittsburgh Press, 1994.

Selfe, Cynthia L. "The Movement of Air, the Breath of Meaning: Aurality and Multimodal Composing." *College Composition and Communication*, vol. 60, no. 4, 2009, pp. 616–63.

Shivers-McNair, Ann. "Making Knowledge: A Kit for Researching 3D Rhetorics." *Enculturation: A Journal of Rhetoric, Writing, and Culture*, Issue 29, 2019, http://enculturation.net/3D_rhetorics.

Stern, Friedel. The Department of Surveys, and the Ministry of Labour. *Israel in Pictorial Maps*. Lion the Printer, 1957.

Unger, Don, and Fernando Sánchez. "Locating Queer Rhetorics: Mapping as an Inventional Method." *Computers and Composition*, vol. 38, 2015, pp. 96–112.

Chapter 6. Social Network Analysis and Feminist Methodology

Patricia Fancher
UNIVERSITY OF CALIFORNIA, SANTA BARBARA

Michael J. Faris
TEXAS TECH UNIVERSITY

We choose to open with the often-cited words of Sara Ahmed on the politics of citation, which she defines as "a rather successful reproductive technology, a way of reproducing the world around certain bodies" ("Making"). By attending to citational practices, Ahmed marks how academic work continues to colonize knowledge production. She also articulates alternative citational practices that reproduce the knowledge of marginalized scholars. She asks us to do the same:

> When we think this question "who appears?" we are asked a question about how spaces are occupied by certain bodies who get so used to their occupation that they don't even notice it. They are comfortable, like a body that sinks into a chair that has received its shape over time. To question who appears is to become the cause of discomfort. It is almost as if we have a duty not to notice who turns up and who doesn't. Just noticing can get in the way of an occupation of space. ("Making")

In both of the research projects discussed in this chapter, we use social network analysis (SNA) as a feminist digital reading methodology that has helped us to ask the question "who appears?" and to sit in that discomfort noting the continued whiteness that occupies feminist and queer spaces. In our use of SNA, we create visualizations that allow us to answer "who appears" within citational practices, wherein we both focused on the reproduction of whiteness through citational practices. Based on these visualizations, we recognize our duty to notice who appears and who does not. We are able to identify whose voices are included, and who is being excluded from academic and professional discourses. This chapter introduces feminist SNA methods and methodologies by putting digital research methods of SNA in conversation with feminist methodological concerns.

In order to theorize the potentials for feminist SNA, we outline the methodological choices we made in our research projects, focusing on each project's goals, study designs, limitations, and challenges. First, Trish outlines methods for digital archival research using SNA to study the practices of solidarity, inclusion, and exclusion within a community of early 20th-century women physicians (published in *Peitho*; access Fancher et al.).[1] The second, conducted by Michael (initial results published in *Peitho*; access Faris), is a citation network analysis of queer rhetoric studies that uses SNA in order to explore citation patterns for how the field builds on the work of scholars of color (or, how it often fails to). Based on these research projects, we outline several affordances of feminist social network analysis for scholars of digital writing and rhetoric, especially centering community, outlining circulation of discourse, and documenting exclusions and marginalization. We recognize that our academic and embodied positionalities inform our research, methods, and analysis. We are both white, queer, feminist scholars who are studying communities that are also predominantly or exclusively white. These positionalities informed the communities we selected for study, the questions we asked, and our methodologies. Our research methods are designed to analyze and redress the racist practices that reinforce the reproduction of whiteness. At the same time, we recognize that our own experiences and biases inform our research, likely creating blindspots or misinterpretations that we are working collectively and individually to assess and redress. Before turning to our specific research projects, we define SNA, situate it in rhetoric and writing studies, and explore how feminist methodological interventions can assist in SNA methods.

What Is Social Network Analysis?

Social network analysis is commonly used to study community formation and dynamics, in and outgroups, organizational communication, and digital communities (especially through social media). SNA approaches these phenomena through the model of *networks*, which Duncan Watts has famously defined as "a collection of objects connected to each other in some fashion" (28). That is, a network consists of two fundamental features: 1) *nodes*, or individual agents or objects (such as people, organizations, social media accounts, texts, and so forth), that are connected through 2) *links* or *edges*, or connections of some sorts.

To help explain social networks, we provide a sample graph in Figure 6.1. This figure shows a citation network of the authors cited by Eric Darnell Pritchard in their 2012 article "Yearning to Be What We Might Have Been: Queering Black Male Feminism." Visualizations of social networks are often displayed as graphs like this one, with nodes represented by dots (or other images or icons) and links or edges represented by lines between those nodes. In this graph, edges connect Pritchard's node to the nodes that they cite using directed edges. Edges are *directed* when there is a unidirectional relationship (like a citation or a reply on Twitter) and are undirected when there is a reciprocal relationship (like two texts that are

---

1.   We follow Jay Timothy Dolmage's model of avoiding metaphors of sight and hearing when referring readers to other sources. In *Academic Ableism*, he uses "access" instead of "see" when suggesting such sources (193n1).

cited together, or two students in the same class in a network of students). Edges can also represent data about the relationship between two nodes. For instance, in this graph, we've increased the width of the edge proportionally for how many texts by an author that Pritchard cited. Pritchard cited 3 texts by E. Patrick Johnson, so that edge is wider than other edges. (This is called an *edge weight*.)

Nodes, too, can be visualized to represent data. In this graph, we've represented each node's weighted in-degree through the size of the node. A node's *degree* is calculated by how many nodes it is connected to. Its *in-degree* is calculated by how many directed edges link to it, and its *out-degree* is a measure of how many nodes it links to. A *weighted* version of these includes the weight of those edges. So, for example, Johnson has an in-degree of 1 and a weighted in-degree of 3. Pritchard, though, because this is a rather simple network, has an in-degree of 0 but has an out-degree of 26 (they cite 26 authors) and a weighted out-degree of 30 (because they cite Johnson three times, Dwight McBride twice, and David Ikard twice).

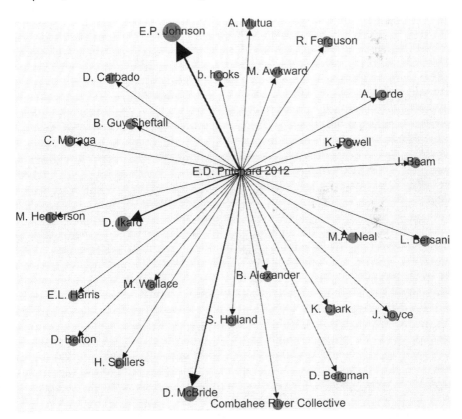

Figure 6.1. A citation network visualization showing what authors are cited by Eric Darnell Pritchard in their 2012 article "Yearning to Be What We Might Have Been: Queering Black Male Feminism."

A few other things to observe about social networks and their visualizations: Graphs can be *unimodal*, meaning they include only one type of node (like a network of students), or *multimodal*, meaning they include at least two types of nodes (like a network of students and teachers). The graph in Figure 6.1 is multimodal: It has a node type that represents specific texts (Pritchard's 2012 article) and a node type that represents cited authors. Network visualizations can also incorporate other features to help creators and audiences understand them, including the use of color (perhaps to visualize communities within a network) or the use of icons to represent different types of nodes.

In addition to visualization techniques, SNA uses algorithms and analytics to understand relationships in a network and the network holistically. Generally, these measurements attend to either 1) "the network as a whole" in order "to see and measure aspects of whole structures" or 2) "the ways that individuals are embedded in networks" (Hanneman and Riddle). Measurements that attend to the whole network typically ask questions of size; density (how well connected are actors in the network); connectivity, or what Robert A. Hanneman and Mark Riddle call the "texture" of the network (patterns of how nodes are connected in the network); clustering; and cliques or subnetworks. Measurements that attend to individual nodes embedded within the network typically ask questions related to how well connected a node is and how authoritative (influential) or central the node is to the whole network or to a subnetwork. Some of these measurements are simple mathematics—like counting a node's degree, or how many other nodes it's connected to—while others require algorithms that recursively go through the data, such as Google's PageRank (which measures the authority of a webpage based on the authority of texts that link to it). (For accessible introductions and overviews of these concepts, access Hanneman and Riddle; Kadushin; Scott.)

SNA has become quite popular over the last few decades—particularly because of the publication of popular books like Duncan Watts's *Six Degrees* and Albert-László Barabási's *Linked*, but also because many digital humanities scholars have found SNA useful as a distant reading method (access Jänicke et al. for an overview of many of these approaches). SNA can highlight trends and patterns that might not otherwise be observed, whereas close reading places those trends in particular historical and embodied contexts. Further, distant reading practices like SNA can afford the opportunity to notice what Matthew Kirschenbaum calls *provocations*, or those "outlier results" that could lead a researcher to attend to questions or aspects of texts or a dataset they might have otherwise ignored (1).

SNA has been deployed as a method or suggested method in rhetoric and writing studies, though much of this work is suggestive, and it has many resonances with the work in rhetoric and writing studies that overlaps with DH methods and considerations (Mueller, *Network Sense*; Ridolfo and Hart-Davidson). In *Digital Rhetoric: Theory, Method, Practice*, Douglas Eyman suggests that

SNA "provides a powerful set of tools for digital writing research" (103). Jordan Frith also advocates SNA as a useful method to complement Actor-Network Theory and Activity Theory in technical communication research, suggesting that its "focus on how people are influenced by their social network" assists in "decentering individuals" and attending to social structures (292).

Scholars in the field have turned to SNA to understand and complicate the concept of student participation in composition classes (Omizo), to visualize and analyze public health communication (Stephens and Applen), and to compare online social networks that emerge during times of crisis (Baniya). And, while not drawing on the methods of SNA for analysis, the Writing Studies Tree (https://www.writingstudiestree.org) visualizes the discipline of writing studies as a network (access Miller et al.). Much of this work helps scholars to develop what Derek Mueller calls *network sense*: "Recognizing forms and patterns in data fosters network sense; we begin to be able to see those distributed, circulating and non-obvious formations previously compromised by a lack of field-wide record keeping" (*Network Sense* 62). While SNA has been among those methods adapted in rhetoric and writing studies, few if any SNA studies in the field are explicitly informed by feminist methodologies.

While these applications of SNA do support a networked sense of rhetoric, Gabriela Raquel Ríos reminds us that metaphors of mapping and ecology erase physical land and bodies as sites of rhetoric. She insists on returning to the land as a site of rhetoric:

> This is an indigenous concept of relationality that is similar to the notion of ecologies—of networked relationships existing among various human and non-human objects—however, this indigenous concept relies on a relational ontology at the level of kinship quite literally. As such, land-based literacies are literal acts of interpretation and communication that grow out of active participation with land. (64)

Our visualizations also remove communities represented from land. However, we do acknowledge the land on which both of us work, live, and write. Trish lives on the unceded territories of the Chumash people. She walks along the shores that the Chumash historically have and continue to embark in *tomols* across the channel rich with life. She puts her hands into the rich soil and grows food on the land that the Chumash cultivated and thrived upon before white colonizers enslaved them to build the Spanish Missions and the colonial infrastructure that continues to attract tourists and school groups into Santa Barbara. Michael lives and works on historic Nʉmʉnʉʉ Sookobitʉ (the Comancheria), the lands occupied by the Nʉmʉnʉʉ (Comanche) in the 19th century. The local vineyards that produce the wine Michael and his colleagues drink, the six-lane roads in Lubbock he drives on, the Spanish Renaissance-style buildings he works in on campus, and the cotton fields he passes while driving out of town all reside on the Llano Estacado (the Staked Plains), where the Numunuu once hunted buffalo before Spanish, Mexican, Texan, and U.S. American settlers brought smallpox and cholera epidemics, wiped out the buffalo, and eventually relocated the Numunuu to reservations after decades of wars. We honor and express gratitude to the Indigenous people who are the rightful stewards of the lands we occupy.

Social Network Analysis and Feminist Methodology

A major challenge that comes with network visualizations is that they are often misread or presumed to transparently represent reality. This challenge is especially significant for feminist researchers who have long critiqued claims of objectivity. Mary Fonow and Judith Cook define critiques of objectivity to be a central tenant of feminist methodology (2213), as does Gisa E. Kirsch's important work on ethics in feminist methodology. Kirsch instead features the subjective, embodied experience of the researcher as central to knowledge claims (4–5).

However, there's a lure to data visualizations that can lead a researcher or a reader to believe they're viewing unmediated reality with what Donna Haraway calls a "gaze from nowhere" (581). As Desiree Dighton explains, drawing on the work of Haraway, Catherine D'Ignazio and Lauren F. Klein, and Johanna Drucker, "visualizations interpellate users into a particular perspective/ideology by a seeming lack of subjective authorship and the illusion that the viewer has control over the display and, perhaps, the underlying data" ("Rhetoric and Feminist"). While Dighton here is explaining the lure of interactive visualizations (which network graphs can be), her point extends to all network graphs: They can be read as unmediated reality without a subjective author and can give readers a sense that they understand the data.

Indeed, in some ways, SNA seems antithetical to methodologies of feminist rhetorical research, which have been so consistently committed to embodiment, particularity, and the nuance of particular people and communities. In her introduction to a collection on feminist methodologies for rhetorical research, Eileen Schell consistently returns to central themes of embodiment and emotion, as well as care (4). To be clear, SNA does not include the nuance of lived experience. Another risk of SNA as a set of methods, like other quantitative approaches, is that it can flatten complex relationships (Frith 295; Fuhse and Mützel 1078). Further, Leah DiNatale Gutenson and Michelle Bachelor Robinson have demonstrated that digital reading methods often replicate and reinforce the erasure of Black women in the archives.

At the same time, while Schell and many other feminists in rhetoric do center emotion and embodiment as key methodological concerns, Schell and K.J. Rawson's collection on feminist methodology has movement as its central theme because feminist methodologies often require us to attune ourselves to movement within communities and require feminist researchers to adjust to adopt ethical, feminist research methods. Importantly, SNA can visualize community dynamics and movement. Given the importance of solidarity and intersectionality for feminist research, SNA is a valuable method for asking questions about solidarity, inclusion, and exclusion. Ultimately here, we follow Sandra Harding, who in her often-cited chapter "Is There a Feminist Method?" warns against defining a method ("techniques of gathering evidence") as feminist or not and suggests instead that the power of feminism lies in methodology, or "theory and analysis of how research should proceed" (2). She suggests that traditional or familiar methods could be deployed (and perhaps even required in some situations) along with "new methodologies and new epistemologies" (2). Thus, we suggest that SNA can be useful as a digital research method in conjunction with feminist methodologies, especially those that attend to questions of power, community, solidarity, justice, and inclusion.

To date, scholars of feminist rhetoric have not used SNA as a method, though we argue that SNA shares many of the same goals and purposes as their feminist methodologies. Feminist methodologies are "oriented toward cohabitation; acknowledge the dynamic construction of relationships within and across locations and between people as constituting knowledge and values" (Ryan et al. 11), while SNA methods "share the view that agency is networked and relational" (Frith 292). SNA can support feminist scholarship on "social circulation," introduced by Jacqueline Jones Royster in *Traces of a Stream* and expanded upon by Kirsch and Royster, which interprets "overlapping social circles in which women travel, live, and work are carried on or modified from one generation to the next and give rise to changed rhetorical practices" (Kirsch and Royster 660). Feminist historiography of rhetoric has increasingly placed an emphasis on recovering not only individual women rhetors but also recovering their networks and analyzing their discourse as ecological (Dingo; Gaillet and Bailey; Graban and Sullivan; Hallenbeck; Royster and Kirsch, *Feminist Rhetorical Practices*; Ryan et al.; Schandorf and Karatzogianni). This shift is critical for feminist research because it situates rhetors within broader communities and social networks, thereby highlighting collective agency, circulation of discourse, and the importance of solidarity. Researching feminist rhetoric from an ecological and networked perspective opens possibilities for drawing on digital humanities methods and adopting distant reading methods rather than traditional close reading methods (e.g., Enoch and Bessette; Gatta; Graban; Losh and Wernimont; VanHaitsma). Further, by combining feminist (especially intersectional feminist) methodologies with SNA methods, we can heed the calls of feminists of color and other critical theorists to put digital humanities and digital rhetoric methods and methodologies in conversation with cultural rhetorics (Cedillo; Haas, "Toward a Digital Cultural Rhetoric," "Wampum"; Sano-Franchini), intersectional feminism (Bailey; Bailey et al; Bianco; DeVoss et al.; Losh and Wernimont; Perez), queer theory (Keeling), critical race theory (McPherson), cultural criticism (Liu; Sayers), and decolonial methodology (Kim; Medina and Pimentel; Nakamura).

SNA may also be of particular interest to feminist scholars who are contributing to emerging research methodologies that utilize digital reading and analysis. Jessica Enoch and Jean Bessette invite feminists doing historiographical work to consider distant reading to generate "evidence, we contend, that might help us track the social circulation of women's rhetorical activity through time and space" (143). Scholars of feminist rhetorics have widely adopted DH methods for feminist historiography and especially for digital archival methods (a few examples include Enoch; Enoch et al.; Graban and Rose; Graban and Sullivan; Gutenson and Robinson; Ramsey-Tobienne). Building on these models of digital feminist reading methods, we offer our research methods as case studies on how SNA can be used to further feminist rhetorical research.

Feminist Networks in Archival Research: Trish's Methods

Over a period of 3 years, I collaborated closely with Gesa Kirsch and Alison Williams to design a feminist digital humanities project studying the writing of women physicians in the *Woman's Medical Journal* (*WMJ*) from 1900–1919. Our co-authored article, "Feminist Practices in Digital Humanities Research: Visualizing Women Physician's Networks of Solidarity, Struggle and Exclusion" published in *Peitho*, presents research from both distant reading and close reading to study the evolving community of women physicians, their rhetorics of solidarity, and the limits of that solidarity, including racist exclusion. Much in the way that contemporary feminists use Twitter or Facebook, these early 20th-century women physicians used the *WMJ* as a social networking site to connect, share, and support each other. Once we began thinking of this archival material as a form of pre-social media, it was then easier to imagine how to use digital reading methods to study the community. Our project is an unusual application of SNA because the source material is historical and archival. SNA is most commonly used to study digital networks, especially on social media. With careful reading and detailed hand coding, we were able to make these archival materials accessible to digital research methods.

This project was inspired by the speculative work on networked rhetorics and digital humanities of Royster and Kirsch, which began well before I began collaborating. Royster and Kirsch imagined the possibilities for using digital tools to facilitate the analysis of social circulation. They imagined that the *Woman's Medical Journal* could be fruitful for a "a rich digital social history project, then, would attempt to identify, aggregate and map women's social and professional circles by creating visual maps (geographical and other), Venn diagrams, bar graphs, and other forms representations" ("Social Circulation" 176). They suggested that the purpose of feminist digital humanities research would be to step "back from the specificity of rhetorical analysis of artifacts and processes of communication to gather other layers of evidence in order to detect larger patterns of action" (176).

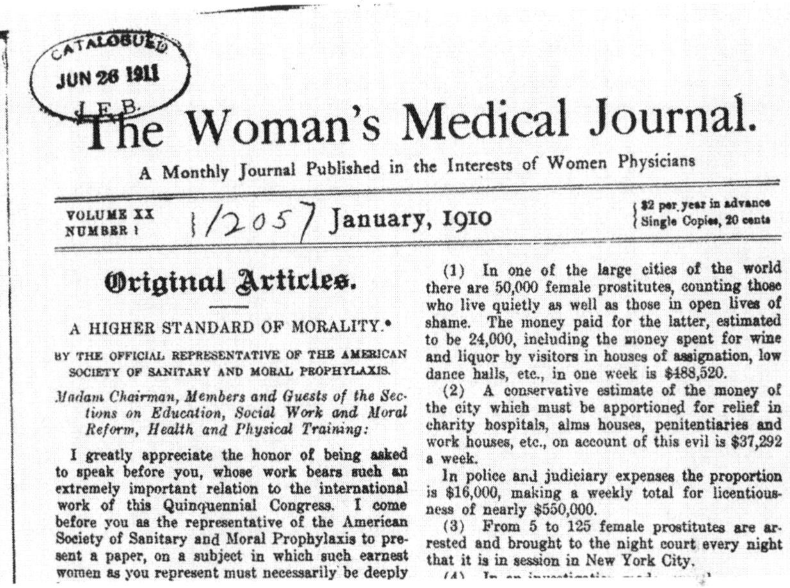

CATALOGUED
JUN 26 1911
J. F. B.

The Woman's Medical Journal.

A Monthly Journal Published in the Interests of Women Physicians

VOLUME XX
NUMBER 1

1/2057 January, 1910

$2 per year in advance
Single Copies, 20 cents

Original Articles.

A HIGHER STANDARD OF MORALITY.*

BY THE OFFICIAL REPRESENTATIVE OF THE AMERICAN SOCIETY OF SANITARY AND MORAL PROPHYLAXIS.

Madam Chairman, Members and Guests of the Sections on Education, Social Work and Moral Reform, Health and Physical Training:

I greatly appreciate the honor of being asked to speak before you, whose work bears such an extremely important relation to the international work of this Quinquennial Congress. I come before you as the representative of the American Society of Sanitary and Moral Prophylaxis to present a paper, on a subject in which such earnest women as you represent must necessarily be deeply

(1) In one of the large cities of the world there are 50,000 female prostitutes, counting those who live quietly as well as those in open lives of shame. The money paid for the latter, estimated to be 24,000, including the money spent for wine and liquor by visitors in houses of assignation, low dance halls, etc., in one week is $488,520.

(2) A conservative estimate of the money of the city which must be apportioned for relief in charity hospitals, alms houses, penitentiaries and work houses, etc., on account of this evil is $37,292 a week.

In police and judiciary expenses the proportion is $16,000, making a weekly total for licentiousness of nearly $550,000.

(3) From 5 to 125 female prostitutes are arrested and brought to the night court every night that it is in session in New York City.

Figure 6.2. Image of the title page of the January 1910 Women's Medical Journal from the digital archive in the HathiTrust Digital Library.

With Royster and Kirch's earlier chapter as an invitation to future research, Kirsch, Williams, and I began to plan how we could visualize women's professional communities. Our collaboration became an exciting challenge and fruitful opportunity to apply digital humanities methods for feminist archival research. While I came with more technical expertise and familiarity with digital research methods, Kirsch has a long career thinking about feminist methods and the ethics of those methods. Her expertise became a key guiding set of questions as we developed our research project and designed the methods.

While we did experiment with several possible visualization models, SNA allowed us to best identify patterns and changes in the community. With SNA, we first began to address questions such as the following:

- Around whom is the community centered?
- Who is marginalized?
- What clusters of actors support each other?
- Who has relative power or influence in the community?
- Because we coded for institutions and we analyzed the social network within historical context, we were also able to address questions like the following:
- What professional or governmental organizations supported or excluded women?
- What historical events corresponded to relative success or struggle for women physicians?

Overall, the goal was to visualize a community, analyze its politics of inclusion and exclusion, and place those dynamics in social and political contexts.

Data Entry: To Code or Not to Code

To create SNA, we first needed to code the *Women's Medical Journal (WMJ)* to isolate the people and institutions named. In order to do this, we made choices about who to include, how to code, and how much content to include. First, we created trial coding strategies and visualization prototypes. We attempted different strategies for coding that initially focused solely on the *WMJ*'s announcements, which often included the highest concentration of names. However, we found that this process excluded too many members of the community and prioritized announcements over scientific articles and editorials. We then shifted to include every person and every institution named. However, this quickly became too time consuming so that the coding process was taking more time than we could allow. Instead, we decided to include a sample size of up to five people and up to five institutions per article, announcement, or report. For most content, this included all people or institutions. However, when coding reports with long lists of names, we excluded some names.

We coded all original content, which included articles, reports, announcements, items of interest, editorials, and abstracts. We did not include advertisements because this is paid content and is less representative of the community of women physicians than the original content. However, the *WMJ* also published a directory of what they considered to be every woman physician[2] practicing medicine in each state. This was an exciting inclusion because it meant that we could create a network that included readers as well as writers and leaders in the professional network. However, there were several hundred women physicians included in the directories. Coding so much content was very time consuming. In the end, we decided not to include the names in the directory network because, while these women were listed as members of the community, they may have been more passive readers and not active leaders in the community. When we included them, the visualization became so dense and diffuse it was difficult to interpret and identify trends. This means that, to save time and identify trends, we excluded readers from the network.

We included all original content for every monthly issue of the Journal for the years of 1900, 1910, and 1919. In total, this included 36 issues, 1017 pages, and 745 separate articles or announcements. We used a Google form that created a spreadsheet to make the coding process easy and consistent. We coded each article for metadata (page, date, link to article in archive). Then we coded for actors, defining actors as both any person who is named in the journal and any institution that is named. Institutions most typically included medical schools

---

2. We later discovered that the directories only include white women. More on the scale of racist exclusion in the section on analysis.

and universities, hospitals, professional organizations, and state and regional medical societies, community groups. To say this was a time-consuming process is an understatement. We spent much of the summer and fall of 2018 coding pages meticulously. I also paid undergraduate research assistants to aid in this work. Even after coding, many hours were spent cleaning up the spreadsheet. Errors in spelling and formatting were present in the original source and were often introduced in the coding process, and these had to be identified and corrected.

Visualizations: Prototyping and Programming

Before programming the final versions of the SNA, we prototyped visualizations using Google Graph. From these prototypes, we were able to ensure that SNA was in fact going to be a useful method to address the questions we were pursuing.

To make the visualizations, we collaborated with recent University of California, Santa Barbara data science student Raul Eulogia, who created the graphs and taught me how to create these as well. I worked closely with Raul on several versions of the visualization to revise the color, proximity, and interactivity of the visual. We processed the data in R using social network analysis and igraph packages. This included loading the igraph, networkD3, and htmltools packages. Programming in R created a still image of the social network. To make the visualization interactive, we added force-network JavaScript.

The SNA graphs the relative power and significance of people and institutions named in the *WMJ*. Each actor is a node in the network. We color-coded the nodes so that people were purple, and institutions were yellow (this is an example of a bimodal network). The location of each node is determined by the number of times they were named in the *WMJ* and by the number of connections, which are represented with the line. Connections were identified whenever people or institutions were named together in the same article or announcement. Therefore, the nodes in the center are people or institutions that are both named frequently and are named along with several other people or institutions.

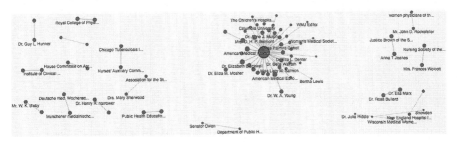

Figure 6.3. Early SNA prototype of just one-month of 1900
Women's Medical Journal *made in Google Graphs.*

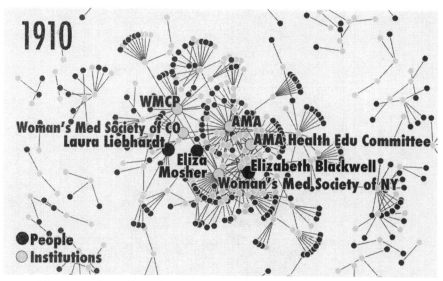

Figure 6.4. SNA of people and institutions who are named in the 1910 issue of the Women's Medical Journal. The nodes in the center were named more frequently and were named in connection with more people and institutions. I added labels to three of the most often mentioned women, who were all key leaders in the professional community of women. I've added labels to the most often mentioned professional communities.

Analysis

As we turned to analysis, we began to look specifically for Black women in this network. From our secondary research, we knew that Black women graduated from the same medical schools as the most famous and well-connected white women (Aptheker; Hine). We know they worked together in the same hospitals and women's clinics. However, not a single Black woman was included in our coding of the *Women's Medical Journal* 1900, 1910, or 1919. In our initial analysis, we thought that this exclusion could be a reflection on our incomplete coding. But no, we were able to search in the digital archive and found Black women were entirely excluded from the *WMJ* during our sample years. From there, we expanded to search the *WMJ* for every single year from 1900–1920. In the 240 *WMJ* issues published between 1900–1919, six African American women are included.

Before completing the SNA, we expected that Black women would be marginalized. Once completed, the SNA helped us to see the exact scale of exclusion, which was total exclusion in the years we included in the SNA. In that way, the SNA offers further evidence of the erasure of Black women from the professional community of women physicians. As Tessa Brown argues in her cultural rhetorics critique of white feminist discourse, there is an "ongoing and unresolved history of white supremacy in the United States women's activism" (234). The

WMJ supported white supremacy, and the SNA is further evidence of this white supremacy. However, it is important to note that we needed to ask those additional questions and expand the scope of our research to fully document the scale of erasure. As Ahmed has taught us, we need to ask, "who appears?" as well as "who does not appear?" ("Making").

SNA was a useful method for visualizing the community, its points of solidarity, and locations of power. It took our experience as feminist researchers to look not only at what was in the visualization but also at who was excluded from the visualization. Gesa, Alison, and I are all three white feminists. And we were studying a community of white feminists. During parts of our research study, we failed to question the whiteness of the community we were studying. However, we benefit from the excellent research of Black feminists who call on us to do better and be accountable for the racist practices of white feminism. We hope to especially account for Audre Lorde's pointed questions, "What woman here is so enamoured of her own oppression that she cannot see her heelprint upon another woman's face? What woman's terms of oppression have become precious and necessary to her as a ticket into the fold of the righteous, away from the cold winds of self-scrutiny?" (63). Our own positionality and awareness of the long history of white feminist exclusion of Black women informed our analysis and the efforts to recenter Black women within a reimagining of the SNA. From this experience, I was also moved to turn the same critical eye to my own syllabus, especially in a writing and gender studies course, and revise the central questions and reading material to center the contributions of Black feminist intellectual and activist traditions. However, I also know that my whiteness can act as a blinder, preventing me from seeing and understanding experiences of racism, and this can shape and inform my own research and analysis. I can commit to continuing to listen, learn, and do better as I move in gratitude for the intellectual and emotional labor of feminists of color in our field and my life.

Queer Co-Citation Analysis: Michael's Methods

In 2015, my coauthor Matthew Cox and I published an ambitious annotated bibliography of rhetoric and writing scholarship that attended to LGBTQ+ issues. I spent much of 2014 reading this scholarship as we worked toward organizing and annotating it. I was, at the same time, also becoming interested in SNA and its possibilities for assisting in understanding networks—whether networks of activity like Twitter conversations or scholarly networks like subfields of rhetoric and writing studies.

My initial experiences with SNA led me to think it might be a useful method for approaching citation practices in queer rhetorical studies. I was curious about citation practices for two reasons. First, as I read all this queer rhetoric scholarship, it seemed that English studies scholars and communication studies rhetoricians were barely in conversation with each other, and I wanted to understand this conversation (or lack of). Second, I experienced a "felt difficulty" (Takayoshi et al. 100) that feminists of color and queers of color were largely being ignored or under-cited in this set of texts Matt and I had collected. As I explain below, my research started to focus on this second question: Was queer rhetorical studies as white in its citational practices as I intuited? Where and how often are scholars and activists of color cited in this field?

So, I turned to citation network analysis as a potential method to explore these questions. I was inspired in part by studies (some formal and some informal) like Dan Wang's co-citation analysis of economic sociology syllabi to determine if the subfield had developed a canon, Kieran Healy's maps of co-citation networks in philosophy exploring conversation within the discipline ("A Co-Citation") and gendered patterns of citations ("Lewis"), Jonathan Goodwin's co-citation network analysis of literary and cultural theory journal citations (which showed that if the feminist journal *Signs* was removed from the corpus, the majority of most-cited authors in the network were men), and others. (Much of this work was introduced to me by Collin Gifford Brooke during his networks and rhetorics workshop at the 2015 Rhetoric Society of America Summer Institute.) Whereas citation network analysis works through networks of who is citing which scholars or texts, a co-citation network analysis studies what authors are cited together (more on this later). My project is still in progress (in 2018, I became writing program administrator of Texas Tech's First-Year Writing Program, so I have been focusing on that instead of finishing this project), but the process has been useful in thinking through feminist methodologies and SNA, and I published some initial results in *Peitho* in 2018 and have continued to update my data (slowly) over the following years.[3]

Data Collection: Defining the Network

An important "first" step for me—which iteratively became a series of steps that were never really "first"—was to define the network. I began by entering data about the works cited and references list for all roughly 200 entries in Matt's and my bibliography. But queer work in the field continued to be published, so I started adding more recent work, as well as work that Matt and I had accidently overlooked. When I first began presenting on this data, I soon realized that I had so many errors (e.g., mistyped names, either because of my data entry errors or because an author had misspelled something) in my spreadsheets that the dataset was likely inaccurate, and any conclusions I might start to draw wouldn't have much validity.

I returned to the spreadsheets and cleaned up the data, and I decided pretty soon that I couldn't possibly make progress if I kept such a large corpus to start with. So, I had to make methodological decisions about what texts to count as

---

3. Studying citation practices is not new in rhetoric and writing studies, though few have used citation network analysis. For previous studies, access Detweiler; Goggin; Mueller, "Grasping"; Phillips et al.; Reinsch and Lewis; Reinsch and Reinsch; Smith, "Points," "Strength."

"queer rhetorics." I first decided that for the time-being, I would focus on schol-ars who identified more with English studies than with communication studies, which isn't a precise science at all (because what about rhetoric departments not housed in English or communication?). And I decided I'd include publications by rhetoricians that were published in venues that weren't rhetoric-centric (which might be impossible to be exhaustive about). A further question I had to address was: what about scholarship that is questionable in its focus on queerness, sexu-ality, LGBTQ+ issues, and so forth? Ultimately, I had to make a lot of decisions about what texts belonged in this network I was calling "queer rhetorics," and I can't make any claims for objectivity here.

Importantly, SNA researchers make many choices about defining networks and analytic approaches. Defining the network was an important choice I made. Determining the boundaries of a network and the types of ties to include is an important methodological choice. Edward O. Laumann et al. provide one of the most useful metatheoretical discussions of defining a network's boundar-ies. The boundaries of a network are anything but self-evident, they argue, and a researcher must be careful about how they are defining those boundaries (64). Laumann et al. explain that there are two general approaches for defining a net-work. First, a *realist* approach determines the network by participant perception. For example, the boundaries of a network of a church choir would be determined by members of the choir. Second, a *nominalist* approach determines inclusion in a network based on the researcher's theoretical concerns (65–66). Building a network based on my perceptions of the subfield of queer rhetorics (what Mueller would call my "network sense" of the field; access also Brooke 100) constitutes a nominalist approach, as I was less interested in whether a scholar identified their publication as queer rhetorics than I was in the question of if their article or book chapter addressed issues of LGBTQ+ rhetorics, sexuality, or queerness. That is, I was defining the network as the researcher (which has its limitations, of course, because of my own situatedness in the field and subject position).

Another aspect of defining the network was what constituted nodes and links or edges in the network. Citation network analysis combines citation analysis from information sciences with SNA approaches from sociology (De Bellis 142–43, 156–66; de Solla Price; Otte and Roussea; Small). A citation network is typically a directed network with author or source text nodes connected to the authors or texts they cite. Co-citation analysis, however, explores relationships between texts or authors that are cited together in the same text. First proposed by Henry Small in 1973, co-citation network analysis is useful in determining which authors or texts are frequently cited together, which can help to understand a field, discipline, or subfield and the circulation of ideas within those networks. After playing with the data, I decided to focus on the co-citation network because it would help give me a sense of which scholars were cited together frequently and which scholars were rarely cited. That is, I could get a sense of what sort of conversations queer rhetoric publications were entering by who these publications were co-citing.

Data Entry: To Code for Race or Not?

As I began to work on this project, I moved away from the first question above (about disciplinarity between English studies and communication studies) for the time-being and focused on the second question about how inclusive citation practices were in queer rhetorics regarding race. Was the field as white in its citational practices as I intuited it to be? A few very important questions emerged as I considered coding the data: I didn't feel I could justifiably code cited authors for race or ethnicity. While many authors publicly state their racial or ethnic identity in publications, for others, I would have to work under assumptions. I knew I couldn't assume anyone's racial or ethnic identity, so I decided I wouldn't code for that and instead I would test what analytic and visualization methods provided with the minimal data provided.

Consequently, my data entry became quite simple: I entered data in a spreadsheet for source text and cited author. Then, for some spreadsheets, I asked a friend who knew Python to write a script that turned these author-text spreadsheets into co-citation spreadsheets, and for others, later in the process, I manually did this myself.

I do want to note that while the data was quite simple, the data collection and entry was quite laborious. I've lost track of how many hours I've spent on entering, organizing, and cleaning up data. There are more automated ways to create data for citation networks if one is defining a different network. For instance, due to indexing by sites like Web of Science, data can be scraped for different journals and then cleaned up by the researcher. But because my network spanned different journals (many of which aren't indexed) and book chapters (few of which are indexed), it was not possible to automate this data collection.

Visualization and Analysis

As I considered how to analyze and visualize this network, I made a variety of choices. First, I chose to use the open-source software Gephi (https://gephi.org) to conduct network analytics and visualizations, mostly because the learning curve was not too steep (especially after watching some online tutorials) and because it was free and open source. Second, I had to decide what I was looking for in this co-citation network in order to explore the prevalence of queers of color and feminists of color in the network. I was, then, mostly interested in questions of inclusion, visibility, and power. I was, to be explicit, interested in citation practices in queer rhetoric because citations have power. As geographers Carrie Mott and Daniel Cockayne write, "Careful and conscientious citation is important because the choices we make about whom to cite—and who is then left out of the conversation—directly impact the cultivation of a rich and diverse discipline, and the reproduction of geographical [or, in our case, rhetorical] knowledge itself" (955). Ahmed, too, has argued that citation practices matter, as we discussed in our introduction (*Living* 15–16; "Making"), and Ange-Marie Hancock encourages us to understand citation practices as a matter of "stewardship," or a matter of caring for the intellectual traditions we are working from and within (22).

Consequently, I decided to do a rather simple network analysis: first, I conducted a raw citation count of authors to determine just who were the most-cited authors in the text. Next, I ran an algorithm to determine who the most authoritative authors were in the co-citation network. Authority in a network is akin to Google's PageRank: a node is deemed more authoritative the more it is linked to by other authoritative nodes (thus the need for an algorithm, which iteratively runs through the data to determine authority; access Kleinberg). Third, I decided to run a community detection algorithm to see if certain groups of cited authors seemed chunked together (this specific one is called modularity class; access Blondel et al.). (I decided on these three after playing with the data and running as many different metrics as possible on the data in Gephi that I could.)

I also made decisions about visualizing the co-citation network. Figure 6.5 shows the entire co-citation network as of September 2019: 2,951 cited authors connected via edges when they're cited together (from 201 journal articles and book chapters published between 1981 and 2017). Importantly, this network is too busy for readers to understand or to make much knowledge from (and indeed, Alexander R. Galloway observes that most network visualizations look the same [85]).

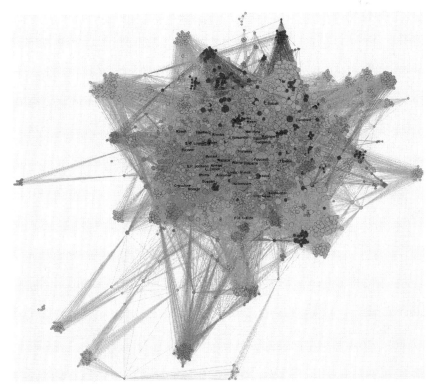

Figure 6.5. The entire co-citation graph, showing 2,951 unique nodes (cited authors) connected by edges marking co-citation.

I also made decisions to make the visualizations accessible for analysis and readers. One choice I made in a conference presentation was to apply a filter to the visualization to show only authors who had an edge weight of at least 3, meaning authors were cited along with another author at least 3 times. I also chose to only label the authors who were most authoritative in the network. (Labeling more would have led to too cluttered a visualization.) This visualization is displayed as Figure 6.6. I also decided it would be worthwhile to share visualizations of communities within the network (Figure 6.7) to show how in the network, scholars of color seem to be clustered together frequently, meaning there seems to be a conversation in the field about "queerness" and "sexuality" and separate conversations about race and queerness/sexuality.

Since I'm still adding to the network and playing with data, I don't want to draw firm conclusions, but I will, as Mueller and Kirschenbaum suggest, point to provocations drawn from the network. That is, following Mueller, I understand visual models not as "proofs, finally, but provocations; not closures, but openings; not conclusions or satisfying reductions, but *clearings* for rethinking disciplinary formations—they stand as invitations to invention, to wonder" (*Network Sense* 4). What sorts of genealogies of queer thinking are queer rhetoricians turning to? Where and how does the field draw on the contributions of queers and feminists of color? (José Esteban Muñoz has observed that too many histories and genealogies of queer thinking ignore the contributions of feminists of color [21–22]). How are scholars acting as stewards of intellectual traditions in ways that honor the contributions of queers and feminists of color? And, if we turn back to close reading, when queers and feminists of color are cited in this body of scholarship, is their work engaged with thoroughly, or is it a passing reference?

These questions continue to drive this project. For now, I can say, given the network I've created so far, that scholars and activists of color are not as authoritative in the co-citation network as white scholars. José Esteban Muñoz, bell hooks, Gloria Anzaldúa, and Audre Lorde are authoritative in the network, but the next most authoritative scholar of color in the network is Jacqueline Jones Royster, ranked at 40th, and then E. Patrick Johnson at 53rd. Surprisingly, Cherríe Moraga is barely cited in the network, and most of her citations are by Eric Darnell Pritchard. The most authoritative authors in the co-citation network (at this point in the study) are largely white scholars who don't make race central to their work (though some do nod to race in important ways). As a white cisgender man, I've found this analysis useful as a teacher and a scholar of queer rhetorics. For instance, when I taught my first graduate course on queer rhetorics in 2015, graduate students observed that the reading list was whiter and more men-centric than they anticipated (and I laud them for this observation). Now, in all my classes, I make explicit efforts (and am transparent with students about this) to include more scholars of color. After all, graduate courses are one of the avenues through which graduate students become enculturated into the conversations and citational practices of a field and consequently build a mental map of the field's network (Brooke 100).

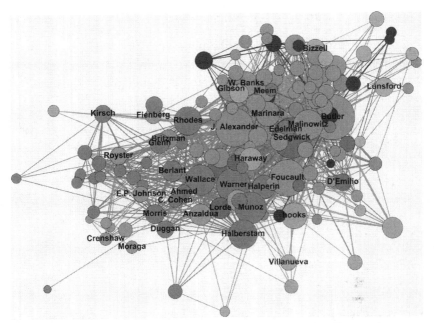

Figure 6.6. The co-citation network graph, filtered to show only nodes that are co-cited at least 3 times. The most authoritative nodes in the network are labeled with their last name.

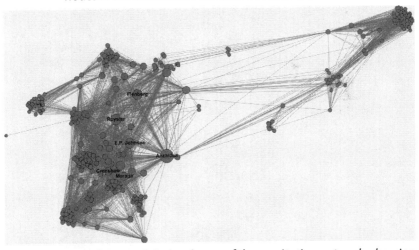

Figure 6.7. One of the modularity classes of the co-citation network, showing that scholars of color tend to be co-cited in clusters or communities. This cluster includes mostly scholars of color: Gloria Analdúa, Cherríe Moraga, Kimberle Crenshaw, Jacqueline Jones Royster, E. Patrick Johnson, Shirley Brice Heath, Roderick Ferguson, Jasbir Puar, Samantha Blackmon, Eric Darnell Pritchard, Karma Chavéz, Adam Banks, Angela Haas, Elaine Richardson, and Gwedolyn Pough (most of whom are unlabeled).

Conclusion

Throughout this chapter, we have stressed that SNA is not simply collecting data and representing the reality of networks but rather a matter of choices researchers make about how to define the network, what data to include, how the data is collected, how the data is organized and coded, how the data is visualized and presented to readers, how the data is analyzed, and perhaps most importantly, what questions are asked of this data. In closing, we want to suggest three key feminist methodological principles for SNA.

First, feminist SNA should attend to *questions of power*—specifically to both examine power and to challenge it. As D'Ignazio and Klein write in *Data Feminism*, a feminist approach to data science "begins by analyzing how power operates in the world" (22) by asking questions of who: Who is doing the work? Who is marginalized and who is recognized? Who benefits and who is harmed within the network? (47). But it is not enough to simply examine power: Feminist SNA must be "commit[ted] to challenging unequal power structures and working toward justice" (49). Feminist SNA can be useful in examining and challenging power by exploring questions of circulation, community formation, ingroup and outgroup dynamics, inclusion and exclusion, and who is central or authoritative within networks and who is excluded and marginalized. However, when SNA is used without asking questions about power and exclusion, the visualizations can be used to replicate inequitable power structures and normalize existing authority.

Second, feminist SNA can attend to *embodiment* and *emotions*. Whereas SNA is typically more data-driven, there are many affordances for feminist SNA for the incorporation of embodiment and emotions. This can be done through aesthetics of the visualization, which can be emotionally evocative. Each time we have presented on our visualizations at conferences, the first response is always to the aesthetics of the visualization. They are appealing because they are pretty. The networks are complex, delicate, and intricate. Before even identifying the trends and patterns, our audiences respond first on an emotional level to the design of the visualizations (access Gaviria on information visualizations as art).

Importantly, we find that, especially when used for feminist research, SNA is most effective when used alongside qualitative network methods and feminist rhetorical analysis, as well as personal narrative that place the trends and provocations within embodied experiences. Together, these multiple methods can help to situate the embodied and emotional experiences within a broader social network as well as grounded in people's experiences. (And, we might add, data visualization for social networks does not always have to be digital; access Gollihue and Xiong-Gum; Haas, "Wampum.") Finally, these methods included significant embodied labor and collaborative labor, which feminist scholars can discuss at length (access D'Ignazio and Klein, chapter 7, on documenting the labor of data collection and analysis). Data do not exist all by themselves. Our labor created and crafted data into usable material for visualizing these communities and framing our research questions.

Third, and relatedly, feminist SNA should *acknowledge and complicate the choices* researchers make in determining and defining a network, collecting and coding data, selecting and deploying algorithms for analysis, and visualizing a network. In her writing about feminist methodologies, Harding urges researchers to place themselves "in the same critical plane as the subject matter, thereby recovering the entire research process for scrutiny in the results of the research" (9). For Michael's project, he quite literally placed himself on the same plane as the subject matter because his work is included in the co-citation network that he studies. Therefore, he includes his own citational practices under critical inquiry within the evolving community of queer scholars of rhetoric. In the archival research, Trish and her co-authors Gesa Kirsch and Allison Williams are separated by 100 years from their subject matter. However, they placed themselves on the same plane as the subject matter by applying strategic contemplation to assess the networks composed in their methods and citational practices. While asking questions about inclusion and exclusion in the *Women's Medical Journal*, they also asked those questions of our own citational practices, recognizing who they were citing most frequently and whose voices we sought to amplify.

We invite future researchers to build upon our early models of feminist social network analysis. We offer these two case studies as instructive examples and realize that both are limited in scope. Future research could use SNA to study feminist communities on Twitter or online professional networks of feminists in rhetoric and composition. A wide array of archival and digital communities could be studied with SNA to study the social circulation, networked rhetoric, and velocity of rhetorical tropes and memes. We hope the SNA methods that we have outlined here will help feminist researchers to continue to foreground questions about community, social network, solidarity, inclusion, and exclusion in feminist rhetorical research.

Works Cited

Ahmed, Sara. *Living a Feminist Life*. Duke UP, 2017.

———. "Making Feminist Points." *feministkilljoys*, 11 Sept. 2013, https://feministkill joys.com/2013/09/11/making-feminist-points/.

Alexander, Jonathan, and Jacqueline Rhodes, editors. *The Routledge Handbook of Digital Writing and Rhetoric*. Routledge, 2018.

Aptheker, Bettina. *Woman's Legacy: Essays on Race, Sex, and Class in American History*. U of Massachusetts P, 1982.

Bailey, Moya Z. "All the Digital Humanists Are White, All the Nerds Are Men, but Some of Us Are Brave." *Journal of Digital Humanities*, vol. 1, no. 1, 2011, http://journalofdigitalhumanities.org/1-1/all-the-digital-humanists-are-white-all-the-nerds-are-men-but-some-of-us-are-brave-by-moya-z-bailey/.

Bailey, Moya, Anne Cong-Huyen, Alexis Lothian, and Amanda Phillips. "Reflections on a Movement: #transformDH, Growing Up." *Debates in the Digital Humanities 2016*, edited by Matthew K. Gold and Lauren F. Klein, U of Minnesota P, 2016,

Chapter 8, https://dhdebates.gc.cuny.edu/read/untitled/section/9cf90340-7aae
-4eae-bdda-45b8b4540b6b#ch08.

Barabási, Albert-Lázsló. *Linked: The New Science of Networks*. Perseus, 2002.

Baniya, Sweta. "Comparative Study of Networked Communities, Crisis Communication, and Technology: Rhetoric of Disaster in Nepal Earthquake and Hurricane Maria." *Proceedings of the 37th ACM International Conference on the Design of Communication*, Association for Computing Machinery, 2019, https://doi.org/10.1145/3328020.3353913.

Bianco, Jamie "Skye." "The Digital Humanities Which Is Not One." Gold, pp. 96–112.

Blondel, Vincent D., Jean-Loup Guillaume, Renaud Lambiotte, and Etienne Lefebvre. "Fast Unfolding of Communities in Large Networks." *Journal of Statistical Mechanics: Theory and Experiment*, 2008, https://doi.org/10.1088/1742-5468/2008/10/P10008.

Brooke, Collin Gifford. "Discipline and Punish: Reading and Writing the Scholarly Network." *Ecology, Writing Theory, and New Media: Writing Ecology*, edited by Sidney I. Dobrin, Routledge, 2011, pp. 92–105.

Brown, Tessa. "Constellating White Women's Cultural Rhetorics: The Association of Southern Women for the Prevention of Lynching and Its Contemporary Scholars." *Peitho*, vol. 20, no. 2, 2018, pp. 233–60, https://cfshrc.org/article/constellating
-white-womens-cultural-rhetorics-the-association-of-southern-women-for-the-
-prevention-of-lynching-and-its-contemporary-scholars/.

Cedillo, Christina V. "Diversity, Technology, and Composition: Honoring Students' Multimodal Home Places." *Present Tense: A Journal of Rhetoric in Society*, vol. 6, no. 2, 2017, www.presenttensejournal.org/volume-6/diversity-technology-and
-composition-honoring-students-multimodal-home-places/.

Cox, Matthew, and Michael J. Faris. "An Annotated Bibliography of LGBTQ Rhetorics." *Present Tense: A Journal of Rhetoric in Society*, vol. 4, no. 2, 2015, www.present
tensejournal.org/volume-4/an-annotated-bibliography-of-lgbtq-rhetorics/.

De Bellis, Nicola. *Bibliometrics and Citation Analysis: From the Science Citation Index to Cybermetrics*. The Scarecrow Press, 2009.

de Solla Price, Derek J. "Networks of Scientific Papers." Science, vol. 149, no. 3683, 1965, pp. 510–15, https://doi.org/10.1126/science.149.3683.510.

Detweiler, Eric. "'/' 'and' '-'?: An Empirical Consideration of the Relationship Between 'Rhetoric' and 'Composition.'" *Enculturation: A Journal of Rhetoric, Writing, and Culture*, no. 20, 2015, https://www.enculturation.net/an-empirical-consideration.

DeVoss, Dànielle Nicole, Angela Haas, and Jackie Rhodes, editors. *Technofeminism: (Re)Generations and Intersectional Futures*, special issue of *Computers and Composition*, vol. 51, 2019.

Dighton, Desiree. "Arranging a Rhetorical Feminist Methodology: The Visualization of Anti-gentrification Rhetoric on Twitter." *Kairos: A Journal of Rhetoric, Technology, and Pedagogy*, vol. 25, no. 1, 2020, https://kairos.technorhetoric.net/25.1/topoi/dighton/index.html.

D'Ignazio, Catherine, and Lauren F. Klein. *Data Feminism*. The MIT P, 2020.

Dingo, Rebecca. *Networking Arguments: Rhetoric, Transnational Feminism, and Public Policy Writing*. U of Pittsburgh P, 2012.

Dolmage, Jay Timothy. *Academic Ableism: Disability and Higher Education.* U of Michigan P, 2017, https://doi.org/10.3998/mpub.9708722.

Enoch, Jessica. "Coalition Talk: Feminist Historiography: What's the Digital Humanities Got to Do With It?" *Peitho*, vol. 15, no. 2, 2013, pp. 40–45, https:// cfshrc.org/article/coalition-talk-feminist-historiography-whats-the-digital -humanities-got-to-do-with-it/.

Enoch, Jessica, and Jean Bessette. "Meaningful Engagements: Feminist Historiography and the Digital Humanities." *College English*, vol. 64, no. 4, 2013, pp. 643–60.

Enoch, Jessica, Jean Bessette, and Pamela VanHaitsma. "Feminist Invitations to Digital Historiography." *DRC: Digital Rhetoric Collaborative*, 28 Mar. 2014, www· .digitalrhetoriccollaborative.org/2014/03/28/feminist-invitations-to-digital -historiography/.

Eyman, Douglas. *Digital Rhetoric: Theory, Method, Practice.* U of Michigan P, 2015, https://doi.org/10.3998/dh.13030181.0001.001.

Fancher, Patricia, Gesa Kirsch, and Alison Williams. "Feminist Practices in Digital Humanities Research: Visualizing Women Physician's Networks of Solidarity, Struggle and Exclusion." *Peitho*, vol. 22, no. 2, 2020, https://cfshrc.org/article /feminist-practices-in-digital-humanities-research-visualizing-women -physicians-networks-of-solidarity-struggle-and-exclusion/.

Faris, Michael J. "Assaying Queer Rhetoric: Distant Reading the Rhetorical Landscape for Queers and Feminists of Color." *Peitho*, vol. 20, no. 2, 2018, pp. 174–81, https://cfshrc.org/article/changing-the-landscape-feminist-rhetorical-practices -new-horizons-for-rhetoric-composition-and-literacy-studies-five-years -later-2/.

Fonow, Mary Margaret, and Judith A. Cook. "Feminist Methodology: New Applications in the Academic and Public Policy." *Signs: Journal of Women in Culture and Society*, vol. 30, no. 4, 2005, pp. 2211–2236, https://doi.org/10.1086/428417.

Frith, Jordan. "Social Network Analysis and Professional Practice: Exploring New Methods for Researching Technical Communication." *Technical Communication Quarterly*, vol. 23, no. 4, 2014, pp. 288–302, https://doi.org/10.1080/10572252.2014 .942467.

Fuhse, Jan, and Sophie Mützel. "Tackling Connections, Structure, and Meaning in Networks: Quantitative and Qualitative Methods in Sociological Network Research." *Quality and Quantity*, vol. 45, no. 5, 2011, pp. 1067–1089, https://doi .org/10.1007/s11135-011-9492-3.

Gaillet, Lynée, and Hellen Bailey, editors. *Remembering Women Differently: Refiguring Rhetorical Work.* U of South Carolina P, 2019.

Galloway, Alexander R. *The Interface Effect.* Polity, 2012.

Gatta, Oriana. "Connecting Logics: Data Mining and Keyword Visualization as Archival Method/ology." *Peitho*, vol. 17, no. 1, 2014, pp. 89–103, https://cfshrc.org /article/connecting-logics-data-mining-and-keyword-visualization-as -archival-methodology/.

Gaviria, Andres Ramirez. "When Is Information Visualization Art? Determining the Critical Criteria." *Leonardo*, vol. 41, no. 5, pp. 479–82, https://doi.org/10.1162/leon .2008.41.5.479.

Gold, Matthew K., editor. *Debates in the Digital Humanities*. U of Minnesota P, 2012, https://dhdebates.gc.cuny.edu/projects/debates-in-the-digital-humanities.

Gollihue, Krystin, and Mai Nou Xiong-Gum. "Dataweaving: Textiles as Data Materialization." *Kairos: A Journal of Rhetoric, Technology, and Pedagogy*, vol. 25, no. 1, 2020, https://kairos.technorhetoric.net/25.1/disputatio/gollihue-xiong-gum/index.html.

Goggin, Maureen Daly. *Authoring a Discipline: Scholarly Journals and the Post-World War II Emergence of Rhetoric and Composition*. Lawrence Earlbaum, 2000.

Goodwin, Jonathan. "Citations to Women in Theory." *Jonathan Goodwin*, 25 June 2013, www.jgoodwin.net/blog/citations-to-women-in-theory/.

Graban, Tarez Samra. "From Location(s) to Locatability: Mapping Feminist Recovery and Archival Activity through Metadata." *College English*, vol. 76, no. 3, 2013, pp. 171–93.

Graban, Tarez Samra, and Shirley K. Rose. "Editors' Introduction: The Critical Place of the Networked Archive." *Peitho*, vol. 17, no. 1, 2014, pp. 2–11, https://cfshrc.org/article/editors-introduction-the-critical-place-of-the-networked-archive/.

Graban, Tarez Samra, and Patricia Sullivan. "New Rhetorics of Scholarship: Levering *Betweenness* and *Circulation* for Feminist Historical Work in Composition Studies." Gries and Brooke, pp. 189–207.

Gries, Laurie E., and Collin Gifford Brooke, editors. *Circulation, Writing, and Rhetoric*. Utah State UP, 2018.

Gutenson, Leah DiNatale, and Michelle Bachelor Robinson. "Race, Women, Methods, and Access: A Journey through Cyberspace and Back." *Peitho*, vol. 19, no. 1, 2016, pp. 71–92, https://cfshrc.org/article/race-women-methods-and-access-a-journey-through-cyberspace-and-back/.

Haas, Angela M. "Toward a Digital Cultural Rhetoric." Alexander and Rhodes, pp. 412–22.

———. "Wampum as Hypertext: An American Indian Intellectual Tradition of Multimedia Theory and Practice." *Studies in American Indian Literatures*, vol. 19, no. 4, 2007, pp. 77–100, https://doi.org/10.1353/ail.2008.0005.

Hallenbeck, Sarah. "Toward a Posthuman Perspective: Feminist Rhetorical Methodologies and Everyday Practices." *Advances in the History of Rhetoric*, vol. 15, no. 1, 2012, pp. 9–27, https://doi.org/10.1080/15362426.2012.657044.

Hancock, Ange-Marie. *Intersectionality: An Intellectual History*. Oxford UP, 2016.

Hanneman, Robert A., and Mark Riddle. "Concepts and Measures for Basic Network Analysis." *The SAGE Handbook of Social Network Analysis*, edited by John Scott and Peter J. Carrington, SAGE, 2014, Chapter 24, https://doi.org/10.4135/9781446294413.

Harding, Sandra. "Introduction: Is There a Feminist Method?" *Feminism and Methodology: Social Science Issues*, edited by Sandra Harding, Indiana UP, 1987, pp. 1–14.

Haraway, Donna. "Situated Knowledges: The Science Question in Feminism and the Privilege of Partial Perspective." *Feminist Studies*, vol. 14, no. 3, 1988, pp. 575–99.

Healy, Kieran. "A Co-Citation Network for Philosophy." *Kieren Healy*, 18 June 2013, https://kieranhealy.org/blog/archives/2013/06/18/a-co-citation-network-for-philosophy/.

———. "Lewis and the Women." *Kieren Healy*, 19 June 2013, https://kieranhealy.org/blog/archives/2013/06/19/lewis-and-the-women/.

Hine, Darlene Clark. "The Corporeal and Ocular Veil: Dr. Matilda A. Evans (1872–1935) and the Complexity of Southern History." *The Journal of Southern History*, vol. 70, no. 1, 2004, pp. 3–34, https://doi.org/10.2307/27648310.

Jänicke, Stefan., Greta Franzini, Muhammad Faisal Cheema, and Gerik Scheuermann. "On Close and Distant Reading in Digital Humanities: A Survey and Future Challenges." *Eurographics Conference on Visualization*, edited by R. Borgo, F. Ganovelli, and I. Viola, The Eurographics Association, 2015, https://doi.org/10.2312/eurovisstar.20151113.

Kadushin, Charles. *Understanding Social Networks: Theories, Concepts, and Findings.* Oxford UP, 2012.

Keeling, Kara. "Queer OS." *Cinema Journal*, vol. 52, no. 2, 2014, pp. 152–57.

Kim, Dorothy. "How to #DecolonizeDH: Actionable Steps for an Antifascist DH." Kim and Stommel, pp. 479–97.

Kim, Dorothy, and Jesse Stommel, editors. *Disrupting the Digital Humanities.* Punctum Books, 2018, https://doi.org/10.21983/P3.0230.1.00.

Kirsch, Gesa E. *Ethical Dilemmas in Feminist Research: The Politics of Location, Interpretation, and Publication.* SUNY UP, 1999.

Kirsch, Gesa E., and Jacqueline J. Royster. "Feminist Rhetorical Practices: In Search of Excellence." *College Composition and Communication*, vol. 61, no. 4, 2010, pp. 640–72.

Kirschenbaum, Matthew G. "The Remaking of Reading: Data Mining and the Digital Humanities." *NGDM 07: National Science Foundation Symposium on the Next Generation of Data Mining and Cyber-Enable Discovery for Innovation*, 2007, https://www.semanticscholar.org/paper/The-Remaking-of-Reading-%3A-Data-Mining-and-the-Kirschenbaum/817296d88c191a307980020ad1d4d58e708ecf46?p2df.

Kleinberg, Jon M. "Authoritative Sources in a Hyperlinked Environment." *Journal of the ACM*, vol. 46, no. 5, 1999, pp. 604–32, https://doi.org/10.1145/324133.324140.

Laumann, Edward O., Peter V. Marsden, and David Prensky. "The Boundary Specification Problem in Network Analysis." *Research Methods in Social Network Analysis*, edited by Linton C. Freeman, Douglas R. White, and A. Kimball Romney, George Mason UP, 1989, pp. 61–87.

Lorde, Audre. "The Uses of Anger." *The Selected Works of Audre Lorde*, edited by Roxane Gay, Norton, 2020, pp. 53–66.

Losh, Elizabeth, and Jacqueline Wernimont, editors. *Bodies of Information: Intersectional Feminism and the Digital Humanities.* U of Minnesota P, 2018, https://doi.org/10.5749/j.ctv9hj9r9.

Liu, Alan. "Where Is Cultural Criticism in the Digital Humanities?" Gold, pp. 490–509.

McPherson, Tara. "Why Are the Digital Humanities So White? or Thinking the Histories of Race and Computation." Gold, pp. 139–60.

Medina, Cruz, and Octavio Pimentel. "Introduction: Coded in Technology Literacy." *Racial Shorthand: Coded Discrimination Contested in Social Media*, edited by Cruz Medina and Octavio Pimentel, Computers and Composition Digital Press, 2018, https://ccdigitalpress.org/book/shorthand/chapter_introduction.html.

Miller, Benjamin, Amanda Licastro, and Jill Belli. "The Roots of an Academic Gene-alogy: Composing the Writing Studies Tree." *Kairos: A Journal of Rhetoric, Technology, and Pedagogy*, vol. 20, no. 2, 2016, https://kairos.technorhetoric.net/20.2/topoi/miller-et-al/index.html.

Mott, Carrie, and Daniel Cocayne. "Citation Matters: Mobilizing the Politics of Citation toward a Practice of 'Conscientious Management.'" *Gender, Place, and Culture*, vol. 24, no. 7, pp. 954–73, https://doi.org/10.1080/0966369X.2017.1339022.

Mueller, Derek. "Grasping Rhetoric and Composition by Its Long Tail: What Graphs Can Tell Us about the Field's Changing Shape." *College Composition and Communication*, vol. 64, no. 1, 2012, pp. 195–223.

———. *Network Sense: Methods for Visualizing a Discipline*. The WAC Clearinghouse/UP of Colorado, 2017, https://doi.org/10.37514/WRI-B.2017.0124.

Muñoz, José Esteban. *Disidentifications: Queers of Color and the Performance of Politics*. U of Minnesota P, 1999.

Nakamura, Lisa. "Indigenous Circuits Navajo Women and the Racialization of Early Electronic Manufacture." *American Quarterly*, vol. 66, no. 4, 2014, pp. 919–41, https://doi.org/10.1353/aq.2014.0070.

Omizo, Ryan M. "Participation and the Problem of Measurement." *The Rhetoric of Participation: Integrating Commonplaces in and beyond the Classroom*, edited by Paige V. Banaji, Lisa Blankenship, Katherine DeLuca, Lauren Obermark, and Ryan Omizo, Computers and Composition Digital Press and Utah State UP, 2019, https://ccdigitalpress.org/book/rhetoric-of-participation/omizo/.

Otte, Evelien, and Ronald Rosseau. "Social Network Analysis: A Powerful Strategy, also for the Information Sciences." *Journal of Information Science*, vol. 28, no. 6, 2002, pp. 441–53, https://doi.org/10.1177/016555150202800601.

Perez, Annemarie. "Lowriding Through the Digital Humanities." Kim and Stommel, pp. 143–54.

Phillips, Donna Burns, Ruth Greenberg, and Sharon Gibson. "College Composition and Communication: Chronicling a Discipline's Genesis." *College Composition and Communication*, vol. 44, no. 4, 1993, pp. 443–65.

Pritchard, Eric Darnell. "Yearning to Be What We Might Have Been: Queering Black Male Feminism" *Palimpsest: A Journal on Women, Gender, and the Black International*, vol. 1, no. 2, 2012, pp. 179–200.

Ramsey-Tobienne, Alexis E. "Archives 2.0: Digital Archives and the Formation of New Research Methods." *Peitho*, vol. 15, no. 1, 2012, pp. 4–29, https://cfshrc.org/article/archives-2-0-digital-archives-and-the-formation-of-new-research-methods-2/.

Reinsch, N. L., and Phillip V. Lewis. "Author and Citation Patterns for The Journal of Business Communication, 1978–1992." *Journal of Business Communication*, vol. 30, no. 4, 1993, pp. 435–62, https://doi.org/10.1177/002194369303000404.

Reinsch, N. L., and Janet W. Reinsch. "Some Assessments of Business Communication Scholarship from Social Science Citations." *Journal of Business and Technical Communication*, vol. 10, no. 1, 1996, pp. 28–47, https://doi.org/10.1177/1050651996010001002.

Ridolfo, Jim, and William Hart-Davidson, editors. *Rhetoric and the Digital Humanities*. U of Chicago P, 2015.

Rìos, Gabriela Raquel. "Cultivating Land-Based Literacies and Rhetorics." *Literacy in Composition Studies*, vol. 3, no.1, 2015, pp. 60–70, https://licsjournal.org/index .php/LiCS/article/view/827.

Royster, Jacqueline Jones. *Traces of a Stream: Literacy and Social Change among African American Women*. U of Pittsburgh P, 2000.

Royster, Jacqueline Jones, and Gesa E. Kirsh. *Feminist Rhetorical Practices: New Horizons for Rhetoric, Composition, and Literacy Studies*. Southern Illinois UP, 2012.

Royster, Jacqueline Jones, and Gesa E. Kirsh. "Social Circulation and Legacies of Mobility for Nineteenth Century Women." Gries and Brooke, pp. 170–88.

Ryan, Kathleen J., Nancy Myers, and Rebecca Jones, editors. *Rethinking Ethos: A Feminist Ecological Approach to Rhetoric*. Southern Illinois UP, 2016.

Sano-Franchini, Jennifer. "Cultural Rhetorics and the Digital Humanities: Toward Cultural Reflexivity in Digital Making." Ridolfo and Hart-Davidson, pp. 49–64.

Sayers, Jentery. "Introduction: 'I Don't Know All the Circuitry.'" *Making Things and Drawing Boundaries: Experiments in the Digital Humanities*, edited by Jentery Sayers, U of Minnesota Press, 2018, https://dhdebates.gc.cuny.edu/projects /making-things-and-drawing-boundaries.

Schandorf, Michael, and Athina Karatzogianni. "#NODAPL: Distributed Rhetorical Praxis at Standing Rock." Alexander and Rhodes, pp. 142–52.

Schell, Eileen E. "Introduction: Researching Feminist Rhetorical Methods and Methodologies." Schell and Rawson, pp. 1–20.

Schell, Eileen E., and K. J. Rawson, editors. *Rhetorica in Motion: Feminist Rhetorical Methods and Methodologies*. U of Pittsburgh P, 2010.

Scott, John. *Social Network Analysis*. 3rd ed., Sage, 2013.

Small, Henry. "Co-citation in the Scientific Literature: A New Measure of the Relationship Between Two Documents." *Journal of the American Society for Information Science*, vol. 24, no. 4, 1973, pp. 265–69, https://doi.org/10.1002/asi.4630240406.

Smith, Elizabeth Overman. "Points of Reference in Technical Communication Scholarship." *Technical Communication Quarterly*, vol. 9, no. 4, 2000, pp. 427–53, https://doi.org/10.1080/10572250009364708.

———. "Strength in Technical Communication Journals and Diversity in the Series Cited." *Journal of Business and Technical Communication*, vol. 14, no. 2, 2000, pp. 131–84, https://doi.org/10.1177/105065190001400201.

Stephens, Sonia, and J. D. Applen. "Rhetorical Dimensions of Social Network Analysis Visualization for Public Health." *2016 IEEE International Professional Communication Conference*, IEEE, 2016, pp. 1–4, https://doi.org/10.1109/IPCC.2016 .7740480.

Takayoshi, Pamela, Elizabeth Tomlinson, and Jennifer Castillo. "The Construction of Research Problems and Methods." *Practicing Research in Writing Studies: Reflexive and Ethically Responsible Research*, edited by Katrina M. Powell and Pamela Takayoshi, Hampton Press, 2012, pp. 97–112.

VanHaitsma, Pamela. "Between Archival Absence and Information Abundance: Reconstructing Sallie Holley's Abolitionist Rhetoric through Digital Surrogates and Metadata." *Quarterly Journal of Speech*, vol. 106, no. 1, 2020, pp. 25–47, https://doi.org/10.1080/00335630.2019.1706188.

Wang, Dan. "Is There a Canon in Economic Sociology?" *Accounts: ASA Economic Sociology Newsletter*, vol. 11, no. 2, 2012, pp. 1–8.

Watts, Duncan J. *Six Degrees: The Science of a Connected Age*. Norton, 2003.

Chapter 7. Recording Nonverbal Sounds: Cultivating Rhetorical Ambivalence in Digital Methods

Kati Fargo Ahern
SUNY CORTLAND

In this collection I am lucky enough to be participating in conversations with new and established scholars whose work is positioned throughout several different areas within digital methods. While some of that positioning comes from personal identity, the work we do is also positioned in place. Therefore, I offer the following land acknowledgment with the understanding that a statement alone is never enough, and we must all actively work to dismantle colonial practices. The work of this chapter has been made possible by my inhabitance at SUNY Cortland, therefore I'd like to acknowledge the land I occupy at Cortland as the traditional, ancestral home of the Haudenosaunee, the People of the Longhouse, and of the Onondaga Nation, whose 2005 Land Rights Action includes the land on which our institution now resides. I take this opportunity to thank the original occupants of this place for their historical and continued stewardship.[1]

In addition to the place from which this chapter comes, it has been influenced by my own positionality. As an able-bodied, white, middle-class, heterosexual, and cisgender woman, I have benefitted from a tremendous amount of privilege. I first became interested in methods and methodologies in an undergraduate college course in 2004 that students had affectionately nicknamed "ERMs" (for Empirical Research Methods.) However, it was not until more recently that I began to think about what sonic methods may mean for the intersection of sound studies, rhetoric, and writing—and in particular, nonverbal soundscapes with attunement to different embodied experiences of such nonverbal sounds and different consequences for soundscape participants. In 2018, I gave a presentation at the Symposium for Sound, Rhetoric, and Writing called "Listening to this Soundscape Six Ways," where I attempted to show different values in comparative methods coming from different disciplines such as material rhetoric, social semiotics, and learning spaces design.

Here I will first review a little bit of that thinking on comparative listening methods. However, my main goal in this chapter is to explore rhetorical ambivalence related to sonic methods. Specifically, I will deal with the ambivalence involved in a particular component of many sonic methods—field recordings.

---

1.   Thank you to my colleague, Dan Radus, for his help in sharing this land acknowledgment.

Rhetorical ambivalence comes from Hillery Glasby's chapter on queer methodologies, which I will discuss in greater detail shortly. While ambivalence is often treated as a negative quality of confusion or contradictory feelings, Glasby (and I by extension) believe that ambivalence can be productive and even necessary to shake us out of a too-neat, post-positivist relationship to method. One of the generous reviewer comments I received for this chapter was the reminder that ambivalence may also be intertwined with power and privilege. While I will be arguing for the messiness of productive "unknowing," vulnerable people do not always have that luxury of unease, contradiction, or unknowing, which might cause their research project to be questioned or misinterpreted. I will return to this complexity and the role of my own privilege in cultivating rhetorical ambivalence in the concluding recommendations in this piece. First, it may be necessary to understand field recordings as a sonic method as opposed to an uncontested research practice.

Using an often-cited argument on methodology by Sullivan and Porter, Jeff Grabill emphasizes the importance of a distinction between method and methodology, where a methodology may involve a component of ideology or values, a component of practices, and finally a set of methods, or tools, for accomplishing the study (211). Using this distinction field recordings could be considered merely the tool or means by which a sonic methodology is carried out—how the data is collected. (This would be similar to the distinction between titration as a methodology versus measuring a liquid from the center of the meniscus as a conventional lab practice.) Here I argue that field recordings are often treated simply as the tool or convention for sonic methodologies, but we may move field recording closer to the methodological by suggesting that there are ideologies, as well as practices involved in field recording sounds.

Field recordings are often used in one of two of the following ways: 1) as a set of audio assets for "making as method" sonic research or 2) as data for qualitative methods involving applying code categories or listening frameworks that may isolate specific categories of sound or consequences of sound. While recordings of participant interviews or conversations present some clear requirements in terms of IRB and ethics, the recording of nonverbal soundscapes, which might include the combination of weather sounds, machine sounds and/or animal sounds with human-made nonverbal sounds (such as sighs, coughs, or footsteps) present a greater sense of uncertainty. I argue that field recordings for nonverbal sounds are fraught with questions of ethics, ownership, IRB-related issues (consent and nonparticipation), and consequence.

In order to address these complications and how to cultivate ambivalence related to recording human-made nonverbal sounds, first, I will briefly explore some of the available methods or listening frameworks that may require or at least make field recording data desirable. Next, I will use two examples of sonic methods projects (one "making as method" and one qualitative coding project) to discuss where ambivalence may fit into choices of whether to record soundscapes.

Finally, I will present a rough heuristic based on Indigenous digital composing and Indigenous sound studies to help researchers think about what it means to truly cultivate ambivalence when using field recordings.

Field Recording in Sonic Methods of Making and Coding

"Sound studies" is an interdisciplinary research area that exists within communication, media studies, critical cultural studies, history, archeology, and so forth, with relatively recent intersections with rhetoric and writing. Jonathan Sterne defines sound studies as reflexive, critical, and conscious of its own objects and methods, such that not all study of sound is "sound studies" (4–5). Joshua Gun et al. have made a similar point that not all studies of sound are sonic rhetoric (486). Therefore, studies in sound, rhetoric, and writing have been conscious of methodologies, even as these have evolved to consider more and more the embodied listening and recording of sounds.

In early research on sound and rhetoric, Greg Goodale made the argument throughout his 2011 book, *Sonic Persuasion,* that to "read" sound or sonic texts was not much different for those engaged in close reading as a method than it was to read other complex texts. To the question of specific approaches, Goodale writes "The viability of a specific method for reading sound is not as important as the greater argument that sound can be read" (12). With her concept of "multimodal listening," and Jennifer Lynn Stoever's "embodied ear," Steph Ceraso has more recently questioned the role of embodiment and materiality in working with sound. (I will return to this embodiment in the subsequent section on listening.) What this means is that 1) sonic methodologies for rhetoric and writing are still in the very early stages of development; 2) not all study of sound is based in rhetoric and writing; and 3) unlike early studies, many recent research projects in rhetoric, writing, and sound are incorporating files of actual sound, often made possible through field recordings.

Field recordings are frequently treated as a transparent or agreed-upon aspect in a variety of sonic methods. Deciding to take a field recording of a place, space, or event might be as "clear-cut" to a researcher as deciding to use a pencil while making a sketch of a learning space or a transcription program for an interview with a participant. By which case, I mean that these are choices still conditioned by disciplinary and personal training, but may not seem to be particularly ethically complicated, and are choices that are in widespread use. However, as I noted above, it is my goal in this chapter to consider what makes field recording nonverbal sounds more of a methodological or epistemological choice—what are the various ways in which concepts such as ownership, consent, or affect impact a researcher's decision to field record nonverbal sounds?

By field recordings, I simply mean a researcher taking a recording device or multiple devices and recording different tracks (or a single track) of a given soundscape for future analysis, coding, or soundwriting/remixing. The act of choosing what to record is another aspect of method—does one leave a recording device literally in the field for hours or days and capture a longitudinal study of the given soundscape, or is the field recording more focused on an a priori, desired sonic phenomenon? What hardware or recording device, microphone type, or windscreen would best be used to capture sounds? How are sounds archived, stored, and possibly transcribed after being recorded? These are all important questions. However, as I mentioned above, I'm focusing even more simply on the question of whether one chooses to field record at all.

It may seem obvious at first why a researcher would want to make field recordings, particularly from novel sonic events or soundscapes to make, remix, or design a project as a method of inquiry. Perhaps misplaced ideals of "authenticity" or a kind of positivist "truth" seem to cling to having audio assets from a particular place, moment, or time. It doesn't seem as rigorous or "sound" (if you pardon the pun), to simply recreate the soundscape of a busy street corner, or protest, or school yard from sounds already recorded in a Creative Commons archive. In essence, "making" or soundwriting as a methodology depends on having the sound of that school yard, that protest, that street corner to mix among other sound sources or moments in field recordings to explore analysis and argument about how the nonverbal sounds are working in that context or in order to answer the research questions we might ask about how sounds function. Support for field recording within sonic methods can be found in several studies and institutes. For instance, the 2018 Digital Field Methods Institute at UT Austin included practice, training, and considerations of field recording to work with sonic data and sonic research practices. Making as method is also discussed from the standpoint of practitioners, such as Victor Del Hierro's study of DJs as technical communicators. Furthermore, many scholars involved in video also focus on audio assets within their video recordings (VanKooten; Halbritter and Lindquist).

Besides making as method of inquiry, field recording can also be used in empirically driven sonic inquiry. In fact, although not often cited in this way, R. Murray Schafer's 1977 book, *Tuning of the World*, includes numerous depictions and discussions of decibel levels, frequency, decay and attack of sounds, as well as a spectrograph of the different bird notes (31). In these ways and others, field recordings allow for sounds to be categorized, even quantified by machine listening and principles of acoustics. This in turn makes possible different quantitative and qualitative methods. In discussing the difficulties of collaborative, feminist methods, Kris Blair and Christine Tulley identify issues in perceptions of rigor and tradition when completing their project within the expectations of a "typical" dissertation process (312). While not the same in terms of purpose or conventions as a dissertation, sonic methods as newly evolving within rhetoric and writing are also subject to objections about rigor, subjective listening, and disciplinary "fit." Field recordings that lend themselves to "traditional" quantitative and qualitative methods can sometimes effectively counter those objections.

In addition to perceptions of rigor or traditions of empirical inquiry, taking field recordings can also be used as a means of invention, to develop new sonic methods through either qualitative coding or listening frameworks. There are many potential ways to analyze the "raw" sonic data of field recordings. Although a discussion of comparative and inventive sonic frameworks is beyond the scope of this chapter, the following are just a set of possibilities for using field recordings to develop new sonic methods:

1. Coding sounds or sonic interactions between two or more sounds based on Theo van Leeuwen's six parameters of sound (outlined in his 1999 book, *Speech, Music, Sound*) from a tradition of social semiotics
2. Coding aspects of materiality involved in a soundscape (by modifying Carole Blair's five questions of materiality)
3. Using Anselm Strauss and Juliet Corbin's grounded theory model for discourse analysis or qualitative coding to develop codes "emerging" from the data
4. Charting multimodal interactions of the kind Sigrid Norris describes based on attention, interpersonal interaction, and placement of the body
5. Mapping or taking counts on the instances of sounds in particular zones of usage, (adapting Adam Bunnell et al.'s "hot spot" model from learning spaces research)
6. Developing a framework for interpreting sonic data that cites cultural rhetoric research, such as Afrofuturism within Black sound studies (Steinskog) or sound studies of the Global South (Steingo and Sykes), or Ecofeminism and technology (Romberger) or Indigenous sound studies (Robinson)

This is by no means an exhaustive list of sonic methods, but merely offered to show the range of possibilities for interpretive or qualitative frameworks when working with field recordings.

Field recordings don't just nebulously heighten the sense of possibility for sonic methods, but also address the idea of listening itself. As I wrote about in "Tuning the Sonic Playing Field," listening presents a position that is complicated by the embodied experience of the listener, as Greg Downey notes in his study of capoeira (Ahern 80–82). More recently Jennifer Lynn Stoever also addresses the fusion of listening with the self in her development of the concept of the "embodied ear." She writes: "I use the 'embodied ear' to represent how individuals' listening practices are shaped by the totality of their experiences, historical context, and physicality, as well as intersecting subject positions and particular interactions with power (the listening ear)" (Stoever 15). In other words, it isn't possible (or perhaps even desirable?) to listen outside of oneself or from an "objective" stance devoid of culture and subject position. However, what does this mean for a researcher interested in "intercoder reliability" (where at least two different people demonstrate statistically that they are able to code data with "enough" similarity?) Even taking seriously Dylan Robinson's point about listening from different subject positions, which I will explore in the subsequent sections, it may be true that access to the sonic, and/or visualized, metadata of field recordings offers different avenues for multiple individuals to reach "close enough" agreement or similarity. This is akin to the principle of tuning where there need not be "perfect" alignment with a particular acoustic measure of pitch, but the possibility of reaching close enough agreement in order to "play together."

Complicating Field Recording with Two Examples

However, just because field recording (whether for making or for coding/frameworks of interpretive listening) offers theoretical richness and possibilities, does not make this an uncomplicated practice within sonic methods. The opportunity to field record may often be presented and framed only in those terms—as an opportunity available for the taking or not. It isn't often that researchers in sound studies have presented instead a complicated decision-making process based on ambivalence and when/if to make field recordings. In this section I will outline two projects that differ in several ways (participants, perception of public/private space, purpose, and method) and that potentially involved the use of field recordings. I am using these examples to highlight some of the choices that may be made about whether or not to record nonverbal sounds, and then will move into further complicating factors that could be involved in other sonic projects.

The first project to be discussed is one that involved making as method and where the field recordings that were collected took place in a public, observational context with no intention of human interaction. The second project is one that involved the IRB-approval process and took place within several discipline-specific writing intensive college classrooms but did *not* ultimately result in field recordings being made.

To Record

In May 2012, following the defense of my dissertation, and in connection to my interest in materiality and memorial construction, I made several field recordings of the Vietnam Veterans Memorial and the World War II Memorial in Washington, D.C. It was a hot day in the beginning of the height of tourist season in D.C., and these field recordings were made by visibly extending my arm, holding up the recorder, and capturing the soundscape for approximately five 2- to 3-minute increments. These field recordings would then be used several years later to mix into an argument about erasure and sonic participation operating differently within each memorial space. (This piece can be found in the soundscapes section in the ebook *Rhetorics Change/Rhetoric's Change*, edited by Rice, Graham, and Detweiler.) At the time, I decided to complete these field recordings based on my understanding that this was a public space, I was not close enough to capture any individual conversations, and no identifying information could be traced back to the participants in the space. In other words, if there were approximately 40 people present at the Vietnam Veterans Memorial it would be impossible to isolate identifying information in individual voices, and no opening of a soda can or footstep, or even cellphone ringtone could reasonably be traced to any specific person. This assumption was also related to the fact that these were outdoor memorials with no prior registration or ticketing to enter, so there was no public record (except for perhaps GPS data?) that could be linked back to anyone being present at the memorials on that day. Additionally, as I could see no means for a participant to "opt out" of contributing to the soundscape or be contacted quickly enough in such a large space, it didn't seem realistic or feasible to try to collect informed consent.

Not to Record

The second project was an IRB-approved, empirical study conducted at my first teaching appointment in which I wanted to observe writing-intensive classrooms across different disciplines to listen to their soundscapes. The IRB approval was sought in summer of 2014, with data collection taking place within seven different classrooms two times apiece during fall 2014. Some of the same complications were involved (such as the issue of opting out), but this was clearly a private space, and one that involved ethical complications, such as perceived differences of power and affect between students and instructors. Additionally, I was only concerned with collecting data on the nonverbal sounds of the classroom, and not any of the exact conversations or dialogue/exchanges within a lesson or activity. In other words, I was outwardly doing something very similar to a traditional classroom observation, but I was solely interested in the exchange of nonverbal sounds in the soundscape. However, unlike the outdoor memorial spaces, I couldn't really capture nonverbal sounds without also capturing individual conversations and class dialogues in my field recording.

In this project, the decision to not field record was made at the request of my institution's IRB. My institution's IRB was concerned over students' rights to their nonverbal sounds and would not approve the project if it involved field recordings because there was no clear way for students to "opt out." It is true that students could be given a consent form, but unlike video recording (which could be directed to specific students or away from others) or the collection of classroom artifacts, the IRB members recognized that students would be unable to prevent themselves from making nonverbal sounds (like coughing or paper flipping) within the classroom soundscape. Furthermore, unlike the memorial visitors, who chose to enter public space, the students would be missing their learning experience if they chose not to enter the classroom space at their private institution on the day of my observations. In other words, opting out would either involve recording students' sounds without their permission, or would interfere with their learning if they chose to be absent. Instead, I was given the option to collect only my own written, listening field notes and an informed consent from instructors (similar to a traditional classroom observation.) At the beginning of each observed class instructors introduced me and the goal of my research based on the script that I provided.

At the time I agreed to this modification of my research project, predominantly because I was only entering my third year of my appointment in a tenure track position, and as a very junior scholar I was also aware of being one of the few people in my English department studying writing, with interest in digital environments, and the only faculty member studying sound. So, while my identity afforded me privilege, at the time my research positionality felt more precarious, and further so exacerbated by being pregnant by the time of data collection. Therefore, I was content to collect written field listening notes, reasoning that I could do more research into IRB protocols and expand/replicate my study with actual field recordings later on. In other words, at that time I perceived my lack of field recording as my own lack and certainly not as a productive, intentional, or ethically motivated choice.

This choice to not field record was one that then caused me to create a focused listening template where I first recorded information such as a quick sketch of the visual and material configurations of the classroom spaces, setup of chairs/seating, and any other notable features (such as windows or placement of technology, classroom projectors, and so forth). From there my listening notes were largely temporally based and descriptive, with occasional time stamps and onomatopoeia-like visualizations for nonverbal sounds. Thus, this data collection affected what I listened for and what I learned, such as ideas about learning space design (in my article "Understanding Learning Spaces Sonically, Soundscaping Evaluations of Place") and the focus on temporal unfolding of genre performances (with Ashley Mehlenbacher in "Listening for Genre Multiplicity in Classroom Soundscapes"). It also affected methodology in that because I had essentially written a moment-by-moment transcript in my field notes, Ashley and I used Nvivo, rather than complicating our coding method based on coding segmented audio files themselves. So, the single choice to abandon the possibility of field recordings in turn influenced and reverberated throughout the research project in unpredictable (at the time, to me) ways.

What both of these examples show is a few of the ideas that I will now unpack further in relation to ambivalence to field recording nonverbal sounds, particularly when those soundscapes involve the "sounding" of human participants. Many of the concepts that will be introduced are ones that scholars have grappled with in a variety of contexts such as WPA work, community-based research, and feminist and queer methods. What I am attempting to do is "listen to the ambivalence" or the questions that arise from taking these concepts seriously when applied to field recordings of nonverbal soundscapes specifically, or nonverbal sonic methods more generally.

Listening for Ambivalence

The importance of the term "ambivalence," is one that Glasby traces in a chapter of *Re/Orienting Writing Studies: Queer Methodologies, Queer Projects*, titled "Making it Queer, Not Clear: Embracing Ambivalence and Failure in Queer Methodologies." Glasby uses both Seigworth's notion of ambivalence as "unresolved, enmeshed, disoriented" and Yagelski's definition of ambivalence as "a troubling space between doubt and committed action . . . a space of both possibility and paralysis" to argue for ambivalence as generative, serving to "diminish authority," and open to "author-ize" an expanded sense of lived experiences (28). It is for these reasons that I similarly believe that field recordings (and perhaps all sonic methodologies as newly developing) might be subject to ambivalence as a kind of messy proving ground for ethical and ideological practices of method. Rather than simply accept the conventions or traditions of making field recordings as a practice that has been used and legitimized within many different sonic methods, it is important to first reinvigorate this conversation about methods and methodologies with the sense of productive not-knowing.

One of the ways in which ambivalence may enter the conversation of field recording nonverbal sounds is through Grabill's discussion of research stance. In his chapter on community-based research in *Writing Studies Research in Practice: Methods and Methodologies*, Grabill presents research stance as "a set of beliefs and obligations that shape how one acts as a researcher" (211). Further he notes that in community-based research this also has to do with two issues—the place of community in inquiry and the importance of relationships (Grabill 213). Although presently I will be discussing purpose as well, research stance seems to encompass a firmer, a priori set of priorities to govern choices within a research project. Another way that research stance could be considered is through the lens of feminist methods and reciprocity. Lauren Rosenberg and Emma Howes offer "lingering on relationships with participants, listening, and co-creating knowledge" as essential principles in a feminist ethos of representation (89). Regardless of framework, however, the field recordings I took from the U.S. memorials did not consider community, relationships, reciprocity, or participants. In fact, my research stance, (if one could even call it that) did more to call into question Rosenberg and Howes' distinction between "the ethnography" vs. "an archive." While they use these terms to literally describe their two projects, conceptually, they raise for me the question of how we treat sounds. Can sounds exist without a community emplacing them? Are sounds more an archive of a place, captured and preserved, (though with other associated ethical concerns and complications—see Stone) or are they always a kind of ethnographic study?

Another key concept to listening for or witnessing ambivalence within the practice of taking field recordings is by interrogating issues of purpose. In relation to WPA work, Douglas Hesse gives us three analytic axes offering different configurations of purpose (identity, instrumentality, advocacy, and integrity); audience (professional or local); and act [of research] (as basic or applied) (153). While Hesse offers these distinctions in Figure 7.1 to name and explore different types of WPA research, his three axes of purpose, audience, and act could also be subsumed under the larger umbrella of purpose/intent since purpose is related to audience and research design. In this way, larger aspects of purpose could help to locate ambivalence or motivation for field recording, rather than simply designing a soundscape study on the prior basis of needing or wanting to make field recordings based on a notion of convention or method (vs. methodology.) In other words, how might a project's field recording of nonverbal soundscapes address purpose in terms of the desired outcome, audience, or dimension of research (basic or applied?)

Perhaps even more obvious than these two overall concepts of stance and purpose, which are in some ways connected, is the issue of how IRB and human subjects research creates ambivalence for making field recordings. In "Digital Spaces, Online Environments, and Human Participant Research" William Banks and Michelle Eble give an extensive reading of the history and requirements of IRB approval, while also noting the messiness that traditional definitions acquire in humanities research, particularly when conducted online. In addition to noting that what constitutes "research" and "generalizable knowledge," can become tricky, Banks and Eble offer another definition within the Code of Federal Regulations based on human subjects and interaction: "Human subject means a living individual about whom an investigator (whether professional or student) conducting research obtains 1) data through intervention or interaction with the individual, or 2) identifiable private information" (32). Under this definition, the field recordings of the U.S. memorials certainly do not constitute human subjects research in that no human subjects were interacted with and that no identifiable private information was recorded. The only possible "interaction" with human-created data would be the recording of human-made nonverbal sounds such as footsteps, coughs, laughter, the pop of a soda can, and so forth, but which could not be attributed to any individuals or identified in any way. However, even though IRB approval may not have been required in a public, unidentifiable aggregation of nonverbal sounds, it still warrants consideration in how Banks and Eble talk about ethical issues of public vs. private and harm to contributors (in their case of digital, online blogs) and in my case, nonverbal sounds.

When it comes to legality and ethics, there is also not much guidance on nonverbal sounds unless they capture conversation, or identifiable, human-made, verbal sounds. Particularly in the current time of protests against police violence and a citizen-led desire to police violent behavior, there are numerous resources on rights related to video recording with audio. However, most of these guidelines are not only state-specific in some cases but focus nearly exclusively on videotaping and the capture of possible, private conversations in public (ACLU PA, "Know Your Rights"). The question then becomes whether the non-video, field recording of nonverbal sounds is subject to the same ethical or legal considerations. If it isn't a publicly held, "private" conversation, but footsteps, coughs, or ringtones, is there less expectation of privacy or consent? For the project out-lined above I might argue that few people would expect to be asked to consent to the recording of their footsteps, however, probably at the same time, equally few would expect that someone would be recording their footsteps in public.

Another related notion to ethics of recording these nonverbal, non-conversa-tion-based sounds is the idea of ownership. In fact, in the example above of whether people would have the expectation of informed consent to record their footsteps, one could just as easily ask how much *ownership* people attribute to their own human-created, nonverbal sounds. Again, the nonverbal sounds of interest to me are ones that humans are involved in making but do not include verbal components like conversation or identity markers, such as "the voice" more broadly. This cate-gory of nonverbal sounds might include human body sounds like yawns or coughs; sounds in motion like footsteps or clapping; or object-assisted sounds like opening a soda can or manipulating a cell phone. I hesitate to say that for the last type of nonverbal sounds we might attribute the sound more to the object (the phone or the can of soda), but logically these sounds are made through human manipulation.

We've addressed above the notion of "is this human subject research?" and now I'm asking even if it is technically not, how much ownership should or does one have over the sounds of their own bodies? This question has of course both a theoretical and a practical component. In her chapter "Multimedia Research," Janice McIntire-Strasburg raises the question of how feasible it is to give or seek informed consent in the context of digital assets (audio and visual) that are being remixed into new works, and then moves on to explore the issue of intellectual property (293–98). In her exploration she covers the idea of citation practices, authorship vs ownership, and differing practices of appropriation (for example "borrowing" code in programming) (298). The problem is that none of these areas seem to apply to ownership over the sound source of one's own footsteps. I can't cite them, they might not fall into the categories of intellectual property, and the only practices or conventions of borrowing are that the field of sound studies seems to have already become quite comfortable with recording soundscapes of busy outdoor markets, cafés, and so forth. However, this doesn't mean that the question of ownership is without ambivalence. In *Hungry Listening*, Robinson discusses at length the Western settler, colonial mentality toward "extractivism" and appropriation (14). Robinson writes:

> In other words, the meeting between listener and listened-to is bounded by a Western sense orientation in which we do not feel the need to be responsible to sound as we would another life. Sound's perceived lack of subjectivity here results in an asymmet-rical relationship where the listener's response can be one where they dismiss, affirm, or appropriate sound as content. (15–16)

Robinson's point that we as researchers do not feel responsible to the sounds we record or treat sounds as involved in a research relationship is well-taken.

However, my question remains whether a person has any feelings of ownership over footsteps or clapping? And if so, what are the conditions or types of sounds that create feelings of ownership? Again, this is even more troubled by the notion of field recordings being used in projects of "making as method" where sounds may be changed, as well. This is not something I covered extensively above, because the field recordings I made involved juxtaposing two different memorial soundscapes without any further editing or remixing such as pitch modification or volume leveling, but such a project could have been done, and thus could have introduced even more ambivalence.

Also related to ownership is the idea of affect. While affect is itself another complex concept filled with nuance (and scholarly research), my more simplistic suggestion is that ambivalence over recording nonverbal human sounds is tied to an implicit sense of whether a sound is laden with affect (such as cries, groans, sobs, or screams) or feels more affectively "neutral" to us, such as a footstep. Perhaps it is the notion of affect that gets more precisely to feelings of a nonverbal sound being "private" or perceptions of ownership over that sound. In the case of my classroom soundscape project described above it was pragmatically my IRB who raised issues over informed consent from students that caused me to not make any field recordings, but also theoretically a sense that students within a classroom were vulnerable and subject to different affects and power structures than a tourist at the World War II Memorial. However, I can guarantee this reaction might have been very different had I encountered in my field recording of memorials any visitors who were crying.

Another complicating factor is that again, Robinson argues that normative settler listening prioritizes listening "well" for content versus listening for "affective feel, timbre, touch, and texture of sound" (38). In other words, as a white, settler-listener, I could be very bad at listening for affect. And even if it isn't as much a matter of being "good or bad," as Janine Butler discusses in her chapter in this collection on transcription of ASL, differences of listening and interpreting present unique complications connected to affect, as well. Queer theory and feminist theory also affirm this. Caroline Dadas and Matthew Cox write about queering professional writing, but making a larger point about normativity, state: "Shifting our frames is essential to reorienting writing studies, to recognize the ways our research methodologies work to reproduce the same knowledge in the same frameworks we're already comfortable exploring" (192). I would argue that perhaps our field recording of nonverbal sounds does the same and hears what we are already comfortable with—neutral affect within field recording.

Finally, one last concept to listen for in the context of field recordings is consequence. Although more of an umbrella term, consequence brings together some of the issues above of "othering": harm, surveillance, and affective results. Much of the work already reviewed above examines the valences of consequence whether implicitly or explicitly. So, in this last section I will consider just a few places where consequence could be unexpected, further the marginalization of communities, or be used for harm. The examples of footsteps, coughing, or the opening of a soda can are ones that I have used somewhat disingenuously above as they seem to offset this dimension of ownership, affect, or identity when considered against some other nonverbal sounds such as laughter, cries, or screams. However, within a recording context, no nonverbal human sound is without potential consequence in being recorded and attributed to a particular location, place, event, or set of practices. First, in the case of footsteps, identifying footsteps and quantifying them could allow for arguments to be made about visitor density, perhaps even directions or pathways of motion, or speed. While this is maybe not the most shocking or harmful use of field recordings of footsteps in the setting of a memorial meant to be visited, a field recording of a street corner or alleyway at night could have an analogous effect to putting down a strip on a road that senses how many cars pass by.

As our field and others become increasingly interested in "big data," our ability to isolate sounds and harness machine listening to make counts could become weaponized in certain arguments. To this point, the sound of coughing, while more neutral in previous times, has become very much a sound of some consequence during the current global pandemic. Not only could it be used in field recordings to map and make arguments about community health, but it could also be used in surveillance and tracking. Just as social media posts recently warned about posting photographs of protesters, which could allow those protesters to be identified and targeted, field recordings involving any coughing among protesters could allow certain groups to double-down on arguments about the dangers of protesting for public health, even though a cough occurs for many other reasons than infection. Thirdly, the example of the sound of opening a soda can could similarly become associated with metrics of obesity, public and community health, or moralistic claims about funding to events or communities. Finally, nonverbal sounds can mean different things to different listeners (as has been cited above) and can enact psychological harm and violence apart even from any sort of potential sonic data mining. In the 2019 Computers and Writing Conference, keynote speaker Chris Gilliard discussed oppressive systems with a sonic example of the development of the automatic door lock and what that sound meant to a Black man walking down the street hearing the cascading sound of ca-chunk, ca-chunk, ca-chunk, ca-chunk of white "fear" inscribing sonic violence in that space, as every driver locked their doors. So, consequence is something that as researchers we must consider for making, archiving, and sharing/remixing field recordings, but also something that is deeply complicated by listener and researcher subject position.

After exploring so many different concepts that make the choice to conduct field recordings feel riddled with ethical complications, messiness, and scholarly ambivalence, it might be questionable why we would *ever* want to use them as method or methodology in the future. So, before moving into my final thoughts, I offer a last caveat about the potential use of field recordings in quantification.

While quantitative studies are not always as popular in our disciplines of writing studies, rhetoric, or sound studies, many theorists of methods and methodologies have argued for their utility. Richard Haswell opens his chapter on the functionality of quantitative methods for writing studies with the reality that in times of crisis we often call on colleagues to share quantitative data on things such as contingent faculty wages, class sizes, and so forth. In other words, one does not need to buy into antiquated and harmful post-positivist notions in order to make quantitative data useful. According to Haswell, quantitative methods can be used for the following purposes: insight (into phenomena that would be hard to observe); transgression (to change the minds and hearts of our audiences and correct misconceptions); challengeability (in regard to method/research design); and persuasion (to intervene, fund, or move stakeholders to change) (188). G Patterson also notes in "Queering and Transing Quantitative Research," that rather than cleaving to mean, median, and standard deviation or some sense of "objectivity," quantitative data can be productive in several different ways including "queering data interpretation" and reading for deviation—making more of the margins of data and who is represented or not (66–72). In conclusion, field recordings allow for many positive possibilities as a methodology, or a method embedded within different research studies. In terms of quantitative methods, field recordings could make possible machine listening to identify acoustic dimensions of sound (such as hertz or decibels) that create quantitative data and invite *positive* interventions and arguments, as well as ones of negative consequence and harm. This is why there may be so much ambivalence and not-knowing involved in the choice to make field recordings.

In this section I have attempted to do some listening for and witnessing of ambivalence, messiness, un-knowingness coming from different methods and methodologies in feminism, writing studies, digital writing, queer methods, and Indigenous theory related to field recordings. In attuning to these places some key concepts such as research stance, purpose, informed consent, ownership, affect, and consequence have emerged. In the final section, I will turn to how we might as researchers *cultivate* that ambivalence rather than ignore or avoid it.

Cultivating Rhetorical Ambivalence

I am calling this final section "cultivating ambivalence" because as Glasby argues, ambivalence is not something we should shy away from or avoid in our methods, and instead is something that can be generative and ethically-guiding (25). Although the choice to complete field recordings might seem like a simple, one-off decision in the life of a research project, I argue that it could instead gain methodological status, by asking us to interrogate the values, practices, and ways of knowing codified within field recording.

In order to dig deeper into what cultivating may be like, as opposed to simply listening to or for ambivalence, I will turn back to Indigenous approaches to both sound studies (Robinson) and digital composing and the assemblage (Arola and Arola). As I have reviewed above, Robinson's book deals with complicated notions of listening subject positions, appropriation/extractivism, and how a sound must be treated—not as an "asset," but as a complicated interplay among things. Robinson states that in order to

> consider intersubjectivity between listener, music, and space and reach beyond adjectival reliance, [he engages] in what [he calls] apposite methodology. Apposite methodologies are processes for conveying experience alongside subjectivity and alterity; they are forms of what is sometimes referred to as "writing with" a subject in contrast to "writing about." (81)

As a musicologist, Robinson is perhaps most focused on laying out a taxonomy of four different forms of musical encounter, however, throughout the monograph he makes the point that sound does not just exist as sound, to be taken up at will of an authorial intent, but among relationships, and based in space or land protocols. Similarly, and in the field of composition and rhetoric, Kristin Arola and her brother, Adam Arola, consider what it means to work with assemblages in ethical, responsible ways for digital composing in their chapter, "An Ethics of Assemblage: Creative Repetition and the 'Electric Pow Wow.'" In drawing on Deleuze, they consider DJs, the refrain, and "creative repetition," saying "yet we want to avoid an understanding of assemblage where cultural appropriation can enter under the auspices of a remix ethos" (209). They ultimately set out a framework in which a "good assemblage" can be assessed through considering if it is innovative, productive, responsive, opens up new ways of living and thinking, and, perhaps most importantly, if an assemblage is interrogating and answering ethically "whom does this assemblage benefit?" (211). I argue that both of these frameworks—the idea of sound, relations, and place, and assemblages of sound as benefit can be brought together in a way that helps sound scholars more fully consider whether or not to engage in even the first step of composing or assembling—the initial field recording of sounds. In Figure 7.1 I have sketched out a possibility for a visual/verbal heuristic that could help us to cultivate this ambivalence:

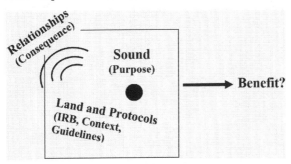

Figure 7.1. Heuristic for Cultivating Ambivalence in Field Recording Nonverbal Sounds

In Figure 7.1, I have chosen an image that uses visual clustering to depict that there are complex considerations among sound, relationships, and land/protocols, and that these complexities must also be weighed against the potential for benefit from making field recordings. In the figure, sounds are aligned with questions of purpose—why is this sound or space being subjected to field recording? Next, the IRB and questions of legal and human ethics of field recording form a kind of connection to the land and the context of place in which sounds are being recorded. Like land protocols may offer guidance, but not in isolation, IRB concerns can be read as the "space" of appropriate recordings and can help sound studies researchers to consider a myriad of complexities that may not immediately seem apparent in the first choices of research design. Finally, relationships are aligned with consequences. Rather than simply plucking sound "out of the air" in a space without context for participants or listeners, consequence asks us to imagine the not yet imagined use of our field recordings. This is also made in the visual metaphor to locate relationships or consequences extending beyond the "box" or boundaries of the research project. Can the field recordings be used for large scale data mining or surveillance? Do the field recordings "other" participants in the soundscape? Do they offer productive or capacious potentials? And finally, my argument is that these questions ultimately are intertwined with Arola and Arola's questions of benefit. To whom is the greatest benefit being conveyed? If the answer is only the researcher in a way that does not positively intervene in communities or impact the public or listeners in ethically expansive ways, perhaps field recording is just that, seeking to strip away sounds from people and places.

While I attempted to visually inscribe some of the complexity of these interplays between sound, relationships, context/land/protocols and benefit, Figure 7.1 could alternatively be configured as a chart to help researchers actively cultivate rhetorical ambivalence. In this way, a chart version could help researchers to inventively brainstorm some of this balancing or complexities that may not otherwise be considered. Such a chart may look like Table 7.1.

Table 7.1. Figure 1 Recording Heuristic in Chart Form

Sounds to be recorded and their purpose	**Land/Space** and **Protocols** considering context, place of recording, and IRB	**Relationships** and consequence for people being recorded and soundscape participants	**Benefit**—who benefits and how/in what ways?
(Space for notes and categories for brainstorming / invention)			

While it is my recommendation that sonic researchers use either the provided visualization or chart format in order to cultivate rhetorical ambivalence around the decision of whether to make field recordings, I'd like to return once again to privilege and vulnerability before concluding. Much of this chapter has considered the vulnerability of those whose nonverbal sounds are being recorded. I stand by that argument and believe it to be important. However, I would also like to acknowledge the vulnerability of BIPOC researchers in cultivating rhetorical ambivalence. As a white researcher, the most negative feedback I have ever previously received for my research into nonverbal sound within an English department has been in the form of being ignored or a gentle ribbing that "I must think I'm John Cage." However, researchers with other positionality must constantly endure microaggressions, questions of competence and rigor, and an assault on their research agendas. As I mentioned above, a reviewer reminded me that in many cases vulnerable researchers cannot afford the uncertainty or productive un-knowing that cultivating rhetorical ambivalence requires. Some researchers might feel pressured to make field recordings precisely because it feels like a conventional step within sonic methods. That is why I would argue that researchers, like me, who have benefitted from a tremendous amount of privilege need to first assume the risk of cultivating rhetorical ambivalence toward making field recordings so that it becomes a conventional practice, a thoughtful and accepted first step in any sonic research project.

In conclusion, Robinson and other sonic cultural rhetorics scholars have discussed appropriation, listening from subject positions that disregard the complexity of sound, and "extractivism." Feminist scholars have noted the importance of relationships and reciprocity. Queer scholars in *Re/Orienting Writing Studies* and Steinskog in *Afrofuturism and Black Sound Studies*, note who is marginalized in our methods and whose voice is left out. I argue that invigorating our sonic methods and methodologies with more ambivalence, particularly for field recording, also takes into consideration contexts of study such as medical soundscapes, cultural soundscapes, and personal soundscapes. While it may be tempting to assert an object-oriented approach to sound that gives weight to the force and potential of the nonverbal sounds "sounding" on their own, decentered from humans, there are often relationships between the sound, sound source, and humans making the sound. So, why listen for and why cultivate ambivalence for field recordings? It may not be that many people will lay claim to their cough, their footfalls, or their flip of a piece of paper. However, these sounds remain embodied as much as they are also dislocated from identifiable bodies. Even when we rely on ethically guided processes such as IRB approval and disciplinary convention, what is "okay" within the guidelines of human subjects research may not encompass the entire complexity and ambiguity of nonverbal sounds. This might be another necessary aspect of our sonic methods and methodologies moving forward—to give more dignity, humanity, and possibility to nonverbal sounds and the humans who make them.

Works Cited

ACLU PA. "Know Your Rights When Taking Photos and Making Video and Audio Recordings." *ACLU Pennsylvania*, 2020, https://www.aclupa.org/en/know-your -rights/know-your-rights-when-taking-photos-and-making-video-and-audio -recordings.

Ahern, Kati Fargo. "Tuning the Sonic Playing Field: Teaching Ways of Knowing Sound in First Year Writing." *Computers and Composition*, vol. 30, 2013, pp. 75–86.

———. "Understanding Learning Spaces Sonically, Soundscaping Evaluations of Place." *Computers and Composition*, vol. 48, June 2018, pp. 22–33.

Ahern, Kati, and Ashley Rose Mehlenbacher. "Listening for Genre Multiplicity in Classroom Soundscapes." *enculturation*, issue 26, 2018, http://enculturation.net /listening-for-genre-multiplicity.

Arola, Kristin L., and Adam Arola. "An Ethics of Assemblage: Creative Repetition and the 'Electric Pow Wow'." *Assembling Composition*, edited by Kathleen Blake Yancey and Stephen J. McElroy, NCTE, 2017, pp. 204–21.

Banks, William, and Michelle Eble. "Digital Spaces, Online Environments, and Human Participant Research: Interfacing with Institutional Review Boards." McKee and DeVoss, pp. 27–47.

Banks, William P., Matthew B. Cox, and Caroline Dadas, editors. *Re/Orienting Writing Studies: Queer Methods, Queer Projects*. Utah State UP, 2019.

Blair, Carole. "Contemporary US Memorial Sites as Exemplars of Rhetoric's Materiality." *Rhetorical Bodies*, edited by Jack Selzer and Sharon Crowley, U of Wisconsin P, 1999, pp. 16–57.

Blair, Kris, and Christine Tulley. "Whose Research Is It, Anyway?: The Challenge of Deploying Feminist Methodology in Technological Spaces." McKee and DeVoss, pp. 303–17.

Bunnell, Adam, Emily Hensley, ReBecca Williams, Russell Carpenter, Kelsey Strong, and Rachel Winter. "Mapping the Hot Spots: A Zoning Approach to Space Analysis and Design." *Journal of Learning Spaces*, vol. 5, no. 1, 2016, pp. 19–25.

Ceraso, Steph. *Sounding Composition: Multimodal Pedagogies for Embodied Listening*. U of Pittsburgh P, 2018.

Dadas, Caroline, and Matthew B. Cox. "On Queering Professional Writing." Banks, Cox, and Dadas, pp. 186–207.

Del Hierro, Victor. "DJs, Playlists, and Community: Imagining Communication Design Through Hip Hop." *Communication Design Quarterly Review*, vol. 7, no. 2, 2018, pp. 28–39.

Downey, Greg. "Listening to Capoeira: Phenomenology, Embodiment, and the Materiality of Music." *Ethnomusicology*, vol. 46, no. 3, 2002, pp. 487–509.

Gilliard, Chris. "Click here if you agree: Opting out of oppressive systems." *Computers and Writing Conference* Saturday Keynote Session, 2019.

Glasby, Hillery. "Making it Queer, not Clear: Embracing Ambivalence and Failure as Queer Methodologies." Banks, Cox, and Dadas, pp. 24–41.

Goodale, Greg. *Sonic Persuasion*. U of Illinois P, 2011.

Grabill, Jeffrey T. "Community-Based Research and the Importance of a Research Stance." Nickoson and Sheridan, pp. 210–19.

Gunn, Joshua, Greg Goodale, Mirko M. Hall, and Rosa A. Eberly. "Auscultating again: Rhetoric and sound studies." *Rhetoric Society Quarterly*, vol. 43, no. 5, 2013, pp. 475–89.

Halbritter, Bump, and Julie Lindquist. "Time, Lives, and Videotape: Operationalizing Discovery in Scenes of Literacy Sponsorship." *College English*, vol. 75, no. 2, 2012, pp. 171–98.

Haswell, Richard H. "Quantitative Methods in Composition Studies: An Introduction to Their Functionality." Nickoson and Sheridan, pp. 185–96.

Hesse, Douglas. "Writing Program Research: Three Analytic Axes." Nickoson and Sheridan, pp. 140–57.

McIntire-Strasburg, Janice. "Multimedia Research: Difficult Questions with Indefinite Answers." McKee and Devoss, pp. 287–300.

McKee, Heidi, and Dànielle DeVoss, editors. *Digital Writing Research: Technologies, Methodologies, and Ethical Issues*. Hampton Press, 2007.

Nickoson, Lee and Mary P. Sheridan, editors. *Writing Studies Research in Practice: Methods and Methodologies*. Southern Illinois UP, 2012.

Norris, Sigrid. *Analyzing Multimodal Interaction: A Methodological Framework*. Routledge, 2004.

Patterson, G. "Queering and Transing Quantitative Research." Banks, Cox, and Dadas, pp. 54–74.

Rice, Jenny, Chelsea Graham, and Eric Detweiler, editors. *Rhetorics Change/Rhetoric's Change*. Intermezzo and Parlor Press, 2018, http://intermezzo.enculturation .net/07-rsa-2016-proceedings.htm.

Robinson, Dylan. *Hungry Listening: Resonant Theory for Indigenous Sound Studies*. U of Minnesota P, 2020.

Romberger, Julia. "An Ecofeminist Methodology: Studying the Ecological Dimensions of the Digital Environment." McKee and DeVoss, pp. 249–67.

Rosenberg, Lauren, and Emma Howes. "Listening to Research as a Feminist Ethos of Representation." *Composing Feminist Interventions: Activism, Engagement, Praxis*, edited by Kristine L. Blair and Lee Nickoson, The WAC Clearinghouse/ UP of Colorado, 2018, pp. 75–91, https://doi.org/10.37514/PER-B.2018.0056 .2.04.

Schafer, R. Murray. *The Tuning of the World*. Knopf, 1977.

Steingo, Gavin, and Jim Sykes, editors. *Remapping Sound Studies*. Duke UP, 2019.

Steinskog, Erik. *Afrofuturism and black sound studies: culture, technology, and things to come*. Springer, 2017.

Sterne, Jonathan. "Sonic Imaginations." *The Sound Studies Reader*, edited by Jonathan Sterne, Routledge, 2012, pp. 1–18.

Stoever, Jennifer L. *The Sonic Color Line: Race and the Cultural Politics of Listening*. New York UP, 2016.

Stone, Jonathan W. "Listening to the Sonic Archive: Rhetoric, Representation, and Race in the Lomax Prison Archives." *enculturation*, 2015, https://www.enculturation.net/listening-to-the-sonic-archive.

Strauss, Anselm, and Juliet Corbin. "Grounded Theory Methodology." *Handbook of Qualitative Research*, vol. 17, no. 1, 1994, pp. 273–85.

VanKooten, Crystal. "The Music, the Movement, the Mix." *enculturation*, 2017, http://enculturation.net/the_music_the_movement_the_mix.

Van Leeuwen, Theo. *Speech, Music, Sound*. Macmillan International Higher Education, 1999.

Chapter 8. Digitally Preserving the Home through the Collective: A Communal Methodology for Filipinx-American Digital Archiving

Stephanie Mahnke
VANDERBILT UNIVERSITY

James Beni Wilson
ARIZONA STATE UNIVERSITY

Land Acknowledgment. Our article relies on the importance of decolonizing methodologies toward revisionist histories and reclamation of land rights. As part of a culture that has been colonized for over three centuries and still struggles to undo the harmful effects of colonialism on our land and people, we are committed to both materialist and discursive approaches to decolonization, and thus acknowledge we are conducting research on Anishinaabe land. We acknowledge and support the sovereignty of the Ojibwe, Odawa and Botawatomi tribes.

The library of the Philippine American Cultural Center of Michigan (PACCM) would seem, upon first glance to the visitor, a storage room: papers hang off the shelves with faded post-its, cardboard boxes filled with documents press against the walls, some closed by the resting weight of tinikling bamboo sticks, and donated books with Catholic covers rest on every seating space. Filipinx American newsletters and history books are stacked out of order, the fate of their intermingling decided only by a donor's casual placement—a drop-off that hints to the conversational tenor of praise for the donated contents, their unanticipated accumulation, and the donor's dismay at being unable to keep them secure. The realized historical import that gradually weighed on many of the donors is another theme we often hear in these conversations at the cultural center. Yet for a center whose collections span the last two decades of Michigan's Filipinx American activity and inherited the previous decades of the community's planning documents, organizational minutes, event artifacts, letters, pictures, and collections from community leaders, the collection of the community's past had continued to both multiply and lay dormant. Their narratives lay in fragments, talking over each other and interrupted by the history of their neighboring artifacts, only remembered by the conversations and lives retained by the cultural center's members.

In 2018, affiliate members of the cultural center and the non-profit organization Filipino American National Historical Society—Michigan Chapter (FAN-HS-MI) spear-headed the digital archiving of the center's artifacts to preserve the objects' present integrity, as well as document and file them for accessible community use. This daunting multi-year project had to confront two critical tasks: how do we create an ongoing and sustainable working infrastructure for archiving such a large set of collections? Further, how do we also incorporate an equally large Filipinx American community in this process, since they are the holders, interpreters, and translators of these memories? Essentially, what these tasks required was a marriage of both an expert and informed approach to digital archiving as well as the expertise and experience of the local Filipinx American community.

Often, in traditional forms of digital archiving, the former eclipses the communal presence, resulting in distilled and "objective" archival narratives that drive decisions around what's deserving of attention based on Western-centric and institutionalized values. Much of what is considered "traditional archiving" today refers to the post-modern archiving methods from the 1970s onward which, though it recognized the pluralism of voices, identities, and histories in our society, "ultimately involved an imposition of the archivist's expertise on records, records creators, and records users" (Cook 11). To address this imbalance and meet our community's needs, many of our methodological answers came from prioritizing the behavioral and value-driven mechanisms of the Filipinx collectivist mentality and localized socio-cultural patterns that were already in place. Though some Filipinx American archives have grounded these cultural values and patterns in a controlled material space, such as a cultural center, we found digital space and methods could also accommodate and resolve our preservation and access needs without sacrificing our local collectivist patterns. What resulted has been a culturally informed working infrastructure for digital archiving exemplifying a community-engaged praxis that adds to a diverse stream of research methods. More specifically, this infrastructure informs approaches to digital archiving that make space for local community dynamics and ecosystems.

Computers and writing as a field has seen an upswing in such archival work and studies, with Kathleen Blake Yancey suspecting that writing studies may be getting serious about an "archival turn" (364). A wide range of research in the field has covered the pedagogical use of archives in the composition classroom (Daniel-Wariya and Lewis; Enoch and VanHaitsma) and developing archival methodologies (Ramsey et al.). The need for methodologically incorporating local contexts and actors who produce archival collections has become a critical focus, a way to correct weak historiography from depending on secondhand readings and postmodern critiques, and instead supply emerging archival practices on which our revisionist histories depend (Ferreira-Buckley 581–82). As studies of archival methodology have shifted from a focus on institutional to social practice (Friedrich 422–23), communal archives that had been previously peripheral to archiving's Western-centric roots have gained more recognition in producing visible histories with culturally distinct archival practices.

Calls from the digital humanities (Posner) and digital rhetoric (Poudyal) to interrogate and rebuild digital archives from its elitist ties have reflected the steady emergence of new archival models (Kurtz; Bastian "The Records"). These non-Western forms of digital archiving have contributed to a growing number of heterogeneous practices for researching and conducting archival work based on a variety of community practices. Many of these culturally curated archives—by nature of their community-centered approaches—have also answered technical communications' call for a collaborative alliance between designers and users (Haas 304; Agboka 4) to further combat erasure, misrepresentation, and dehumanization of marginalized communities within digital writing and rhetoric. Similarly, cultural rhetoricians have argued the methodological importance of including community stakeholders in the digital archiving process by re-centering cultural processes of knowledge-making (Ridolfo, Hart-Davidson, and McLeod; Cushman).What has often resulted are archival methodologies that not only blur the lines between archivists and users, but ultimately rely on a network of participant-archivists who record, preserve, and make meaning of their own histories within their communal and cultural logics.

In the following sections, we provide the research backdrop within which we situate our own Filipinx American archival process for our cultural center in Michigan, a process which strives for dynamic preservation and access policies that reflect the community's values and practices. By looking at the methodological nature of research and archival processes in the broader fields of digital rhetoric and archival studies, and Filipinx American archiving specifically, we begin to establish how our cultural center's particular archival process contributes to emerging and diverse practices as well as distinct forms of Filipinx American archiving as fitted for localized contexts.

Community Archives in Rhetoric and Archival Studies

Given the influx of diverse forms of community archiving processes, community archives—or autonomous archives created, managed, and sustained by communities often apart from mainstream or institutionalized archives—have marked the most recent paradigmatic shift of archival identity. Diverse archival processes have broadly exposed the imperial logics of traditional Western-centric archives, a process Ellen Cushman outlined as operating through a Western tradition and timeline, and de-contextualized methods of collecting and viewing artifacts that reinforce a subject/object dichotomy (121). At the core of this exposure is a re-consideration of Western standards of legitimacy and validity. The community-participatory model has interrogated and revised archives and archival processes to specifically question what archivists consider to be legitimate authentication of evidence through such long-standing methodological factors such as evidence, memory, and provenance (Cook 114–115).

For example, one major impact of the community archiving model has been its reexamination of the term *provenance* which ties notions of authenticity to original order. According to the International Council of Archives, provenance refers to the "agency, institution, organization, or individual that created, accumulated, and maintained records . . . prior to their transfer to a records centre/archives" (qtd. in Sweeney 194). Typically a means of grounding claims of legitimacy, terms like provenance have been transformed by varied claims of authentic order and origin within the hands of communities. For instance, ideas of authenticity have shifted to incorporate Indigenous voices through parallel provenance (Hurley), descendants of records (Bastian), cultural networks (Battley 61) and ethnicity (Wurl). Like provenance, other processual practices and principles such as appraisal, collection development, arrangement, and access have typically leaned into newer democratized forms dictated by each community archives' own terms (Poole 663). As a result, looking merely at the records of a community archive does not provide the full picture of the value networks guiding and assessing cultural objects (Battley 60). Instead, taking stock of the localized rhetorical process which ascribes a particular logic of order, value, and legitimacy to archived objects can tell researchers, archivists, and users of object meanings within the cultural systems they are situated.

Today, community archives with their own systems of archival method/ologies have shown to achieve several goals in line with social justice and activism work, the root motivation that had spurred community archiving movements in the 60s and 70s (Poole 658; Flinn and Stevens 6). Based on their social politics, these archives have addressed and filled gaps in historical records, addressed unequal representation in the landscapes of our national memory, and grounded priorities on the collective memory and concerns of the people. In interviews with 17 community archive participants, for instance, Cifor et al. found most community archivists wear many hats such as activists, advocates, and community organizers as they stay close to public engagement and ethical and inclusive orientations to archival methodologies. Finally, community archives have shown to generate "representational belonging" for communities, a form of empowerment through representation that serves as a counterweight to what Michelle Caswell termed *symbolic annihilation* from memory institutions (Caswell et al. 75). The field of cultural rhetorics has explored similar affordances to community-driven archival work, with notable methodological examples and commentaries on such community archives as Cherokee digital archives (Cushman), a Samaritan digital archive (Ridolfo et al.), and the Lesbian Herstory Archive (Narayan).

Filipinx American Historiography and Community Archiving

Filipinx American communities have added to these culturally distinct and community-centered forms of archival models, and their epistemologies have driven unique models that not only break from Western institutional archiving processes, but also provide diverse method/ologies from within Filipinx or Filipinx American contexts. Many Filipinx American community archivists have emphasized their methodological approach, underscoring that the process be taken as seriously as the product (see Stoler 83; Ruskin). Grounding more resources within community perspectives, Filipinx and Filipinx American researchers' methods have often involved the consultation of oral histories, Filipinx publications, personal family histories, decolonized interpretations of Filipinx psychology,[1] and proposed history-writing in Filipinx language,[2] For archives specifically, Filipinx and Filipinx American community archivists have reclaimed the documentation of their histories through various rhetorical strategies around narratives and place/space.

Narratives

Following the direction of more Filipinx-centric histories and narratives, the broader impulse of Filipinx historiography in the last five decades has leaned on *Pantayong Pananaw*, or the "for-us-by-us" perspective, which involved Filipinx cultural perspectives for documenting Philippine history to respond to a number of predominant themes, such as colonial influence, discovery, reaction, and the "first Filipinos" (Reyes 243). In the U.S., projected themes around Western contact have carried into Filipinx American collections and archives which are often read in terms of the influence of colonialism, the attendant cultural loss, and a multiculturalism which "presumes the centrality of the U.S. nation-state" in incorporating different groups (Fujita-Rony 4–5). Filipina researchers such as Dorothy Fujita-Rony have suggested lenses to nuance and problematize the assimilationist-leaning themes of Filipinx archival readings. For instance, she offers the lens of "militarized rupture" to show ways in which imposed war and militarization complicate the seemingly positive social scientific narratives. Similarly, the Manilatown I-Hotel Archives resurrects Filipinx American narratives around the anti-eviction movement of San Francisco's International Hotel (I-Hotel), an erased chapter of *manong* and Filipinx American history documenting the community's fight against corporate displacement (Wong et al. 124). Both approaches to Filipinx American archives allow for fuller and reclaimed perspectives on these narratives from the community.

Place/Space

Filipinx American community archives have continuously pushed against institutional and Western archiving roots not only in the way they seek to be narrativized,

---

1. See *Sikolohiyang Pilipino* movement, which revised literature on Filipinx psychology from Western authors to account for Filipinx ontology.

2. See the *Pantayong Pananaw* movement, which stressed "for-us-from-us" historical perspectives written in Filipinx language.

but also in imposing their own terms around space, particularly on the grounds of access and autonomy. Often to address the common community archiving challenges of balancing sustainability and autonomy (Poole 672–73), many of these Filipinx American community archives have partnered with academic and library institutions who serve as custodians of the collected materials, but with the insistence that the gathering of materials stays autonomous for the community. Filipinx American community archives such as the *My Baryo, My Borough* project housed at Queens Library, and the Archiving Filipino American Music in Los Angeles (AFAMILA) project housed in the UCLA Ethnomusicology Archive are examples of institutional partnerships who use major institutions to archive and house materials collected by communities' digital copy donations (Schreiner and de los Reyes 2) or gathered by Filipinx American graduate students who serve as community liaisons (Ruskin). Similarly, UC Davis's *Welga Digital Archive* which is housed in the Bulosan Center for Filipino Studies is run by an entirely Filipinx American personnel, and the center's archivist inputs digital copy donations from local Filipinx Americans. Though the sustainability and legitimacy of these archives are bolstered by institutional partnership and its attendant formalized space for collections, the partial autonomy has also led to issues of limited access and use from the very Filipinx American communities that contributed the majority of the collections (Ruskin).

Some Filipinx American archives have taken to digital platforms as a means of using virtual space to solve the issue of sustainability and autonomy. In one example, The Manilatown I-Hotel Archives, run by grassroots activists, their cultural networks, and the non-profit Manilatown Heritage Foundation, did not have a physical space to safely house their materials on the I-Hotel anti-eviction movement. So, they showcased their materials on a *blogspot* to make it accessible to the Filipinx American public. Prioritizing public engagement and easy access, the group also took to social media to highlight the materials and spark discussion of a Filipinx American movement that has often been erased from the history books (Wong et al. 125–26).

Though the above Filipinx American archives have faced different affordances and limitations in terms of physical and digital spaces, one of the leading models that resolved these issues of sustainability and autonomy comes from one of the largest and well-known Filipinx American community archives in America. The National Pinoy Archives (NPA), founded by Dr. Fred Cordova and affiliated with the Filipino American National Historical Society (FANHS) formed in 1982 (Fujita-Rony 12; Monberg 197). Communal and participatory archiving serves as the foundation of the NPA, and the community archive's main principles for sustainment include remaining independent and locally accessible. Determined to stay housed within FANHS' Seattle office for accessibility reasons, the archival material on Filipinx American history includes hundreds of oral histories, newspaper clippings, and boxes of objects labeled by subject. As part of its communal participatory approach, Filipinx Americans are invited to visit the archives, as well as create their own files to contribute. According to Terese Monberg's interview with Dr. Fred Cordova, the NPA's materials are ninety-nine percent derived from community members whose contributions far outnumber those of academic contributors. To keep it community driven, Cordova insisted on specific terms of access and space:

> To be community-based, in Fred's eyes, means that community members have physical access to one another's research, artifacts, and publications. No institutional affiliation or identification card is required, no minimum age applies, no user's fee is charged—though donations are encouraged. This community-based model is enacted through the National Pinoy Archives (NPA), housed with the FANHS National Chapter in Seattle. Here, students, community researchers, and other folks interested in Filipino American history not only have full access to the archives, they are led through the archives by community researchers who know the materials, their origins and interconnections, exceptionally well. These archives facilitate the kinds of sharing that is central to the philosophy behind FANHS. The archives become a physical, social, and virtual space for sharing and networking. (Monberg 197)

The NPA remains an exemplary model of Filipinx American methodologies that incorporate autonomous, accessible, and entirely community-run participatory archiving, and much of these features are facilitated by communal logics and considerations.

Each of the above examples add to a tapestry of methodological approaches that are anchored on localized contexts and needs, while also feeding into an interdependent network of constitutive possibilities for more responsible archival infrastructures. Amongst the wide array of community archival models and research, Filipinx American community archives, driven by their collectivist values, have provided some localized methodological solutions to key challenges consistent to community archiving. Alex Poole's review of community archives research spanning from 1985 to 2018 highlighted several common issues, some of which included the lack of sustainable resources, outreach, and intracommunity and intercommunity tensions. In response to these challenges, Filipinx American archives have implemented institutional partnerships bridging expert and community ties, thus tapping into more sustainable resources and grounding stakeholder relationships on mutual trust and rapport, as well as creating their own autonomous and Filipinx-run collections powered by internal cultural networks. We add to the current literature on community archiving methodologies by discussing our FANHS Michigan chapter's distinct approach to communal digital archiving. We offer insight as to how our chapter addressed the above challenges through our own approach to local collective-driven decisions around narrative and place/space. More specifically, it is our choice of digital methods that allows an excess of voices in our collection, overlaid by a communal approach to tagging and metadata, as well as our unique grounding of archival content and participation through the physical space of our cultural center. Further, our methodology also offers pathways to address other common challenges to community archives more broadly, such as outreach, sustainability, and succession.

We begin by discussing the background history, partnerships, and working infrastructure of our community archive. Then we outline the model's successes and challenges, followed by a discussion of implications for community archival practices. For the Filipinx American culture whose knowledge production is often inherently communally-centered, our *Filipinx Americans in Michigan Historical Archive* demonstrates a digital archival model that continues to push against archives/databases that are written *about* racial communities rather than *with* them, allows communities to engage with their own histories in ways that align with their own epistemologies and localized contexts, and contributes to a heterogenous history of decolonizing practices for ethical digital cultural heritage production.

The Collections of Filipinx American History in Michigan

The conception of *The Filipinx Americans in Michigan Historical Archive* began in 2018 when discussions between staff and elders at the Philippine American Cultural Center of Michigan (PACCM) and members of FANHS–Michigan Chapter (FANHS-MI) identified the need to preserve and organize the large collection of historical documents sitting in PACCM's library and offices, which, at that point, had largely been in the care of the center's elders.

Officially opening in Southfield in 2001, PACCM was a near seven-decade pursuit by the Filipinx Americans of Michigan to find a centralized space for gathering and sustaining their heritage. Given the decades-long, cumulative effort, which included a tremendous amount of volunteer hours and the sacrifices of board members, youth, Filipinx American community, presidents, and fifty-one Filipinx American organizations, PACCM gained its own building and now serves over 4,000 community members of every age who are looking to get closer to Filipinx heritage and find community with other Filipinx Americans in the state. PACCM remains entirely volunteer-run, including their culture and language program, Paaralang Pilipino, which teaches classes to youth and adults every Sunday. It also serves as a shared and centralized space for Filipinx American college groups, organizations, folk dance groups, and social justice organizations to hold meetings and events.

Many of the documents were donated or compiled throughout the center's years, much of which predate the center and encompass the decades of multi-organizational planning for a centralized space for Michigan's Filipinx American communities. Michigan's only Filipinx cultural and language school, the multiple Filipinx American organizations that formed, fell, and spawned newer organizations, and the collection's vast assortment of minutes, letters, historical photographs, brochures, personal notes, sketches, newsletters, and mini biographies provide an intimate history of Michigan's Filipinx American communities from the 1940s to the present day.

The Need for a Digital Community Archive

Initial ideas for the collections' preservation included organizing the library so the collections would be displayed and easily navigable, but given the limited space of the library in comparison to the number of boxes and donations, as well as the already visible signs of aging and wear from the repeated handling of the documents, our members realized we also needed better protocol for preservation. Not only was there a need to preserve the quality of the documents, but also the stories and meanings behind them, many of which were lost due to poor organization and labeling of boxes. The center's elders often provided this context, but with the rapidly aging population of our center's elders, we were further pressed to find a way to preserve the material and document their communal meanings.

The most immediate answer to the above needs became the idea of digitizing the documents and housing them in a digital archive. Though a digital archive couldn't replicate the material artifacts, it could preserve digital surrogates of the documents in their present quality and provide promise of greater participation and access to the Filipinx American community.

Our Positionality

A critical part of this history and project's methodology requires a reflection and acknowledgment of our—James and Stephanie's—positionality as members and researchers and how that affects the nature of involvement in the archival project. We take seriously such questions as our impetus to speak and commitment to accountability, or more precisely, what LuMing Mao asks us to question: "What right, for example, do scholars have to represent this or that culture and its rhetorics? From what vantage point do they position themselves, and how does their position in turn shape and influence the outcomes of their studies?" (42). Asking such questions of ourselves and the possible epistemological effects of bringing in our lenses, ideologies, and individualized contexts, whether consciously or unconsciously, was the first critical step in prioritizing the community's values, especially in our representation of them.

James is a Filipino American adoptee who came to the center in 2007 during his late adolescence to get closer to his roots. He enrolled in the language school, Paaralang Pilipino, and eventually went on to become the director of Paaralang Pilipino, lead facilitator for Filipino Youth Initiative (FYI), and secretary of FAN-HS-MI. The complexities of his transracial experience, cultural disconnect and upbringing, and identity affects his relationship with his position at the center.

As someone personally impacted by estrangement from his Filipinx roots and community due to the colonial dynamics intrinsic to transnational adoption processes, he leads the center's Filipinx youth in weekly digital archiving of our center's artifacts with a commitment to decolonizing and reclaiming our own cultural approaches to empowerment, knowledge-making, and historiography. He also brings to the project an intimate knowledge of the center's local culture, the needs of the community, and history of many of the center's members, activities, and donated collections.

A relatively new member, Stephanie joined the cultural center in 2017 while attending graduate school in the writing, rhetoric, and American cultures program at Michigan State University. As a mestiza (half white, half Filipina) and part of the 1.5 generation of Filipinx Americans who were born in the Philippines but later immigrated to the states, she continuously negotiates how much space she takes up in Filipinx American spaces like the cultural center. Three features of her positionality directly affected her decisions to responsibly enter the cultural center's space and eventually develop methodology and consult on the archival project. The first was her Filipinx American identity from which she inherited specific cultural experiences and collectivist values in line with the PACCM community's heritage and values. It is also an identity marked by a commitment to decolonization. After witnessing her mother, a Filipina immigrant and fierce journalist who advocated for Filipinxs in the Philippines, experience shame and erasure of her Filipinx heritage in her new American life, Stephanie devoted herself to teaching and service that contributed to the cultural empowerment of vulnerable and marginalized communities to help counter this common dynamic.

The second and third features of her positionality that affected engagement in this process include her white identity and identity as a temporary resident of Michigan. As someone who is half white and an academic—both privileged identity markers in the Filipinx American community—and as a non-local to Michigan and metro Detroit, she resolved to not taking up leadership space at the center and within the archival project, except in a supporting and consulting role. As a result, she has worked as a grant writer, website developer, and guest speaker for PACCM and FANHS-MI, working closely with both groups to support their mission and goals and incorporating feedback loops on all projects so that the community signs off on all representations of themselves. Additionally, acknowledging she's not native to the area and the center, and anticipating she would move again after graduation, Stephanie limited her role on the archival project to that of researcher and consultant as it's a role that can be continued remotely without violently impacting the community and project upon abrupt departure.

The Working Infrastructure of Our Community Archive

As a historical society, FANHS-MI led the project of digitizing and archiving PAC-CM's collections. After PACCM and FANHS-MI member—and then, doctoral student in rhetoric and digital humanities—Stephanie consulted with staff at Michigan State University's digital humanities program about feasible next steps, FANHS-MI board members decided to move ahead with the suggested platform Omeka, as it was well-known, accessible, and affordable for our immediate needs. Omeka allowed our community to easily upload scanned documents, create multiple user accounts to archive and input metadata, privatize the collection from the wider public, and immediately generate a searchable collection based on tags before curating exhibits for later archiving stages. Omeka's pages for generating metadata followed the standard Dublin Core model, which we decided to adopt because of its simplicity and familiarity to mainstream archivists and librarians who we anticipated needing for guidance, and for the possibility of partnering with a larger repository in the future should we be unable to financially sustain the digital archive.

In the project's second phase of development, we created a training process for collectivist-driven archiving on Omeka which would gradually decentralize authority and distribute expertise to Filipinx American members of the PACCM community. We decided on a training model that began with training FANHS-MI board members first, who consist of academics, young professionals, and long-time Filipinx American metro Detroit residents of all ages. In July of 2019, Stephanie led the archival training of the board members, and the group archived their first few historical documents while working through decisions around standardizing the metadata for consistency. The FANHS team then created a Google Drive to upload scanned documents before archiving, to keep community-established archiving instructions, and to serve as a back-up repository for surrogate copies. The Drive also became an easy way to track which uploads were archived by having the participant-archivist move the uploads into collection folders once they're archived into Omeka.

By January of 2020, board members trained the youth from our Paaralang Pilipino school and Filipino Youth Initiative (FYI), who would then consult with the elders on 1) which materials needed to be archived, 2) the stories surrounding the archived objects, and 3) the description and purpose of the archive for curation of the landing page. Led by James, Director of Paaralang Pilipino and FYI, the youth spent the last half hour of their weekly schooling dedicated to archiving PACCM's material. The students work in three teams: the website, Google Drive, and archiving team—though with the possibility to rotate among them. The Website (Omeka) Team is the "face" of the archive. They control what visitors see, understand about the purpose and values of our archive, and how to navigate the pages. The Google Drive Team maintains the Drive folders, maintains protocol for scanned and archived materials, and scans and uploads materials to the Drive. Finally, the Archiving Team archives the scanned material from the Drive and establishes and maintains a consistent system for metadata. Each team was supervised by a FANHS-MI member.

The center's community—whose members include the youth who archive materials, the FANHS-MI members who archive and guide the process, and the elders who provide guidance and consultations—are the ones who more consistently provide additions to the collections. Additionally, Filipinx American locals complete this loop by contributing materials through the cultural center's network of connections (see Figure 8.1). Since March 2020, members of the Filipinx American community of Michigan have volunteered objects to be added to the archives, often by reaching out to FANHS-MI board members who then individually archive the material or add it to the Google Drive.

Successes: Collectivist-Driven Narratives, Shared Place/ Space Identity, and Intergenerational Sustainability

As a collectivist culture grounded on the concept of *kapwa* (fellow being), stressing the values of unity and oneness, Filipinxs tend to operate through their cultural networks and have an intrinsic sense of shared identity. According to EJR David, what springs from the core sense of *kapwa* are further Indigenous values such as *utang na loob* (sense of inner debt and gratitude) and *pakikisama* (companionship, maintaining harmony for the group) (108). Many of these Filipinx values have been retained, drive the underlying local motivations for the volunteer-led communal archiving project, and have steered the networked and intergenerational model that allows our participants to also be users and archivists. Like its peer Filipinx American archives, *The Filipinx Americans in Michigan Historical Archive* challenges Western-centric and institutional models through localized, collectivist-driven narratives and attention to place/space, contributing to a plurality of archival practices within American and even Filipinx American contexts while grounded in the discursive field of a specific locale (the cultural center).

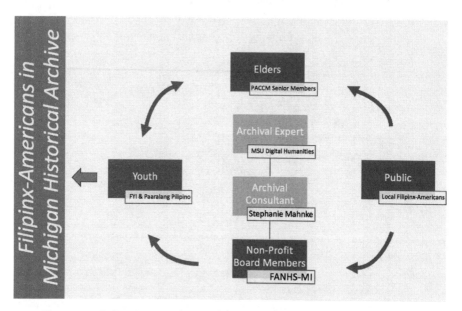

Figure 8.1. Collectivist working infrastructure and flow of archival data.

Guiding Narratives

One way our community has guided the archive's narratives is by communal decisions over collection development. Though largely guided by the center's elders who donate and steer other participant-archivists towards certain materials, our democratized form of collection development relies on an excess of voices to tell a story about a specific collection. Thus, rather than a curated or partial view of Filipinx American history typical in more institutionalized archives, our accumulation of narratives complements and sometimes complicates essentializing categories or descriptions. For instance, the collection on PACCM's history includes original documents from its planning days, such as minutes and financial reports, but also secondary and reflective pieces, such as a dissertation chapter on the history of PACCM written by a Filipinx student, as well as oral history recordings of the center's previous presidents as they reflect on their terms. Some of the oral history testimonies and more personalized items (e.g., handwritten notes and letters) further contextualize other documents pertaining to the planning years, but they also provide different perspectives and conflicting histories. One example of this are the tensions between the PACCM board and the churches which were used or vetted as potential places to house the center and the language school. Though some of the interviews attest to mainly needing an autonomous, affordable, and larger space for PACCM, the inclusion of a letter articulates concerns over upkeep and even a 1996 town hall meeting document reveal community concerns over the safety of the location and a church's concern that the center's purposes would be more cultural than religious. The decision to include a plurality of documents and voices allows for more nuanced and collectively driven histories instead of a monolithic narrative, thus allowing an archival experience that is fuller, textured, and dynamically incomplete.

The choice of sources privileges the excess of narratives to a collection, and additionally, the communal input of metadata and tags allow members to collectively add to these narratives through the addition of key terms, elements, and descriptive notes. To help with discovery and access to archived objects, metadata describes these objects in terms of elements. Though we chose Dublin Core's model of metadata for its easier learning curve and potential for cross-cultural interoperability with other entities (such as institutions, museums, larger archives, etc.), we didn't necessarily privilege rich metadata under the same mindset. In other words, we avoided leaning toward highly descriptive elements under the common principle of avoiding assumptions or predictions of general users' search terms. Instead, participant-archivists were guided toward basic descriptive elements and tags they believed would be relevant to them and the local Filipinx American community. For example, one digitized document of the center's minutes from the 1990s has accumulated tags and details from different participant-archivists emphasizing various aspects of the meeting notes, such as the specific people involved who might be of interest or familiar to the local community, the legacy of a specific fundraising event, the emphasis of the center as a home, or the pursuit of a centralized place/space. In this instance, the description is listed briefly as "Minutes from board meeting on November 3, 1996 at St. Anne's school," but includes community-oriented tags such as the names of attendees and mentions, the popular "Valentine's Ball" fundraiser, and even "land" to highlight meeting discussion of finding a location for PACCM. Using tags, the participant-archivists privilege familiar community-centered narratives in anticipation of what might be useful or of interest to local Filipinx American users.

Afterall, much of the ongoing communally developed metadata is intergenerational, reaching members across the center and its affiliated organizations. Many of the descriptions of the collections are crafted by the youth and FANHS members, usually after discussing the materials with elders and PACCM staff. This communal guidance not only steered the development of the metadata and descriptions, but also affected these choices of tags or keywords from a collectivist perspective in terms of what is worth noting. Even in some instances, participant-archivists developed tags such as "Vincent Chin" for a newsletter which mentioned him, the names of key PACCM members, or specific Filipinx dances or folk terms that the students recognized from the materials, though they aren't mentioned explicitly on the materials themselves. Since Omeka offers the accumulated tags as options when inputting metadata, the community could rely and build upon the community-archivists' collection of focal terms, having an auto-populated repository of terms for additional collectivist consideration. Thus, the communal process itself of inputting metadata and crafting item descriptions not only captures the local Filipinx American history, but the specific community's forms of remembering, interpreting, and emphasizing certain aspects of these artifacts.

Place/Space

As mentioned earlier, attention to place/space in the archival process has influenced Filipinx American archival decisions around access and autonomy. Place holds a particular importance to Filipinx history when considering the centuries of multiple colonizations of the Philippines, and decades of displacement, gentrification, and removal of ethnic enclaves in America. *The Filipinx Americans in Michigan Historical Archive* has not only grounded the archive and its materials on local Filipinx history in the state, but on place, the cultural center specifically, and the history of the Filipinx American communities who have conceived, fundraised, built, and maintained it as a greater community.

Like the National Pinoy Archives, the material collections remain at the cultural center instead of an outside institution because it is the most accessible to the Filipinx American locals who contribute to and use the historical documents. Many locals and Filipinx American groups see PACCM as the nexus of Filipinx events, meetings, and general congregations in the state, as most Filipinx American residents reside in metro Detroit and Wayne County. The center also does not charge a fee, and prides itself on welcoming anyone with even an "ounce of Filipino blood" to visit. The digital archive, as an organized extension of the housed material collections, has amplified this notion of access for users to participate and find items remotely through granted permission from the center's cultural networks. To keep the artifacts private and belonging to the local Filipinx American community and particularly those affiliated with the cultural center, elders in charge of the project insisted the digital archive remain private, at least for now, and only accessible through permission. Our digital methods and platform allow for this tempered and slower form of access to respect the insular and private nature of the local community and its items, and it's the social and discursive field of the cultural center that grounds the range of this access.

As the materials are housed at the center and the digital archive run by the center, collection development and authenticity of archived materials is also grounded in the place/space. The focus on the cultural center not only ties our archival community together by our ethnic background and values, but by the shared space itself. Each participant-archivist weighs in on the materials or consults with other members through the shared intimacy and sense of identity around having been part of the center's history at some point. This sense of belonging and accompanied authenticity crosses over into the handling of the center's material history; the legitimacy of evidence is not only dictated by decisions from the collective and with the collective in mind but has also been established by participant-archivists' knowledgeable relationship with the cultural center.

Thus, the layers of shared identity around culture and place/space help to ease intra- and inter-community tensions, a common challenge of communal archives which cite tensions around identity, ideology, or group loyalty (Poole 673). Our digital methods allow for both the need to privatize the collections to our cultural center's community, but also to extend participation and access as a matter of degrees to members of our internal networks. To accommodate additional users to maintain the archive, the Omeka platform facilitates these networked permissions and extensions to access by allowing users to sign up and manage the digital archive as "admin," "researcher," or "contributor." FANHS-MI board members have control over who gets access and the type of access they are allowed for the archival site, as well as the option to remove users who misuse their privileges or modify the status of users whose use of the archive has changed.

As our archival project continues the work of guiding culturally authored narratives of our Filipinx American history and strategically leveraging strengths around shared place/space, it has also shown positive results around sustainability of human resources, or more particularly, outreach and intergenerational succession which are other commonly cited issues of community archives.

Outreach

After we contemplated the most effective ways for engaging the community to bring more awareness to the archives, we eventually relied on our built-in cultural networks which involved the center's connections through individual members, scholarly circles, and organizational circles. The bulk of the archive includes the processual contributions from the youth, elders, and FANHS members, but individual members who are encouraged to donate have also opened pathways to material contributions that tell a broader story of Filipinx American history in the state. The wider Filipinx American community is included through personal outreach and discussion with family members. Everyone is a part of the collective, each with their own narratives, histories and herstories that converge into the Filipinx American diaspora. Prospective donations of their material data and material lineages are crucial to our archive's collection. A few examples in the local Detroit Filipinx American community are within the familial history of Nanette Maranan Green. Like many other Filipinx Americans, Nanette and her parents have accumulated aged photos stemming from her family's local Filipinx American restaurant. The Maranan family were the original owners of Royal Kubo, which was the first Filipinx American bar with karaoke in the state of Michigan. Dating as far back as 1990, these photos encompass some of the histories of the local Filipinx community organizations in Michigan. Our digital archive is further incentive for individual donations as a method of preservation against unforeseen problematic cases in preserving material history and the occurrence of inevitable catastrophes. In the case of Fe Rowland, one of the past directors of Paaralang Pilipino, much of her own collection of involvement within the Filipinx American community has endured a basement flood.

Another way we developed outreach was to extend the archive to another group of common archival users and contributors, the local Filipinx American college students. The organizational multilayering and multilateral community involvement from both FANHS-MI and Pilipino Student Associations from local universities have helped in facilitating classes at PACCM on most Sundays throughout the academic school year. This built-in partnership with the Filipinx American college groups has allowed for shared discussions around the importance of material archives and its history, a type of reflection that becomes a search for personal relevance with both individual and collective narratives, and importance of intergenerational participation in accepting collective responsibility over the longevity of these material objects.

Finally, outreach through our cultural networks extended to connected organizational groups. FANHS National, the umbrella group under which our FANHS-MI chapter is situated and the owners of the National Pinoy Archives, calls for chapter reports of each of its regional and chapter organizations biannually. Outreach of our localized archive extends to other chapters and Filipinx Americans across America, opening the possibility of receiving donations from those with ties to Michigan, as well as the possibility of collaborating within a larger network of developing communal archives in different states. Though our model strongly believes in designing archival methods and infrastructures that are immediately influenced by localized needs and resources, with the compilation of Dublin Core metadata, our model is still conducive to uptake into a larger, consolidated repository of a FANHS chapter archival network. Through this form of outreach to other FANHS communities, we can share our archival methodologies in incorporating this type of working model, while simultaneously strengthening the greater network of Filipinx American communities' material history.

Intergenerational Succession

Another indicator of the archive's sustainability is the prioritization of the collective in our infrastructure which naturally fosters intergenerational succession. Researchers have cited that across the many forms of community archives, succession and intergenerational engagement has remained one of the greatest concerns for the longevity of these archives (Poole 676). PACCM's elders had long been on board to preserve the center's material history, and with the key guidance of the FANHS-MI members and PACCM staff, our community saw the archival project as an opportunity for youth involvement that could both cement their key role in the succession of our center and history, as well as strengthen the community's relationship to each other and the individual knowledges that piece together the mosaic of this history. The Filipino Youth Initiative (FYI), an intergenerational, community-based class, which is offered at Paaralang Pilipino Language and Cultural School program at the Philippine American Cultural Center of Michigan, shares the goals as emphasized by Melissa Sia, a former facilitator of FYI: "We hope to generate self-awareness and confidence in the youth . . . to have a better understanding of Filipino American history and contemporary issues as well as personal recognition of one's place as a member of the Filipino American community" (Sia). Our intergenerational programs became an easy way to involve the youth at documenting and contributing to our Filipinx American material lineages.

For example, the students are asked first to bring an item from home that is culturally important to them or their family, such as an heirloom. The relevance of "cultural artifacts" helps establish its proper relationship to material lineages whereas in these types of workshops, while it challenges the students and facilitators to reflect and discuss aspects of identity, it also generates crucial intergenerational dialogue through the utilization of material history. Additional workshops provided by PIN@Y Educational Partnerships supplement these methods of building relevance while contributing to cultural material lineages. Some workshop presentations such as *Mapping Your Family's Journey* emphasizes documenting intercultural dialogue from their family members and immigration pattern via oral history or spoken word answering the question "Where are you from?" (Tintiangco-Cubales et al.), and observing the accumulation of letters, photos, and personal documents such as shipping tickets. Cultural artifacts such as these are crucial to be donated to the archive.

These intergenerational programs and workshops have developed their curriculum for recognizing and engaging the youth by not only positioning the youth as audience and "learners" in this approach to history, but also re-centering the power balance between student-facilitator and allowing students to understand their role and responsibility in building and maintaining the material history of our Filipinx community. Some of the elders who serve as a part of the board membership of PACCM engage with the FYI students on what materials are most crucial to be included in the archive. These may include and are not limited to the proper arrangement of board meeting minutes, flyers, brochures, financial statements, and of course, photographs, as well as how to designate and arrange the artifacts under specific collections. The archive's collection development, metadata, tagging, descriptions, multi-user access, and arrangement are in continual flux and revision to accommodate emerging communal stories, shifting consensus, and needs.

Challenges: Remaining Issues of Access and Sustainability

Some of our archive's challenges revolved around negotiating forms of access, and archive longevity in terms of financial sustainability.

Negotiated Forms of Access

For most Filipinx American archives, offering easy access for the Filipinx American communities who are documenting the histories and using the archived materials is a priority. Open access would be the easiest answer for an archive in digital form, but many of the documents contain private information, such as addresses, phone numbers, and sensitive financial information belonging to the center and staff. In light of this concern, the Omeka platform allowed us to privatize the archive in its entirety—although not individual items—which made it accessible only to those with usernames which were given editing, viewing, or contributing permissions. Consequently, the access and outreach became limited to only those connected to the cultural center, FANHS-MI, and our cultural networks. Since the elders steered the decision to privatize the archive to protect some of the information, having to negotiate the extension of access to outside community members became a challenge with these concerns in mind and with the idea that extending access would need collective consent, which is a slow and informal process.

As a result, FANHS-MI members had to carefully oversee the youth's work on the archive, making sure the archiving process occurred at the center with the staff and elders present. All members were also instructed not to give out login information, or researcher or contributor access without consulting the other FANHS-MI members and PACCM elders. There are many drawbacks to these precautions. First, as the community grows, these precautions will be more difficult to control. Secondly, gaining the collective consent to extend username access to the archive takes time, and could prevent the wider community from participating and using the archive if they're meant to wait an extended period. Finally, it limits the scope of documented Filipinx American narratives in Michigan and participation to only those connected to the cultural center in some capacity.

Financial Sustainability

Though the archive's sustainability of human resources benefits directly from PACCM as an already established place/space for Filipinx Americans in Michigan, the shared ethnic background of its members, and the archival process's reinforcement of ties to the center and its members, financial sustainability remains a difficult task. FANHS-MI is a non-profit chapter of the national FANHS organization and must continually generate funds to keep the Omeka platform as our digital archive on a yearly basis. Much of FANHS-MI chapter's limited funds come from a portion of yearly membership dues, and donations from cultural events. Additionally, as the number of items in the archive grows, thus demanding the purchase of more space, the cost of keeping the Omeka platform and our community's accumulated work on the metadata, descriptions, and arrangement of collections will keep rising.

In anticipation of the potential loss of the archival platform in the future, our community relies on the Google Drive, which will remain a stable backup repository for our digitized items. As another safeguard, the choice of the Dublin Core format for our metadata was also in anticipation for the possibility of moving our archive into a more stable repository with a partner institution or organization. The possible depositing of the archive's collection to be housed by an outside entity could greatly impact autonomy and access for our community—not to mention make the cultural values behind our processual model less apparent or tied to the artifact meanings—so financial sustainability is a looming concern for our continued work and ownership of the archive.

Conclusion

Filipinx American community archives continue to challenge traditional or institutionalized notions of the archive and its attendant processes. Finding its natural form in community archives, Filipinx values of *kapwa* and emphasis on the collective steer processual archival models that continue to ask and push in the direction of "how do we serve our local community's needs, the very members who create, use, and are empowered by these histories?" In approaching and revisiting this question, Filipinx American archives, such as our own, have frequently circled the same concerns around the rhetorical curation of narratives, the influence of place/space on autonomy and access, the ways of reaching a wider net of Filipinx Americans, and how to sustain the community archive so it remains within the community's hands and cultural processes.

The Filipinx Americans of Michigan Historical Archive grounds itself on a decolonial and collective methodology that utilizes methods of prioritizing the community and maximizing opportunities for intergenerational involvement. Our unique approach leverages the strength of our centralized place/space, the cultural center, and incorporates an intergenerationally-layered training and working model which is facilitated by the multi-user and generative metadata functions of our digital platform Omeka. We do not offer our archival model as a prescriptive approach to be adopted in its entirety, as one of the key strengths of community archives are their ability to respond to the localized needs and resources of a community and its history. Instead, our archival model demonstrates the diversity of archival approaches, and the heterogenous practices that thrive even within the array of Filipinx American archives.

Works Cited

Agboka, Godwin Y. "'Subjects' in and of Research: Decolonizing Oppressive Rhetorical Practices in Technical Communication Research." *Journal of Technical Writing and Communication*, vol. 51, no. 2, 2021, pp. 159–74, https://doi.org/10.1177/0047281620901484.

Bastian, Jeannette. *Owning Memory: How a Caribbean Community Lost Its Archives and Found Its History*. Libraries Unlimited, 2003.

———. "The Records of Memory, the Archives of Identity: Celebrations, Texts and Archival Sensibilities." *Archival Science: International Journal on Recorded Information*, vol. 13, 2013, pp. 121–31, https://doi.org/10.1007/s10502-012-9184-3.

Battley, Belinda. "Authenticity in Places of Belonging: Community Collective Memory as a Complex, Adaptive Recordkeeping System." *Archives and Manuscripts*, vol. 48, no. 1, Mar. 2020, pp. 59–79, https://doi.org/10.1080/01576895.2019.1628649.

Caswell, Michelle, Marika Cifor, and Mario Ramirez. "'To Suddenly Discover Yourself Existing': Uncovering the Impact of Community Archives." *The American Archivist*, vol. 79, no. 1, 2016, pp. 56–81.

Cifor, Marika, Michelle Caswell, Alda Allina Migoni, and Noah Geraci. "'What We Do Crosses over to Activism': The Politics and Practice of Community Archives." *The Public Historian*, vol. 40, no. 2, 2018, pp. 69–95.

Cook, Terry. "Evidence, Memory, Identity, and Community: Four Shifting Archival Paradigms." *Archival Science*, vol. 13, 2013, pp. 95–120, https://doi.org/10.1007/s10502-012-9180-7.

Cushman, Ellen. "Wampum, Sequoyan, and Story: Decolonizing the Digital Archive." *College English*, vol. 76, no. 2, 2013, pp. 115–35, https://www.jstor.org/stable/24238145.

Daniel-Wariya, Joshua, and Lynn C. Lewis. "The Possibilities of Uncertainty: Digital Archives as Cunning Texts in a First-Year Composition Curriculum." *Pedagogy*, vol. 20, no. 1, 2020, pp. 141–48.

David, E.J.R. *Brown Skin, White Minds: Filipino American Postcolonial Psychology*. Information Age Publishing Inc., 2013.

Enoch, Jessica, and Pamela VanHaitsma. "Archival Literacy: Reading the Rhetoric of Digital Archives in the Undergraduate Classroom." *College Composition and Communication* vol. 67, no. 2, 2015, pp. 216–42.

Ferreira-Buckley, Linda. "Rescuing the Archives from Foucault." *College English*, vol. 61, no. 5, 1999, pp. 577–83.

Flinn, Andrew, and Mary Stevens. "'It is noh mistri, wi mekin histri.' Telling Our Own Story: Independent and Community Archives in the UK, Challenging and Subverting the Mainstream." *Community Archives: The Shaping of Memory*, edited by Jeannette Allis Bastian and Ben Alexander, Facet Publishing, 2009, pp. 3–28.

Friedrich, Markus. "Epilogue: Archives and Archiving Across Cultures—Towards a Matrix of Analysis." *Manuscripts and Archives: Comparative Views on Record-Keeping*, edited by Alessandro Bausi, Christian Brocckmann, Michael Friedrich, and Sabine Kienitz, De Gruyter, 2018, pp. 421–45.

Fujita-Rony, Dorothy. "Illuminating Militarized Rupture: Four Asian American Community-Based Archives." *Journal of Asian American Studies*, vol. 23, no. 1, 2020, pp. 1–27.

Haas, Angela M. "Race, Rhetoric, and Technology: A Case Study of Decolonial Technical Communication Theory, Methodology, and Pedagogy." *Journal of Business and Technical Communication*, vol. 26, no. 3, pp. 277–310, https://doi.org/10.1177/1050651912439539.

Hurley, Chris. "Parallel Provenance: What If Anything Is Archival Description?" *Archives and Manuscripts*, vol. 33, no. 1, 2005, pp. 110–45.

Kurtz, Matthew. "A Postcolonial Archive? On the Paradox of Practice in a Northwest Alaska Project." *Archivaria*, vol. 61, 2006, pp. 63–90, https://archivaria.ca/index.php/archivaria/article/view/12535/13675.

Mao, LuMing. "Writing the Other into Histories of Rhetorics: Theorizing the Art of Recontextualization." *Theorizing Histories of Rhetoric*, edited by Michelle Ballif, Southern Illinois UP, 2013, pp. 41–57.

Monberg, Terese Guinsatao. *Re-positioning Ethos: Rhetorics of Hybridity and the Filipino American National Historical Society (FANHS)*. 2002, Rensselaer Polytechnic Institute, PhD dissertation.

Narayan, Madhu. "At Home With The Lesbian Herstory Archives." *enculturation*, no. 15, 2013, http://www.enculturation.net/lesbian-herstory-archives.

Poole, Alex H. "The Information Work of Community Archives: A Systematic Literature Review." *The Journal of Documentation*, vol. 76, no. 3, 2020, pp. 657–87, https://doi.org/10.1108/JD-07-2019-0140.

Posner, Miriam. "What's Next: The Radical, Unrealized Potential of Digital Humanities." *Debates in the Digital Humanities 2016*, edited by Matthew K. Gold and Lauren F. Klein, U of Minnesota P, 2016, http://dhdebates.gc.cuny.edu/debates/text/54.

Poudyal, Bibhushana. "Building Critical Decolonial Digital Archives: Recognizing Complexities to Reimagine Possibilities." *Xchanges: An Interdisciplinary Journal of Technical Communication, Rhetoric, and Writing Across the Curriculum*, vol. 14, no. 1, 2018, pp. 1–16, https://xchanges.org/building-critical-decolonial-digital-archives-14-1.

Ramsey, Alexis E. Wendy B. Sharer, Barbara L'Eplattenier, and Lisa Mastrangelo, editors. *Working in the Archives; Practical Research Methods for Rhetoric and Composition*. Southern Illinois UP, 2010.

Reyes, Portia L. "Fighting Over a Nation: Theorizing a Filipino Historiography."
   Postcolonial Studies, vol. 11, no. 3, 2008, pp. 241–58, https://doi.org/10.1080/1368
   8790802226645.
Ridolfo, Jim, William Hart-Davidson, and Michael McLeod. "Rhetoric and the
   Digital Humanities: Imagining the Michigan State University Israelite Samaritan
   Archive as a Thriving Social Network." *Journal of Community Informatics*, vol. 7,
   no. 3, 2011, https://doi.org/10.15353/joci.v7i3.2586.
Ruskin, Jesse. "Collecting and Connecting: Archiving Filipino American Music in
   Los Angeles." *Pacific Review of Ethnomusicology*, vol. 11, 2006, https://ethnomusi
   cologyreview.ucla.edu/journal/volume/11/piece/514.
Schreiner, Maggie, and Claro de los Reyes. "Social Practice Artists in the Archive:
   Collaborative Strategies for Documentation." *Urban Library Journal*, vol. 22, no.
   2, 2016, pp. 1–8, https://academicworks.cuny.edu/ulj/vol22/iss2/1.
Sia, Melissa. "Filipino Youth Initiative - More Than Just Being Pinoy, It's About
   Empowering Our Youth." *Pilipinas*, vol. 9, 2010.
Sweeney, Shelley. "The Ambiguous Origins of the Archival Principle of 'Prove-
   nance.'" *Libraries and the Cultural Record*, vol. 43, no. 2, Mar. 2008, pp. 193–213.
Stoler, Ann Laura. "Colonial Archives and the Arts of Governance: On the Content
   in the Form." *Refiguring the Archive*, edited by Carolyn Hamilton et al, Kluwer
   Academic Publishers, 2002, pp. 83–101.
Tintiangco-Cubales, Allison, Kimmy Maniquis, and Gwen Agustin. "Mapping Your
   Family's Journey: From the Philippines to the U.S. to All Around the World."
   Pin@y Educational Partnerships: A Filipina/o American Studies Sourcebook Series,
   vol. 1, Phoenix Publishing House Intl., 2007, pp. 191–96.
Wong, Vivian, Tom Ikeda, Ellen-Rae Cachola, and Florante Peter Ibanez. "Archives
   (Re)Imagined Elsewhere: Asian American Community-Based Archival Orga-
   nizations." *Through the Archival Looking Glass*, edited by Mary A. Caldera and
   Kathryn M. Neal, Society of American Archivist Press, 2014, pp. 111–42.
Wurl, Joel. "Ethnicity as Provenance: In Search Principles for Documenting the
   Immigrant Experience." *Archival Issues*, vol. 29, 2005, pp. 65–67.
Yancey, Kathleen Blake . "From the Editor: A Blueprint for the Future: Lessons
   from the Past." *College Composition and Communication*, vol. 63, no. 3, 2012, pp.
   361–64.

Chapter 9. Counter, Contradictory, and Contingent Digital-Storytelling through Minimal Computing and Community-Praxis

Bibhushana Poudyal
UNIVERSITY OF TEXAS AT EL PASO

> How do strategies of representation or empowerment come to be
> formulated in the competing claims of communities where, despite
> shared histories of deprivation and discrimination, the exchange of
> values, meanings, and priorities may not always be collaborative and
> dialogical, but may be profoundly antagonistic, conflictual, and even
> incommensurable?
>
> *- Bhabha 2*

Through philosophical and methodological discussions of minimal computing and community-praxis, the chapter offers possible methods and methodologies of a counter, contradictory, and contingent storytelling through digital archives with epistemically, epistemologically and structurally marginalized, excluded, and absented voices. My chapter emphasizes the ethics of digital-storytelling and theorizes ethics through dialectical relationship-building, availability of dialogic room for the Other, and deconstructive approaches (Spivak *The Spivak Reader*; Spivak "Translator's Preface"). The chapter also critically discourses precarities and affordances of digital archiving with and from "radical exteriority, that is, thinking *from* and *with* the living configurations and excluded lineages and histories of those considered peripheral" (Vallega 6). To exemplify, I will present theories, praxes, and ethics of the two methods involved in my critical digital archiving project titled, *Rethinking South Asia from the Borderland via Critical Digital A(na)rchiving*.

In my project, I am building a digital archive of my street photography that I had taken in 2017 in Nepal on a CMS platform Omeka through participatory design frameworks with Nepali communities. My open access archive is available at http://cassacda.com. In this project, I am building, documenting, and theorizing a journey of building a digital archive as a Nepali doctoral student from the location of the Mexico-US borderland university, The University of Texas at El Paso, with a determination of exploring and sharing ways of combating colonial-patriarchal gaze and epistemic injustices. And I cannot begin do so without acknowledging the "unceded Indigenous land" I am building Nepal's digital archive and writing this chapter from:

DOI: https://doi.org/10.37514/PRA-B.2022.1541.2.09

205

[I] would like to recognize and pay my respects to the Indig-
enous people with long ties to the immediate region: Lipan
Apache, Mescalero Apache, Piro, Manso, Suma, Jumano, Ysleta
del Sur Pueblo, Piro/Manso/Tiwa Indian Tribe of the Pueblo of
San Juan de Guadalupe, and Tortugas Pueblo. [I] also acknowl-
edge the nations whose territories include present day Texas:
the Carrizo and Comecrudo, Coahuiltecan, Caddo, Tonkawa,
Comanche, Alabama-Coushatta, Kickapoo, and the peoples of
Chihuahua and northern Mexico from whom most/many of
[UTEP's] students descend, such as the Rarámuri, Tepehuan,
Wixarrika and Nahuatlaca peoples. ("College of Liberal Arts
Land Acknowledgement Statement")

Figure 9.1. Image of Kathmandu Streets in 2017.[1]

Besides my situatedness as a doctoral candidate in UTEP's rhetoric and composition program, I am also honored to be serving as an executive member of

---

1. The images woven in the chapter are taken from my digital archive, http://cassacda
.com. Their existence in this chapter is not always meant to validate or represent the texts
they accompany but their existence here is the rhetorical choice I am making to constantly
connect the chapter to Kathmandu streets, from where this journey began and is continuing. I invite the readers to allow these images to function not as a representation of Kathmandu but as an invitation and provocation to deconstruct any such representation. My
digital archive and the photographs are not disruptive in themselves, but the disruption
depends on what we do with them.

an indigenous student organization, Academic Revival of Indigenous Studies and Education (ARISE), a community which has taught me a lot about how our knowledge systems and meaning-making must be accountable to the land, people, and their knowledge systems. I am an international student in this land and learning from this community to listen to and be humble toward the voices and experiences that might not be my own but are excessively crucial to all of us if we are to transform our vision of a justice-oriented future into lived experiences. The experiences with ARISE also gradually started informing how I understand, interpret, and envision digital archives. To me, the ethical and justice-driven archive-building performance did not seem possible without meaningful participation of Nepali communities. As a way to begin the journey toward archival justice, I started conducting UX research since the beginning of the project to co-design and co-curate the archive and find ways of listening to the communities whose voices and experiences are not only different than my own but challenge my research pre-concepts and hypotheses as well. At the same time, I am working on this archive from a space which currently does not have any infrastructural support for digital projects merging humanities and humanistic social sciences. As I go deeper into the chapter, my positionality and the situatedness of this project will continue leaking more as they directly inform how I understand, interpret, and practice minimal computing and community-praxis.

By introducing some grounded examples from the project, I will discuss how the philosophy and practice of minimal computing and community-praxis become both necessity and choice in the projects which frustratingly suffer from the lack of necessary resources and yet stubbornly insist on subverting privileged structures' discourses and gaze through digital-archival storytelling. This chapter is written from the intervening interstices of the following conflicting scenario: on the one hand, digital writing and research infrastructures, initiatives, and programs are becoming more popular in many (well-funded) academic institutions in the Global North and on the other hand, many spaces and communities with interest in digital projects lack access to not only resources, capacity, and institutional support for their work but are excluded from the definitions of digitality, digital archives, and digital methods and methodologies. We must notice two aspects of this scenario: first, minoritized and marginalized voices, in the first place, have limited to no access to the resources required to participate in digital storytelling against power centers' essentializing metanarratives and gaze. And this continuing (infra)structural inequity, uneven development of DH[2] "centers"

---

2. While I am using the terminologies digital humanities (DH) in this chapter, I use it both to talk about the field which is very much invested in archival works and to indicate the research or an epistemological performance conducted by using, reflecting upon, and/or developing digital tools and methods to engage in dialogues emerging from humanities and humanistic social sciences. In this chapter, I understand DH in the following two senses: i) humanities and social sciences' epistemic practices conducted using digital

and digital writing and research "labs," and thus, exclusion of voices continues to impact the documented lack of inclusion and sustainability for minoritized communities (Earhart and Taylor; Risam; Callaway et al.).

Inequitable distribution of voices in digital narrativization directly translates into a terrifying absence of participation of (intersectionally) disadvantaged communities in online and digital spaces in knowledge-making and meaning-making performances, which I will refer to as epistemological performances. But no less disturbing is the second one: the projects and stories that already suffer from (infra)structural inequity not only do not have sufficient resources to translate their narratives digitally but even when they write with digital tools, new media, and multimedia, with whatever means available, they are not recognized as digital praxis. And the consequence is further silencing of these narratives and knowledge systems while the power centers' gaze continues being amplified. In short, within computers and writing studies, digital writing, and computing-related fields, there is still a lack of minoritized and marginalized voices, limiting diversity in demographic, geographical, discursive, definitional, philosophical, theoretical, methodological, political, and ethical terms.

As "[d]igital spaces are increasingly becoming the ones where human knowledge is produced, disseminated, and amplified" (Risam 139), the continuation of these inequities perpetuates the dominance of privileged socio-symbolic order and its law and language and further subalternizes the voices of minoritized and marginalized groups of people. And it only postpones all the possible digital initiatives to anti-imperialize, anti-colonize and de-patriarchalize ontological categories and epistemological performances on local and global levels. In this context, with a profound frustration intricately woven with bits of hope, this chapter is written through an embodied knowledge of what minoritized students and researchers face while trying to digitalize counter-narratives from the spaces with little to no support for digital works. And with that knowledge, I explore what theories, praxes, initiatives, and alliances look like while trying to work digitally, ethically, and critically toward "epistemico-epistemological transformations" (Spivak, *An Aesthetic Education* 41) from and with Othered spaces.

When the representations (and distortions) of the Other—both globally and regionally between and within the "Global South" and the "Global North"—have been ported over the digital realm, it is necessary not only to study that transportation but also what it looks like when the Other writes their stories digitally as resistance against digital gaze. This chapter is mostly about the latter. Though my archival project is focused on the geographic location of Nepal and South Asia, the goal of my project is anything but to portray or build "true" knowledge about Nepal or South Asia. It is neither to offer a manifesto on the "correct" way—I doubt if that even exists—of building, for instance, anticolonial, antiracist, and

---

methods/tools and ii) as a discipline that intersects with rhetoric and composition, technical communication, digital storytelling, and digital archival studies.

feminist digital archives. What I am hoping to do is explore possible methods and theories that can be incorporated, adapted, or experimented with while building digital archives about, for, with, and as the Other. Before moving ahead, I would like to present what I mean by the Other in the context of my research and this chapter:

> The Other can have layered and multiple meanings . . . [T]he Other is the other of the imperial, colonial, capitalist, neo-liberal, heteropatriarchal Self. The Other is an object of inquiry, exploration, and discovery of hegemonic discourses of socio-symbolic order . . . The Other is archived to serve the interest and match the limited imagination of the Self. In those archives, the Other is discoursed, constructed, constituted, distorted, absented, represented, portrayed, or even 'benevolently' spoken for, but is absent/ed from the dialogues that would challenge the knowledge, imagination, and comfort of the Self. (Poudyal, "The "Nature" of Ethics" 179–80)

I offer this brief definition as an invitation to contemplate upon the Other with all complexities and heterogeneities it embodies. Each of us is an inter/play of both the Self and the Other. Here, what we must understand is that how-much-of-what varies in each individual, community, and individual situation, and that dissimilitude makes a lot of difference. This chapter continues with that recognition and with an invitation to recognize that.

Contextual Overview: When Precarities Become Exigencies

As a researcher and teacher whose epistemological performances are rigorously and self-reflectively committed to interfering with the top-down model of representing ("portraying" and "speaking for") the Other, the thought about working on a critical digital archiving project, not only on a theoretical level but also by building my own digital archive, is genuinely a distressing act. This archive-building performance is enveloped in a profound ethical dilemma that when I decided to build one, almost a culprit-like feeling started creeping in. As Mathew Kurtz notes, "[T]he archive . . . is a literal re-centring of material for the construction and contestation of knowledge, whereas postcolonialism often works toward a figurative decentring of that same material" (25). By building a digital archive, I was knowingly putting myself in the most uncomfortable state. In this journey, I am problematizing and deconstructing everything the moment I (plan to) perform it. Here, I request the readers to take a moment to meditate upon this state to truly understand this dilemma I am talking about. Amidst this dilemma, the only thing that keeps me going is by openly talking about it and the problems in my project and by inviting others to deconstruct this archival performance alongside. Therefore, writing this chapter is crucial. It is an extended part of my project. It is another way of inviting and provoking extended audiences to deconstruct my project—or any digital archival project for that matter—and to imagine narratives and ontologies beyond what is present and visible.

On top of everything else, another issue I was dealing with has largely to do with the locations that I am building the digital archive about and from. I am building a digital archive about one of those locations (Nepal) whose non/digital portrayals are often infused with simplistic generalizations, linear narratives, and epistemic injustices. And I am building this archive from one of those locations (the US) that produces or has the power to produce such problematic portrayals, disseminate, and amplify them. This sense of precarity is critical and inexpressible because of the long history of various forms of oppressions that have carved the relationships between West and non-West. But if I try to translate these precarities into words, the questions I face include: What if I end up being a native informant? What if I begin this journey and reach nowhere? What if I end up harming and hurting while my intention is of healing? What if justice and ethics get suffocated by these definitional, material, infrastructural, and historical conditions and "will-to-knowledge and will-to-power" (Poudyal, "The "Nature" of Ethics" 180)? After all, how can we expect the master's tools to dismantle the master's house?

Since the beginning of this project, the overlapping precarities—ethical, infrastructural, definitional, and locational—have always made me nervous in undertaking the project of building a digital archive of street photography in Kathmandu. And, ironically, the same precarities became strong reasons for me to undertake this work. The narration, documentation, and theorization of these precarities are necessary to demonstrate the problems strongly and explicitly in the mainstream narratives of digital archiving, digitalism, design, knowledge, and information. Building an archive and documenting the process is not enough as the constant theorization of every aspect of this process is a crucial part of my project. Or how else to know the situatedness and purpose of the methods and methodologies?

In the rest of the chapter, I will attempt to demonstrate what the methods of an academic with years of contemplative engagement with anti-heterosexist, anti-racist, and anticolonial criticisms through deconstructive approach look like while building a digital archive about Nepal from the location of the US without infra/structural backing. My methodological discussion will revolve around the following two questions:

1. Given the historical and contemporary infra/structural inequities between and within the "Global North" and "Global South," (how) can digital archives still be a dialectical space to deconstruct representation of the Other?

2. What can be the possible theories, methods, methodologies, strategies, and alliances, to build a digital archive ethically and critically with

and about underrepresented communities and from under-funded and under-resourced spaces?

While addressing these questions, this chapter emerges from the intersections of the fields and subfields of rhetoric and writing studies, international technical communication, critical archival studies, and critical digital humanities. In the following sections, I discuss the theoretical-practical aspects of minimal computing and community-praxis to convey what I mean by these two methodologies and how I am working with these methodologies for my research on critical digital archival studies. After doing the ethical, theoretical, and methodological discussions of my project and analyzing the findings, I conclude the chapter by inviting readers to listen to the call of justice through radical initiatives in digital praxis and radical humbleness toward community-voices.

Minimal Computing as Bricoleur Activity of the Other

Figure 9.2. Images of Kathmandu Streets in 2017

As I am insisting in this chapter, discussing definitions of tools, methods, and methodologies are important while practicing them. Very often, as definitions powerfully exist to keep humanity from imagining and participating in a justice-oriented future, we cannot allow ourselves to ignore the rhetoric of their definitions. That's why I am beginning with the definitional aspect of minimal computing. There are multiple definitions of what minimal computing is or what it is not, which also points to who has the privilege and access to choose, define, and make it more inaccessible or accessible. To make digital theory-praxis more accessible and ethical, I strategically exploit the following statement: "In general, we can say that minimal computing is the application of *minimalist applications to computing*. In reality, though, minimal computing is in the eye of the beholder" (Gil and Ortega 28). When I am talking about minimal computing, it can be anything that allows a researcher to compose and conduct research digitally without having to rely on institutional and infrastructural assistance that is not available. One must understand the exploitation of the statement, "minimal computing is in the eye of the beholder," as a strategic method of the Other to punch a hole on the digital frontier and the practice of gatekeeping in the fields related to computing and digital writing and research. One must approach methods and methodologies by rupturing the theory-practice binary. How one practices methods heavily depends on how one defines it or which definition one adopts. And without redefining and retheorizing the method, practicing it differently is not possible. Without revisiting our digital praxis, subverting gatekeeping culture is not possible either. Hence, when I began my digital archiving project without "sufficient" computing-related skills, training, and resources, I had to constantly push and pull at the definitional frontiers of digital methods. When tools are not available, I must, at least, make definitions available to myself so that the privileged definitions of digitality, design, and digital storytelling do not keep me from embarking on this journey.

I prefer to define minimal computing as bricoleur activity, which means doing what is needed to be done with whatever is available (see Derrida's *Writing and Difference* to further understand my approach to bricoleur activity). If we go by this definition, even the tools, definitions, or the power to develop and control those tools and definitions ab/used by the privileged structure are also bricoleur activity. But the only difference is that this structure has more resources available to establish itself as a seamless absolute structure whose definitions are considered unimpeachable. I am connecting minimal computing to bricoleur activity to stress that as the privileged structure is using whatever is available to them to impose and perpetuate different forms of injustices, the margin should not be afraid or hesitate to engage in bricoleur activity to turn the things around and to write our stories. It is apt remembering some of the crucial and provoking questions posed by Matthew Applegate while discoursing minimal computing:

> What must I give up and what must I ignore in the effort to meet my needs? How do I meet my needs without reproducing the antinomies I oppose? If the master's tools are the only tools available, am I willing to wield them against the contemporary political economy of their use? Any response to these questions is radically contingent-dependent on the context of minimal computing's employ—and extend to feminist, decolonial, and Marxist iterations of the task. (146)

I connect these questions to the question that prompted this chapter: What can be the possible theories, methods, methodologies, strategies, alliances, and tools to ethically and critically build counter, contradictory, and contingent storytelling (under-funded and under-resourced) digital archives? Because those stories cannot be told or heard by remaining obedient to the tools of masters. Hence, it is not only about what it is being told but also about how it is told. Does it mean counter-stories cannot use larger-scale tools, resources, and funds? It definitely does not mean that. What it actually means is such binary definitions should not decide the course of these stories. The use of "right," "correct," and "accepted" methods, tools, vocabularies, and definitions to whatever is available is our digital theory-praxis of counter-storytelling. And the first step for me was to overcome the burden of rhetoric such as imparted by Stephen Ramsay at the 2011 annual Modern Language Association convention when he declared, "If you are not making anything, you are not . . . a digital humanist" (qtd. in Gold x). Overthrowing this burden was (and still is) difficult. Even after deciding to work on a critical digital archiving project, it took me months to actually start building one. I was intimidated by my "reality" of not having "sufficient" technical and computing skills or infrastructural support to do such projects. Even if I was planning on problematizing dominant narratives, I could not escape the privileged definition of digitalism, design, and digital archive myself.

Eventually, the insurgent dreams and desires started becoming more powerful than lack (of confidence, courage, and materiality). The questions such as "What do we need?" (Gil and Ortega) and "What don't we need? . . . What do we want? . . . What don't we want?" (Sayers "Minimal Definitions (tl;dr version)") became more important than what is not available to me and what I cannot do. For that reason, my digital praxis entails "learning how to produce, disseminate and preserve digital scholarship ourselves, *without the help we can't get*" (Gil). It involves experiments and necessary messiness.

When I finally mustered some courage to begin a building performance by hosting my own website, I started working on the Content Management System (CMS) platform I was much familiar with, i.e., WordPress (WP). After starting to work on WP, the first dilemma that stared right at me was related to the decisions concerning the selection of photographs. In 2017, I had taken thousands of photographs of the Kathmandu streets, which, I would say, is still not close enough to tell many stories about this city and its streets. Worse still, I had to select from that already limited collection to accommodate photographs in the lowest of the paid storage plans available there, an inescapable compromise that comes with the financial condition of a full-time international graduate student. So, the multidimensional stories that I was committed to bringing in my archive already felt compromised. It does not mean the flood of money, resources, and "expertise" would have made my archive less compromised. Digital or not, archives are always conditioned and compromised by their multiple ecologies. Through the discussion of my project, I am only trying to make it evident.

After gaining relatively a little more confidence to play in digital spaces, I started conducting a landscape analysis of other digital archives. A landscape analysis is an overview of specific products, services, or platforms currently available to facilitate a specific activity. In this case, I conducted a landscape analysis to learn about available platforms for digital archiving, tracing their affordances and constraints. The other reason for exploring available CMSs was caused by my dissatisfaction regarding how my pages were looking on WP. The pages were too linear for my purpose, and I did not have the "coding literacy" to change the way it looked. I was just creating long pages of texts and photographs without the interactivity I was envisioning for my project.[3] Even though I like the way those texts and photographs were appearing on the WP pages, and I am planning to continue working on it, I wanted my archiving to be more non-linear and interactive. In the meantime, I was regularly in touch with Professor Scott Kleinman, the director of the Center for the Digital Humanities at the California State University, Northridge. I had met him in Nepal while participating in his DH seminar-workshop (#DHNepal2017) in 2017. When I expressed my frustration and told him about my plans, he recommended the CMS platform Omeka. Then, I visited the archives built on this platform and found them to be like digital archives I had come across while doing landscape analysis. They were relatively non-linear and interactive with plugins that could somehow facilitate in materializing my vision. And I bought a domain name in Omeka through the web hosting company Reclaim Hosting (where I already had my WP website).

But right after creating a domain on Omeka in July 2018, there was another problem waiting for me. I would upload photographs, but I could not make them visible on the archive. When I contacted the technology helpdesk at my university, everyone responded that they do not know anyone familiar with Omeka. It took me more than 10–15 days to make an image appear in my archive due to some technical issues in the ImageMagick Directory Path. After multiple correspondences with Scott, Omeka Forum, and Reclaim Hosting, I finally figured out the problem and the way to fix it. It's just one of the tiny obstacles I came across in this archive-building journey. And not to forget about the lack of confidence such encounters without any immediate infra/structural help can cause. So, when I borrowed the phrase radical exteriority from Alejandro Vallega at the beginning of this chapter, I am happy to assume that it might make one romanticize a revolution from the margin, but I am here also to be honest about the moments when I just wanted to give up. For instance, when some participants, during my first UX research, pointed out the usability concerns regarding the multiple clicks they had to do to reach the pages with photographs, I neither had skills that could fix it nor access to the resources that could help me fix it. It took a lot of time, so many how-to-do Google searches, some coding lessons, and a lot of those episodes when I just wanted to change my research project. This journey of digital archiving from the margin is very non-linear and fraught with all sorts of emotions. The only thing that is keeping me going is my conviction that what is needed to be done has to be done. If the Other does not disturb the frontiers that keep justice away, who will? For any research and academic "center" to be an ethical, critical, and justice-driven space, it needs to listen to, collaborate with, and be deconstructed by the *margins*. In the ethos and methods of minimal computing, especially in the way it is theorized by some of the scholars mentioned above, I could envision the glimpse of an understanding and acknowledgment of this necessity.

Among many perspectives that Sayers highlights concerning minimal computing, I would like to move ahead with one of its visions, and that is maximum justice. Minimal computing, as per Sayers, "[r]educe[s] the use of technological, cultural, social, and economic barriers to increase entry, access, participation, and self-representation in computing and to also build systems/projects premised on social justice and difference, not white supremacy and settler colonialism" ("Minimal Definitions" tl;dr version). When digitality, design, and digital writing are freed from the clutch of power centers (one may call it utopia, but utopia is what we must demand), it will change the top-down model of power centers representing diversity. Maximum accessibility, both definitional and methodological, can ensure a path toward maximum justice creating spaces for diverse problem solvers.

At this point, I want to bring my experience of working with diverse community members in Nepal from my capacity as an Honorary DH consultant at the Center for Advanced Studies in South Asia (CASSA) since 2017. When I started planning my digital archive project, I started sharing my ideas and plans with students, researchers, and educators in Nepal. I also started sharing information about the resources that were available to me. I recognized early on that in my individual project, however successful (or unsuccessful) it becomes, the anti-oppressive struggle is not as powerful unless it is done collectively with the community with the sense of solidarity (I am remembering Sara Ahmed's interpretation of solidarity here). My project may succeed in telling something, but without initiating this movement as a community, the anti-oppressive agenda could not be envisioned. And therefore, I started inviting diverse voices and experiences to not wait for infrastructural support and power center's validation to start writing their narratives digitally. Matthew Applegate sees the very possibility of agonistic work in these acts of cooperation and writes, "Minimal computing manifests in and through our shared capacities to think and produce in common [and it] asks that we maintain a diversity of tactics for producing these shared capacities . . . to surpass dichotomous thinking (theory/practice, hack/yack, virtual/real)" (146). The reason why I adopted the values of minimal computing while working on my project and with Nepali communities is due to the possibility of a justice-driven goal of "meeting needs, collectively articulated and collectively made" (Applegate 146). A bricoleur activity in solidarity with the community for a justice-driven present and future!

Some of the other definitions, features, and ethos of minimal computing are as follows: maximum access, maximum accessibility, maximum negotiation, minimalist design, minimalist dependencies, minimal maintenance, minimal internet, minimal connectivity, minimal space, and minimal technical language (for more on this, see Sayers "Minimal Definitions" tl;dr version). This list should make minimal computing and thus, the theories, definitions, and methods of digital engagement for research and writing more accessible to under-funded and under-resourced institutions, communities, and individuals. Similarly, GO::DH defines minimal computing as "computing done under some set of significant constraints of hardware, software, education, network capacity, power, or other factors." Minimal Computing also "takes a different approach to 'innovation' in digital humanities projects and practices for low-income and low-bandwidth environments" (Risam 43). As many Nepali researchers' and my projects are situated in similar ecologies, we need to not only tackle this material lack but also with exclusionary rhetoric of digital praxis. Therefore, in this context, the ethos of minimal computing demystifies the assumptions that digital praxis needs to be large-scale tools, teams, resources, funds, and projects. As emphasized earlier, it is about using whatever is available to make social justice initiatives with and from marginalized spaces and voices. This ethos invites researchers, educators, and scholars around the world to make their contributions to digital praxis from where they are and what they have.

In a tentative nutshell, starting with what we have to solve problems and to create space for diverse problem solvers is what needs to be done. Learning to work with communities with what we have should be digital archivists' perseverance. Learning to listen and be humble toward the stories that could not be *spoken* and *heard* should be an unconditional persistence. Only then, we will be able to tell stories in a manner that threatens the colonial mechanism and its metanarratives. And the reason I chose to talk about minimal computing with structurally marginalized communities (that I am part of) is not to create another definitional or methodological frontier. It is to tell; let's use whatever is available to us such as free or affordable digital platforms and softwares, CMS digital archival platforms (such as Omeka and Mukurtu), static site generators (such as Jekyll and its theme ED for minimal editions), other digital platforms, analog platforms, etcetera. Let's share our skills, tools, theories, philosophies, methods, and methodologies across regional, geographical, institutional boundaries. Let's extend alliances. Let's make it easier to seek alliances. Let's build these alliances to rupture digital frontiers and power mechanisms that perpetuate social injustices.

Community Praxis Through Participatory Design Approaches

Regarding community-based participatory design, Rebecca Walton et al. write, "well-designed, well-conducted community-based research encounters

unexpected challenges and serendipitous surprises because power is not centralized with researchers and because complex, dynamic local contexts are informing the work" (64). Well-designed, well-conducted community-based research
is research where relationship building *with* the community is prioritized·over
knowledge building *about* the community. And when I say relationship building,
I mean a relationship where dialogues are possible. Many times, while glorify-
ing relationship-building uncritically, we let the power dynamic and hierarchy
in that relationship go unexamined. Without the possibility of counter, contradictory, and contingent dialogues, the relationships can be hierarchical and end
up becoming a dangerous perpetuation of violence. It is even more dangerous
because hierarchy, power dynamics, and domination are masked under the pre-
tense or impression of relationship and social justice. Deconstructing relationship-building while conducting research, Gesa E. Kirsch observes, "Indeed, the
more successful I was at forming good relationships with interviewees, the more
I felt like a voyeur" (xi). Therefore, when I say relationship, I want to insist on
a dialectical relationship as opposed to a voyeuristic gaze in the name of relationship-building. And those dialogues emerging through dialectical relationship-building are not always necessarily harmonious, cordial, commensurable, or
compatible. They can be very contingent, conflicting, and contradictory, resisting
every risk of essentialization of diversity. In the following paragraphs, I will present some grounded examples of how I am practicing community-based participatory design frameworks in my project.

Figure 9.3. Image of Kathmandu Streets in 2017.

While working on this archive, I am drawing on methods within UX research such as discover, decide, make, and validate frameworks of 18F Methods. Since a very preliminary stage of building the archive, I started conducting UX research with South Asian communities largely consisting of Nepalis. Some of the methods I used are usability testing, visual preference testing, dot voting, affinity mapping, landscape analysis, and user interview. The tentative ways of working with these tools are available at https://methods.18f.gov.

In this section, I will present the results of two of the methods I used during my three UX research projects since 2018: dot voting and user interview. In the dot voting study, the participants were given dots of three different colors to put on the back of the printed photo: green if they wanted the photo to be uploaded in the archive, yellow if they weren't sure, and red if they didn't think the photo should be uploaded. For each of their answers, they would also stick a note with the reason written on it. The first UX research was conducted virtually with the participants of CASSA conference held in Nepal in 2018. The second was conducted in-person in 2019 with the participants of the workshop-seminar, "Critical Digital Humanities and Participatory Design," that I was co-conductor and coordinator of. And the third UX research took place virtually (also due to the pandemic) with the Nepali academics in the US. The participants consist of academics and other professionals. Some of the questions asked to the participants were: Would you like this photograph to be in the archive, and why? What kinds of photographs would you recommend me uploading, and why? Which photographs should remain in the archive, and which should be removed, and why? The questions were drafted to give enough space for the participants to critique my work. The conversations, which will be partly manifested in this section, were so intriguing and important that as a next step in my project, I am planning to invite willing Nepali collaborators to fill out metadata spaces the way they like. With the help of the results of these methods, this section focuses on harmonious and not-so-harmonious dialogues and conversations that took place during my UX research when we attempted co-designing and co-curating the archive.

Even before I started the UX research, I knew that there would not be consistent answers among participants. Yet, each time I started the UX research and conversations with Nepali communities, I was hoping these conversations would help me in making multiple archival decisions. But the moment conversations around photographs through archival perspective started taking place, it became evident that these conversations are not going to help me find a uniform answer which would linearly result in making those specific decisions regarding my archive. The UX research helped me rethink design decisions more than making these decisions. Rather, the impossibility of building a "harmonious" and "organized" archive started becoming more evident. For example, the images where women are making and selling tea and other food items attracted various conflicting responses (for instance, Figure 9.3). While some saw stereotypical gender roles (cooking) assigned to these women in these images, others saw professional women who were using traditional gender roles to do something that is not so traditional, i.e., earning money. In the same way, while some said the images of a jumble of unruly matted wires hanging above the Kathmandu streets or the roads in poor condition and lacking basic safety features should go in the archive, other participants voted them out saying they would portray Kathmandu in a negative light. Some of the participants wanted my archive to capture Kathmandu streets in their rawness and without any censorship steered by certain ideology or philosophy, others wanted me to be extremely cautious while selecting photos so that the archival photographs do not end up inviting a colonial mindset to stereotype us any further. Some participants criticized uploading the images of religious spaces and sculptures, others emphasized there must be more photographs of the art spaces related to goddess culture. Some participants critiqued the photographs of narrow alleys of old towns or the photographs that show old, antique, dilapidated, dirty, disorganized, and religious aspects of Kathmandu. Other participants, during the conversations that followed the dot voting method in the 2019 in-person UX research, countered with something like: "Why on the earth do we have to keep on looking at ourselves through the eyes of the West and build our archive thinking about them? Can't we, for once, do it for ourselves?" Some participants remain indecisive. During a virtual user interview in 2018, one of the participants had made a very crucial point that many of us could relate to:

> You as a Nepali should be able to relate to the experience (and postures) in the photographs, unlike the western photography that religiously selects experiences and postures which are not intrinsic to Nepali sentiments, but used to ridicule or exoticize Nepal or what is Nepali. (Examples: Photographs of delousing, snots running down noses of little children. They may tell a story of poverty, but usually is an incomplete one.) Such photographs tend to stereotype, perhaps negatively.

Through these conversations, what was becoming evident was as South Asians and our shared concerns and experiences in terms of colonialism, neocolonialism, and cultural imperialism, we also share the fear of representation, especially as my digital archive is being built from the location of the US. We share our fear situated in the historical and structural violence and exclusion caused by colonialism, neocolonialism, and cultural imperialism. We also share our excitement when we saw a ray of hope that maybe we have an agency to make a postcolonial dent in this scenario and to find a decolonial option in digital archives. But that does not mean we share some essential features that define our desires, our politics, our ethics, and our aesthetics. The conflicting responses that I was getting were "rupturing the essentialist foundation of identity construction" and we were witnessing "multidimensional, contingent, and contradictory narratives of

South Asia and the deconstruction of identities categories right there" (Poudyal "Digital Activism"). And this moment was also corroborating one thing that the events and episodes like these are "the proof that the moment one tries to identify South Asians and/or Non-Westerners, they dismantle the stability of that identity right away. Because identity is always already dismantled" (Poudyal "Digital Activism"). So, an ethical way of building digital archives should begin with a determination to *anarchive* any identity constructions and such *anarchiving* cannot always be cordial, harmonious, structured, ordered, and organized. "Harmonious archives" are built on an exclusion that remains unacknowledged. Archival harmony can only be possible through the violent exclusion of the Other voices, narratives, politics, and ethics. Such archives are possible only when conflicting stories are crushed.

"Harmonious archives" tend to bulldoze over complexities and heterogeneities and end up essentializing diversity. Essentializing diversity means portraying diverse groups by implying in such a way that individuals within that community share certain essential features that define them all. Even if the intentions are, otherwise, this kind of rhetoric of diversity will reduce the existence of the Other to some essential modifiers and can run the risk of not only postponing the translation of our social justice dreams into lived experiences but rather perpetuating epistemic violence in the name of justice. Elsewhere, I have defined epistemic violence in the context of digital archiving in the following manner:

> When the pluralities and heterogeneities of the Other and their epistemologies and ontologies are reduced to some single narrative to serve the interest and match the limited imagination of the privileged structure, I am calling it epistemic violence. When will-to-knowledge about the Other becomes the driving force instead of dialogues, love, care, embrace, reciprocity, and respect towards the Other, that is epistemic violence. When there is no space for dialogue or no attempt to create a dialectical space while designing technology and building archives, there is a danger of committing this epistemic violence. (Poudyal "Building Digital Archive" 2)

Therefore, digital-archiving and digital-narrativization about diverse communities are not enough. Assuming all Non-Westerners are bound by a certain essential feature that defines them all will only support oppressive rhetoric. Assuming everyone's insurgent dreams are similar is not only insufficient but unethical too. While building digital archives to create a space for counter-texts that tell narratives about diverse communities, digital storytellers must learn to pay attention to the heterogeneities within that diversity. Because we cannot forget that almost all forms of structural violence are inflicted and justified based on hermetically sealed identity constructions. If our digital archival resistance "relies on the same essentialist epistemology and ontology, which is the tool of violence," we will end up "persisting the same tool of violence confirming that even if the violence is not right, the foundation of violence is" (Poudyal "Digital Activism"). As Diane Davis says in *Breaking Up [at] Totality*, we need to venture into the zones of the abstract and provoke a radical rupture. I is possible only when we learn to really listen to all kinds of narratives, ideas, philosophies, ethics, and politics that come from those Othered spaces. To be committed to this ethics of listening, while uploading various kinds of street photography in my digital archive, as my next step, I am planning to collaborate with other Nepali participants to populate the metadata spaces in my digital archive with pluriversal dialogues and conversations so that no photograph, collection, or exhibit tell a single narrative and the linear, unapologetic representation and categorizations of Nepalis and South Asians are shredded into pieces. I have invited willing Nepali participants to collaborate with me and populate metadata spaces in my archive the way they want so that we move toward, as Ellen Cushman et al. would say, *"imagining pluriversal possibilities"* (3). Only then, digital archives can provoke one to imagine plural realities and heterogeneous narratives of the communities that are essentialized, silenced, and absented by privileged structure. And these community-based participatory research frameworks enable researchers to examine "the hermeneutics of 'lived realities' and ask not 'what does it mean' but 'what can we do'" (Jones et al. 241; see Saukko 343). The participatory design frameworks (such as 18F Methods) allow designers to journey toward an equitable relationship with communities (Rose and Cardinal; Agboka; Walton et al.) and to really listen and engage in a relentless dialogue with humans and contexts to build a digital archive that is ethical and critically responsible. These frameworks enable digital archivists to learn to work with and learn from minoritized and underrepresented spaces so that digital archives can be, not exactly a repository for historically, culturally and evidentiary valuable and rare artifacts for permanent or long-term preservation (after all, the question that must be asked is, who gets to decide what's rare and valuable artifacts that get to participate in the future world), but a space of dialogues, possibilities, heterogeneities, pluralities, complexities, surprises, contradictions, counter-narratives, and contingencies.

Conclusion: A Call of Justice

This chapter's theoretical and methodological discussions of digital archives and digital storytelling is a humble and stubborn attempt to imagine the possibility of transforming digital archives into an inviting, safe, and hospitable space for historically and structurally marginalized, disadvantaged, absented voices, and experiences. The way I approached, theorized, and practiced minimal computing and community-praxis in my project and this chapter is a genuine attempt to transform digital-archival justice into lived experiences of the Other. Such transformation demands radical initiatives and radical humbleness from digital archivists and storytellers.

Radical initiatives call for not only making digital tools, methods, and methodologies accessible to the Other but also rupturing definitional frontiers. Only that will allow digital praxis and digital archives to create space for the Other to participate as problem-solvers and storytellers rather than only privileged structure solving problems for and constructing narratives about the Other. And radical humbleness means digital archivists remaining true to "the call of justice—which comes from outside of 'the record,' outside of any archival or record-making theory" and this call "is a calling more important than any other calling" (Harris 248). Only it will enable digital archivists to remain humble toward and strive for "impossible archival imaginaries" (Gilliland and Caswell). As per Anne Gilliland and Michelle Caswell, these imaginary archival imaginaries may work in situations where "the archive and its hoped-for contents are absent or forever unattainable" and "can provide a trajectory to the future out of a particular perspective on the past and may build upon either actual or imagined documentation and narratives" and "to instantiate the possibility of a justice that has not yet arrived" (61–65). While trying to build a dialogic room for counter-stories and counter-texts, digital archivists should also strive to imagine the stories that could not make it this time. Because these stories are not always locatable, recordable, writable, and knowable. They are either inaccessible (because no stories are completely accessible) or made inaccessible (by matrix of oppression).

Figure 9.4. Image of Kathmandu Streets [Source: http://cassacda.com]

Works Cited

18F Methods. 18F, https://methods.18f.gov. Accessed 22 Jul. 2020.

Agboka, Godwin Y. "Participatory Localization: A Social Justice Approach to Navigating Unenfranchised/Disenfranchised Cultural Sites." *Technical Communication Quarterly*, vol. 22, no. 1, 2013, pp. 28–49, https://doi.org/10.1080/10572252.2013.730966.

Ahmed, Sara. *The Cultural Politics of Emotion*, 2nd ed. Routledge, 2014.

Applegate, Matthew. *Guerrilla Theory: Political Concepts, Critical Digital Humanities*. Northwestern UP, 2020.

Bhabha, Homi. K. *The Location of Culture*. Routledge, 1994.

Callaway, Elizabeth, Jeffrey Turner, Heather Stone, and Adam Halstrom. "The Push and Pull of Digital Humanities: Topic Modeling the 'What is Digital Humanities?' Genre." *Digital Humanities Quarterly*, vol. 14, no. 1, 2020, http://www.digitalhumanities.org/dhq/vol/14/1/000450/000450.html.

"College of Liberal Arts Land Acknowledgement Statement." *UTEP College of Liberal Arts*, https://www.utep.edu/liberalarts/statements/college-of-liberal-arts-land-acknowledgement-statement.html. Accessed 17 Mar. 2021.

Cushman, Ellen, Rachel Jackson, Annie Laurie Nichols, Courtney Rivard, Amanda Moulder, Chelsea Murdock, David M. Grant, and Heather Brook Adams. "Decolonizing Projects: Creating Pluriversal Possibilities in Rhetoric." *Rhetoric Review*, vol. 38, no. 1, 2019, pp. 1–22, https://doi.org/10.1080/07350198.2019.1549402.

Derrida, Jacques. *Writing and Difference*. Translated by Alan Bass. Routledge, 1978.

Davis, Diane. *Breaking Up [at] Totality*. Southern Illinois UP, 2000.

Earhart, Amy. E. and Taylor, Toneisha. L. "Pedagogies of Race: Digital Humanities in the Age of Ferguson." *Debates in the Digital Humanities 2016*, edited by Matthew K. Gold and Lauren F. Klein, U of Minnesota P, 2016, https://dhdebates.gc.cuny.edu/read/untitled/section/58ca5d2e-da4b-41cf-abd2-d8f2a68d2914.

Gilliland, Anne J., and Michelle Caswell. "Records and Their Imaginaries: Imagining the Impossible, Making Possible the Imagined." *Archival Science*, vol. 16, no. 1, 2016, pp. 53–75, https://doi.org/10.1007/s10502-015-9259-z.

Gil, Alex. "The User, the Learner and the Machines We Make." *Minimal Computing*, 21 May 2015, http://go-dh.github.io/mincomp/thoughts/2015/05/21/user-vs-learner/.

Gil, Alex and Élika Ortega. "Global Outlooks in Digital Humanities: Multilingual Practices and Minimal Computing." *Doing Digital Humanities: Practice, Training, Research*, edited by Constance Crompton, Richard J. Lane, and Raymond G. Siemens, Routledge, 2016, pp. 22–34.

GO::DH. "About." *Minimal Computing*, https://go-dh.github.io/mincomp/about/. Accessed 23 Jun. 2020.

Gold, Matthew K., editor. *Debates in the Digital Humanities*. U of Minnesota P, 2012.

Harris, Verne. *Archives and Justice: A South African Perspective*. Society of American Archivists, 2007.

Jones, Natasha. N., and Walton, Rebecca. J. "Using Narratives to Foster Critical Thinking about Diversity and Social Justice." *Key Theoretical Frameworks: Teaching Technical Communication in the Twenty-First Century*, edited by Angela Haas and Michelle Eble, Utah State UP, 2018, pp. 241–67.

Kirsch, Gesa E. *Ethical Dilemmas in Feminist Research: The Politics of Location, Interpretation, and Publication.* SUNY, 1999.

Kurtz, Matthew. "A Postcolonial Archive? On the Paradox of Practice in a Northwest Alaska Project." *Archivaria*, vol. 61, 2006, pp. 63–90, https://archivaria.ca/index.php/archivaria/article/view/12535/13675.

Poudyal, Bibhushana. *Rethinking South Asia from the Borderlands via Critical Digital A(na)rchiving*, http://cassacda.com.

———. "Digital Activism: Strategic, Inessential, and Inenarrable Alliances for an Ethical and Political Imperative." *Gayle Morris Sweetland Digital Rhetoric Collaborative*, 1 Dec. 2019, http://www.digitalrhetoriccollaborative.org/2019/12/01/digital-activism-strategic-inessential-and-inenarrable-alliances-for-an-ethical-and-political-imperative/.

———. "Building Digital Archive through Collaborative UX Research: Relationship-Building with the Community or Knowledge-Building about the Community?" *SIGDOC '20: Proceedings of the 38th ACM International Conference on Design of Communication.* Oct. 2020, pp. 1–9, https://doi.org/10.1145/3380851.3416767.

———. "The "Nature" of Ethics While (Digitally) Archiving the Other." *Across the Disciplines*, vol. 18, no. 1/2, 2022, pp. 177–90, https://doi.org/10.37514/ATD-J.2021.18.1-2.14.

Risam, Roopika. *New Digital Worlds: Postcolonial Digital Humanities in Theory, Praxis, and Pedagogy.* Northwestern UP, 2018.

Rose, Emma. J. and Alison Cardinal. "Participatory Video Methods in UX: Sharing Power with Users to Gain Insights into Everyday Life." *Communication Design Quarterly*, vol. 6, no. 2, 2018, https://doi.org/10.1145/3282665.3282667.

Saukko, Paula. "Methodologies for Cultural Studies: An Integrative Approach." *The Sage Handbook for Qualitative Research*, 3rd ed., edited by Norman K. Denzin and Yvonna S. Lincoln, Thousand Oaks, 2005, pp. 343–56.

Sayers, Jentery. "Minimal Definitions (tl;dr version)." *Minimal Computing*, 3 Oct. 2016, https://go-dh.github.io/mincomp/thoughts/2016/10/03/tldr/.

Spivak, Gayatri Chakravorty. "Translator's preface." *Imaginary Maps*, by Mahasweta Devi, Routledge, 1995, pp. xxiii-xxx.

———. *The Spivak Reader*, edited by Donna Landy and Gerard MacLean. Routledge, 1996.

———. *An Aesthetic Education in the Era of Globalization.* Harvard UP, 2013.

Vallega, Alejandro. A. *Latin American Philosophy from Identity to Radical Exteriority.* Indiana UP, 2014.

Walton, Rebecca, Maggie Zraly, and Jean Pierre Mugengana. "Values and Validity: Navigating Messiness in a Community-Based Research Project in Rwanda." *Technical Communication Quarterly*, vol. 24, no. 1, 2015, pp. 45–69, https://doi.org/10.1080/10572252.2015.975962.

Contributors

Kati Fargo Ahern is Associate Professor of English in the Professional Writing and Rhetoric Program at SUNY Cortland. Her research focuses on the intersection between sonic rhetoric and writing theory, in particular "rhetorical soundscape studies." Her work appears in journals such as *Computers and Composition, Composition Studies, enculturation*, and *Journal of Basic Writing*.

    Diane Quaglia Beltran studied Rhetorics, Communications, and Information Design at Clemson University. Her dissertation develops and applies a novel method of reading, interpreting, and responding to memory texts. Her continued research focuses on the intersections of rhetorics, architecture, and memory texts in public locations, especially in locations with tense memories and historical pasts.

    Janine Butler is Assistant Professor at Rochester Institute of Technology (RIT), where she primarily teaches composition courses for the National Technical Institute for the Deaf, one of the colleges of RIT. Her teaching and scholarly interests center on access, multimodal communication, and embodiment. Her research projects explore strategies for improving access to digital media and compositions, particularly through captions. Her writing has appeared in *Kairos, Composition Studies, Rhetoric Review, Composition Forum, Present Tense*, and *Computers and Composition*.

    Todd Craig serves as Associate Professor of English at The Graduate Center of the City University of New York, Medgar Evers College (CUNY), and teaches in the African American Studies Department at New York City College of Technology (CUNY). Craig's publications include the multimodal novel *tor'cha*, a short story in *Staten Island Noir* and essays in scholarly journals including *Fiction International, Radical Teacher, Changing English, Modern Language Studies, Sounding Out!, Kairos* and *Composition Studies*. He teaches courses in writing, rhetoric, and Hip-Hop Studies while being clear with the field that he can't be no bird in a cage (Rapsody).

    Victor Del Hierro is Assistant Professor of Digital Rhetoric and Technical Communication in the English department at the University of Florida. His work focuses on the intersection between Hip-Hop, Technical Communication, and Community. Victor is an Associate Director of TRACE Innovation Initiative.

    Patricia Fancher teaches and researches digital media, technical rhetoric, and feminist rhetorics. Her research on gender and digital media has been published in *Peitho, Rhetoric Review, Present Tense, Composition Studies, Computers & Composition*, and *enculturation* in addition to several edited collections. Her book project, *Embodying Computing*, locates a queer techne in the history of the invention of digital computing. She is from South Carolina but lives in Southern California. She's an aspiring essayist with work in *Catapult* and *Atavist*.

Michael J. Faris (he/him/his) is Associate Professor in the Technical Communication and Rhetoric program at Texas Tech University where, as assistant chair of the English department, he co-administered the First-Year Writing Program (2018–21). His work has appeared in *College Composition and Communication, Kairos: A Journal of Rhetoric, Technology and Pedagogy*, the *Journal of Business and Technical Communication, The Journal of Multimodal Rhetorics*, and *Peitho*. Along with Courtney S. Danforth and Kyle D. Stedman, he co-edited the collections *Soundwriting Pedagogies* (Computers and Composition Digital Press, 2018) and *Tuning in to Soundwriting* (enculturation/intermezzo, 2021).

Stephanie Mahnke is the director of LGBTQI Life at Vanderbilt University. Previously, she has served as Assistant Professor of English and Literature at Utah Valley University, diversity and inclusion consultant at Utah State Board of Education, and board member of Philippine American Association of Utah and Filipino American National Historical Society—Utah and Michigan Chapters. She continues to work with nonprofits and cultural centers across various states to educate on cultural conceptions of gender and sexuality, and promote digital cultural literacy and heritage work. Her research is on digital and cultural rhetorics, with an emphasis on Filipinx-American and place/space rhetoric.

Temptaous Mckoy, from Spring Lake, North Carolina, is Assistant Professor of English with a focus in Technical and Professional Communication, as well as the Coordinator of Graduate Studies in the Department Language, Literature, and Cultural Studies at Bowie State University. Her research focuses on redefining the field of TPC and challenging it to be more inclusive of the (in)formal communicative and learning practices as found in Black communities, such as HBCUs. She is an HBCU alum (Elizabeth City State Univ.) and a member of Sigma Gamma Rho Sorority, Inc. She is the author of a three-time award-winning dissertation: "Y'all Call It Technical and Professional Communication, We Call It #ForTheCulture" as well. Recently, she served as chair of the CCCCs Black Technical and Professional Communication Task Force and co-editor of the *Technical Communications Quarterly* Black Technical and Professional Communication special issue. Finally, she is the Associate Editor of the journal *Peitho*, where she aims to prioritize new titles for review that are published by historically marginalized scholars to leverage *Peitho's* platform to take tangible steps toward a more inclusive field of scholarship in the feminist history of rhetoric and composition.

Eda Özyeşilpınar is Assistant Professor of Rhetoric and Composition in the English Department at Illinois State University. Her research broadly focuses on the intersection between border rhetorics, digital-cultural rhetorics, rhetorics of maps and mapping, and non-Western rhetorics. Her academic and creative work has appeared in *The Routledge Handbook of Comparative World Rhetorics, Kairos, Immediacy*, and *Rhetorics Change/Rhetoric's Change*.

Bibhushana Poudyal is a doctoral candidate and Assistant Director of the First-Year Composition program at the University of Texas at El Paso. Currently, she is working on a digital archival project titled, *Rethinking South Asia from the*

Borderlands via Critical Digital A(na)archiving, where she employs social justice approaches and explores the precarities, negotiations, and affordances of building a digital archive through community-based participatory approaches and design justice commitments. She is also working on her monograph, *Gendering South Asia in Global Capital: Non-Phallic Bodies in Invisible and Visible Spaces*, which is under contract with Routledge. Through her work on anti-imperialist feminism, global rhetorics, and digital rhetorics, she is exploring ways to put intellectual labor, digital tools, and research methodologies into the service of underrepresented communities and intersectionally disadvantaged groups of people and build healing spaces in and through academia.

Ann Shivers-McNair is Associate Professor in the Department of English at the University of Arizona, on the lands of the Tohono O'odham and Pascua Yaqui Peoples. Her book, *Beyond the Makerspace: Making and Relational Rhetorics*, is available from the University of Michigan Press, and her work has appeared in journals such as *Across the Disciplines, College English, Computers and Composition, enculturation, Kairos, Programmatic Perspectives*, and *Technical Communication*, and in edited collections and conference proceedings. She is an associate editor of *Technical Communication Quarterly* and a co-organizer of UX@UA, a user experience community in Tucson, Arizona.

Crystal VanKooten is Associate Professor of Writing and Rhetoric at Oakland University in Rochester, Michigan, where she teaches courses in the Professional and Digital Writing major and in first-year writing and serves as co-managing editor of *The Journal for Undergraduate Multimedia Projects (the JUMP+)*. Her work focuses on digital media composition through an engagement with how technologies shape composition practices, pedagogy, and research. Her publications appear in journals that include *College English, Computers and Composition, enculturation*, and *Kairos*. Her digital book, *Transfer across Media: Using Digital Video in the Teaching of Writing*, was funded by a Conference on College Composition and Communication Emergent Research/er Award and is available online from Computers and Composition Digital Press.

James Beni Wilson is a documentary filmmaker from Metro Detroit. He received his Bachelor of Science in Sociology at Arizona State University and currently works as the Learning Assistant Coordinator for the Michigan Association of Certified Public Accountants (MICPA). He is a Board Member and Youth Chair Liaison of the Filipino American Community Council of Michigan (FIL-AMCCO). He also serves as a Board Member of the Philippine American Community Center of Michigan (PACCM), and Secretary of the Michigan Chapter of the Filipino American National Historical Society (FANHSMI). He is an assistant director of Paaralang Pilipino (Filipino School) at the Philippine American Cultural Center of Michigan (PACCM), where he is also the lead facilitator and teacher for the class, Filipino Youth Initiative (FYI). Lastly, he serves as a Board Member for American Citizens for Justice (ACJ).